£18

3

PERSPECTIVES ON SOCIAL MEMORY IN JAPAN

PERSPECTIVES ON SOCIAL MEMORY IN JAPAN

Edited by

TSU YUN HUI

National University of Singapore

JAN VAN BREMEN

Leiden University

EYAL BEN-ARI

Hebrew University of Jerusalem

**GLOBAL
ORIENTAL**

PERSPECTIVES ON SOCIAL MEMORY IN JAPAN

Edited by Tsu Yun Hui, Jan van Bremen and Eyal Ben-Ari

First published 2005 by
GLOBAL ORIENTAL
PO Box 219
Folkestone
Kent CT20 2WP
UK

www.globaloriental.co.uk

© 2005 Global Oriental Ltd

ISBN 1-901903-24-9

British Library Cataloguing in Publication Data
A CIP catalogue entry for this book is available
from the British Library

Set in 9/11pt Stone Serif by Servis Filmsetting Ltd, Manchester
Printed and bound in England by Cromwell Press Ltd, Trowbridge, Wilts

Contents

Preface

Papers in this volume were originally presented at the International Japanese Studies Conference on Monuments and Memory Making in Japan organized by the Department of Japanese Studies at the National University of Singapore in 2002. The idea of having the conference first emerged in email exchanges between Tsu Yun Hui and Jan van Bremen. Once the two decided to go ahead, they invited Eyal Ben-Ari, a mutual friend, to join the team. The idea was to invite participants from different disciplines and countries in order to obtain as many perspectives as possible on the themes to be dealt with at the workshop. Along these lines, we invited historians, anthropologists, a sociologist, an art historian, and scholars of religious studies and literature from Australia, Britain, Israel, Japan, the Netherlands, Singapore and the United States. A bilingual policy was adopted to facilitate communication between speakers of English and Japanese. The result of this eclectic approach was most satisfying: there was lively discussion and the resulting collection of articles stretches the concept of social memory in different directions while opening up the field to include topics hitherto little explored in terms of memory, monuments and memorialization.

The conference was held over three days in an informal and relaxed atmosphere, allowing ample time for paper presentation and exchange of opinions. The official program also included an excursion to the Japanese Cemetery, the War Memorial and a Second World War battle site in Singapore. Besides providing opportunities for taking photos, the tour also inspired comparison of memory/history making in Singapore and Japan. The conference was made possible by two generous grants from the Toshiba International Foundation and the Japan Foundation. The grants came through the Department of Japanese Studies, NUS, through which Tsu submitted the applications. The Department of Japanese Studies, workshop participants and editors wish to express their appreciation to these organizations. Last but not least, the editors wish to thank Ong Hui Bee and Lee Bee Ling for handling administrative matters in a professional and efficient manner.

TYH
JVB
EBA

Memory, Scholarship and the Study of Japan

EYAL BEN-ARI, JAN VAN BREMEN AND TSU YUN HUI

INTRODUCTION

The essays in this volume deal with social memory in Japan. By social memory we mean the various forms – intentional and unintentional, public and private, material and communicative, consensual and contested – through which peoples are shaped by the past (Olick and Robbins 1998: 112). Indeed, it is hard to disregard the plethora of public events and scholarly works that have appeared in regard to these issues in Japan during the last decade or so. Probably the most striking example is the fifty year anniversary of the end of the Second World War, which aroused interest through films about Pearl Harbor (Chalk 2002), exhibitions about the dropping of the atomic bombs (Yoneyama 1997), the portrayal of the war in textbooks (Hein and Selden 2000), literary works about Hiroshima and Nagasaki (Treat 1995), rituals of commemoration for the war dead (Harootunian 1999), or revelations about the atrocities committed by Japan during the war (Harris 2002). Yet the interest in social memory appears to have struck a wider resonance as the 1990s have seen a surfeit of books and articles related to the complex interrelations between history, memory and identity. One case is Ohnuki-Tierney's (1993) volume on Japanese identities through time. Another is the collection edited by Vlastos (1998) that explores how various past traditions – of labor relations, legal procedures, or the martial arts for instance – were invented as part of the project of modernity in Japanese society. Yet another case in point is Tanaka's (1993) book and Mehl's (2000) essay about the emergence of the discipline of Japanese history as an integral part of the search for Japanese identity. Finally, the recent collection edited by Gong (2001b; and 2001a) attempts to link issues of memory and history to issues of strategy and international relations in East Asia.

What are the reasons for this rather extensive and consistent preoccupation with the past and with memory in Japan? To follow Winter (2000), who writes about the Euro-American context, the upsurge in the concern with memory has occurred because the impulses behind it add up to a whole greater than the sum of its parts. In the Japanese case, we suggest a number of interrelated sources. First, as Ohnuki-Tierney (1993: 123) suggests, a crisis often intensifies the search for a past because it is a time that people are no longer sure of themselves and thus need to rethink their identities and civilization. Such a crisis was precipitated by Japan's 'economic miracle' (and ironically intensified by the current economic downturn) when many people in this society began to look for 'the' past as it was 'retained' in the countryside and in peasants' lives, in themes related to the *furusato*, or 'hometown' or 'old homeplace' (Ivy 1995). Thus, Kelly (1986) argued that a nostalgia borne of Japan's successful modernization clouds the relationship between the local and the national by decontextualizing local practices in the service of a generalized 'folk tradition' of the past. Indeed, as Robertson (1992: 14) argues, the dominant representation of *furusato* is infused with a nostalgia and dissatisfaction with the present on the grounds of a remembered or imagined past plenitude. Since the 1970s, academics and intellectuals, government officials and party activists, as well as ordinary citizens have begun to call for a resolution to these circumstances through such projects as *komyuniti-zukuri*, the creation of community (Ben-Ari 1991, 1992; Bestor 1992; Nussbaum 1985). This term revolves around the notion of remaking the past as the condition for bringing about a social transformation in the present. The idealized characteristics and practices of the 'village of the past' are used as prescriptions for creating a similar set of traits and conventions in contemporary communities (Robertson 1992:9).

The second source, as Robertson (1998) notes, is closely related to the first. Japan's internationalization and the concomitant search for the distinctive cultural identity of Japan in contrast to other nations and cultures has, perforce, involved a turn to its past and to its traditions. What seems to be happening during this historical period is that issues of face-to-face cross-cultural contacts are a central element in constructing personal accounts. Overseas assignments, intercultural contacts, and tours abroad have turned into regular events which prompt people to make various kinds of identity claims and to ask and evaluate such questions as 'who are they?' and 'where are they going?' (Ben-Ari 1998). This point is heightened in the case of Japan, as Befu and Manabe (1991: 110) note, because, when compared to Americans, foreigners have always been very important for self-definition in Japan. Whether through the sale of best-sellers by foreign experts or more humdrum questioning of outsiders about their opinion of Japan, the opinions of 'aliens' have always been important in Japan. Thus in an ironic manner, the turn outwards from Japan has also involved an impulse to explore its distinctive past and traditions.

The third source, perhaps more a precondition, for a preoccupation with the past is the affluence brought about by Japan's economic success. This prosperity has allowed the establishment and immense expansion of a host of local historical circles, photography and film clubs, study groups or communal and family associations. While these associations and activities associated with the past have long existed in Japan, they have been considerably expanded in the previous twenty or so years. Disposable income, more leisure time and increasing numbers of university trained people have formed the base – as in other industrialized countries (Eley 1997; Winter 2000) – for Japan's 'memory boom.' Complementing these developments have been the activities of the popular press, the mass media, and the tourism industry which cater to the tastes and demands of many Japanese seeking to explore their pasts, their links to *furusato* and to Japanese heritage (Ivy 1995).

The fourth and more proximal prompt for remembering are the death of the Shōwa Emperor and the cycle of anniversaries related to World War Two as they have taken place in Japan and outside of it (Evans and Lunn 1997: xv; Harootunian 2000). As Schudson (1995: 350) suggests, 'anniversaries or commemorations of events forty and fifty years in the past become especially significant, as the possibility of living memory fades and the only memories that remain are those culturally institutionalized'. In this way the death of the emperor can be seen in three ways: first, as a marker of a much wider demographic trend within which many of the survivors of the war are slowly dying away; second, as a special event that brought to the fore a reckoning and reflection with what 'his' historical period represents; and third, as many of the first hand witnesses of the war are dying out the efforts to remember and access it are taken up by other groups in society such as scholars, political commentators and politicians. Intensifying these trends has been the recession of the 1990s, then the Kōbe earthquake and the Sarin gas attacks. These events have further undermined the self-confidence of many Japanese and spurred them to look for ways of making sense of the world often with a serious turn to 'their' past.

The fifth source of remembering is external influences on Japan in regard to the politics of identity and the place of narratives of the past within it. Such influence is apparent in diverse sites that include museum exhibitions, repertoires of fashionable singers, the erection of monuments, the recording of oral testimonies, or the activities of popular movements. As Eley (1997: vii) suggests, in today's world

[A]n anxiety about the loss of bearings and the speed and extent of change, in which representations of the past, the narration and visualizing of history, personal and collective, private and public, spell the desire for holding on to the familiar, for fixing and retaining the lineaments of worlds in motion, of landmarks that are disappearing and securities that are unsettled. In this understanding, 'memory' becomes the crucial site of identity formation in the late twentieth century.

Sixth, and no less important, are developments within the scholarly disciplines involved in 'Japanese Studies.' To begin with, the study of both contemporary history and of oral history have – as in other places (Eley 1997: viii) – gained their credentials and been accepted as legitimate scholarly undertakings. But also significant are the ways in which disciplines within the humanities and the social sciences have begun to borrow and apply concepts and frameworks developed outside of them. One example is the interrelations that have developed between the anthropology and history of Japan. Another one is the emergence of cultural studies in regard to 'things Japanese'. Cultural studies have provided one of the main frames for the growth of memory as an academic preoccupation. With its focus on public fields of representation and its interdisciplinary base cultural studies has enhanced and expanded our perceptions of the past. It is within this broad multi- and inter-disciplinary field – in Japan as elsewhere (Maclear 1999) – that elements of the past and of memory have emerged as a central issue.

SCHOLARLY APPROACHES

But what is it that characterizes academic studies of the Japanese past? There seem to be a number of interrelated approaches that bear mention in this regard. The first explores the complex intertwining of remembering and forgetting in interpretations of postwar themes. Kushner (1997; also Buruma 1994) shows how the Japanese adopted Anne Frank as an acceptable and accessible figure in the 1950s since her gender and age accented the themes of victimhood and the stress on a hope for the future rather than a sense of guilt for the past. Yoneyama (1999), demonstrates how monuments built to commemorate the dropping of the Atomic bombs on Hiroshima and Nagasaki were created in a rather certain manner. In these monuments the suffering caused by the war and the responsibility of the perpetrators are forgotten in the name of conjuring up the 'bright' postwar themes of peace and prosperity. Igarashi (2000) for his part contends that Japanese society downplayed its traumatic experiences of the war through narrative devices that centered on the country's history as a teleology of progress. Piper (2001) examines how adopting a victim identity allowed many Japanese to forget their role as perpetrators of violence and the existence of other victims.

The second approach attacks the conceptual underpinnings of historicity, truth, and identity, to raise questions about the links between memory and power. Fujitani (1996), to take one example, uses the framework of invented tradition – first developed outside of Japan – to examine the various kinds of imperial pageantry that were invented in modern Japan. In this manner, he underscores how the 'naturalness', the very taken-for-granted-ness, of the imperial institution is a rather modern fabrication. In a different manner, Yoneyama (1999: ch 5) explains how conscious and intentional acts of remembrance by Korean survivors of the bomb are indicative of how they made their plight suddenly visible and opened up questions about the ownership of memory. Similar efforts have been carried out in regard to the reminiscences and voices of comfort women (Keller 1997) and victims of the Rape of Nanking (Chang 1998). In this way, this approach critiques official historiography as a source of cultural domination and challenges dominant historical narratives in the name of repressed groups. It also underscores how memory is used to shape belonging, exclusivity and social hierarchies in Japan.

Finally, the third perspective provides a contest-based account of the politics of memory. Thus, for example, Gluck (1993) outlines the main disputes between four groups of 'custodians of the past' in contemporary Japan. These disputes center on the ways in which the war is to be interpreted in terms of the long-term development of Japanese society. Seraphim (2003), for her part shows how the competing historical memories of the war influenced the ways in which 'democracy' was understood and adopted in Japan. Hein and Selden (1997) show how two 'official' narratives of the atom bombs and their effects emerged in Japan and the United States but never monopolized what they call 'nuclear consciousness.' Thus despite these official narratives, Japanese writers, artists, and critics have repeatedly used the Atom bomb as a means to question Japanese colonialism, aggression, atrocities, rearmament and the Japan-United States security treaties. What all these approaches share is the underlying assumption about the essentially labile, constructed and political nature of memory and identities. According to this set of approaches, such identities are no longer conceptualized as a given but rather as an assortment of typifications and images that are constantly negotiated and struggled over.

LEARNING DISCIPLINES

It is against this background that the specific contributions of this volume should be understood. Arrayed along an axis between memorials and monuments, the volume presents analyzes of a substantial variety of phenomena centered on social memory such as music and poetry, artifacts and tools, oral testimonies and written documents, stones and performances, rivers and earthquakes, animals and belongings, ritual and ceremonies, or artists and art. These events, forms and activities are treated from a multi-disciplinary perspective that includes anthropology, sociology, history, literature, music, art history, folklore, and cultural studies. Why, readers may well ask, publish such a volume at this point of time? The reason centers on the fact that previous works on social memory and monuments have tended to focus on either rather isolated issues or overwhelmingly on the Second World War. This collection explicitly aims to cast a much wider substantive and analytical net.

Let us be more specific. First, from the perspective of social memory studies, the choice of Japan allows the essays in this volume to examine a very different array of phenomena to those that have been explored in past studies of memorialization (overwhelmingly centered on Europe or America). Thus for instance, cases by which inanimate implements, equipment and tools form the objects for veneration and remembering offer a distinctive perspective on what is involved in memorialization (Nakamaki). Similarly, the essays that deal with animal mortuary rites (Nakamaki, Knight, van Bremen, Veldenkamp) attest to the sheer extent and breadth of commemoration involving Buddhist temples and Shinto shrines, tens of thousands of commemorated pets and animals used in biomedical research, and the extensive amount of resources dedicated to these activities. The essay by Knight on the ways in which the ruthless character of wolves is handled, adds a crucial dimension to previous studies of 'bad' reputation which have focused exclusively on humans. Another fascinating case (Bambling) centers on the emotional and behavioral implications of memorializing individuals that carry on the traditional arts while they are still alive.

Second, this volume presents a distinctive perspective on the project of modernity in Japan. This point is most pronounced in Takagi's contribution in which he shows how the Meiji government sought to find, establish and legitimize an ancient past as part of the grand project of building the Japanese nation-state. Bambling's composition also deals with the project of modernity through the state-mandated project – the Living National Treasure Program – that was specifically aimed at protecting the traditional arts of Japan. Yet, as the essays demonstrate, critiques of the excesses of modernization and modernity appear in a variety of guises such as ironic rock ballads (Bourdaghs), the promotion of intangible cultural resources (Bambling), or a harking back to a purported river culture of times gone by (Tsu). The idea here, to follow Zelizer (1995: 218), is that remembering is 'a process that is constantly unfolding, changing and transforming' (Zelizer 1995: 218).

Third, this collection illuminates how models of memory travel across national and cultural borders. To be sure, scholars of social memory have long contended that 'memory is a process, not a thing, and it works differently at different points of time' (Zelizer 1995; Olick and Robbins 1998). Yet the transnational and transcultural 'migration' of models of remembering and commemoration have hardly received significant scholarly attention. In this respect, precisely because Japan has a relatively long 'modern' history, and has had intense relationships with other societies, it provides very good cases for exploring these issues. Thus some essays in this volume explore what may be called globally available models of memory work. What they show is not just cases of locally available models for commemoration, but rather the interaction of these models with external ones that opens up dynamic possibilities. The primary example here is Bourdaghs' piece about how, in order to understand Japanese and British music, one needs to take into account their links to American music and how it portrays elements of the past.

Fourth, this volume juxtaposes both English language and Japanese scholarship about memory and monuments. Japanese studies have always applied concepts and theories developed in the English speaking world to cases drawn from this society. Recent examples are the introduction of issues related to the 'body' and to 'globalization' in ways that have enriched our scholarly endeavors. At the same time, however, relatively little Japanese scholarship is being published in English. This volume not only includes contributions by leading Japanese scholars such as Takagi and Nakamaki but also essays in which Japanese scholarship is consciously used to construct arguments (van Bremen, Veldenkamp). Take the example given by van Bremen about the Japanese folklorist Kon Wajirō who created a new discipline in the 1920s and 1930s. Contrasting it to archeology, Kon suggested the utility and importance of studying things and life in the present – what he called 'modernology.' In contrast to the folklorists of his day who were preoccupied with attempts to preserve and conserve what they saw as a 'disappearing world,' he was interested in describing the present as a storehouse of memory for the future.

THE PAPERS

Jan van Bremen's contribution is entitled **Monuments for the Untimely Dead or the Objectification of Social Memory in Japan**. It deals with the kinds of memorials, cemeteries, and monuments that have been erected in modern Japan to commemorate the untimely dead. These relatively permanent mortuary architectural objects of varying sizes and shapes honor those individuals that have not died a natural death: soldiers who were killed during military service or in battle, individuals who have died in disasters such as fires or earthquakes and the unknown dead whose bodies have never been recovered. As he shows, it is the souls of these latter persons who pose the greatest symbolic threat as they remain unsettled according to the beliefs of many Japanese.

Van Bremen's analysis neatly fits into the investigations of such critical sociologists as Charles Tilly (1985) or Anthony Giddens (1985) who argue that war and the institutions of war-making are integral to the creation of states and to the mobilization of social resources. Such scholars have done much to uncover the main social and (especially) political mechanisms – recruitment, taxation, or propagation of ideologies of citizenship, for example – by which war has become a routine part of the very dynamics of contemporary countries. In the Japanese case it has been Kurimoto (2000) who has shown the way in which the military was a major mechanism for the creation of the modern Japanese nation-state through conscription and the militarization of the nation. What van Bremen's essay adds is the contention that the modern Japanese state was created – among other *cultural* means – through the establishment of cemeteries and the glorification of death in the service of the state.

But his essay raises another point. We usually look at cemeteries and monuments as rather permanent, relatively enduring types of commemoration. Yet in tracing out the historical development of what may be called the 'sacred map' of military monuments and cemeteries around Japan and Asia, van Bremen shows how even these relatively stable phenomena wax and wane according to historical circumstances. One such example is the complete erasure of Japanese cemeteries in contemporary Hong Kong that has been brought about for various historical and political reasons. In addition, he shows how such comparatively long-lasting sites may be transformed as in the case of some memory locations that have been turned into peace museums. As he argues, the reason for this change is related to the strength of the Japanese peace museum movement and to how it seeks not to glorify war but to learn and disseminate lessons learned from it.

Nakamaki Hirochika's paper is entitled **Memorial Monuments of Interrupted Lives in Modern Japan: From *Ex Post Facto* Treatment to Intensification Devices**. Based on a large-scale survey conducted by the National Museum of Ethnology in Ōsaka, it deals with the ways in which monuments help people to adjust to, behave towards and give meaning to interrupted lives: that is, unexpected deaths brought about by battle, traffic accidents, sickness, abortion and (historically) executions. Concretely, Nakamaki's focus is on the devices – the memorial monuments and services – that are used to deal with these premature deaths and the social and psychological consequences of loss and mourning that they bring about. In his intricate analysis, he demonstrates the multiplicity of possibilities involved in such monuments. For example, he shows how shrines for the war dead may transmit messages 'justifying' death by stressing either glory or anti-war messages.

Yet perhaps the wider import of Nakamaki's analysis for social memory studies lies in the way he links memorials established for humans to the kinds of monuments and services held for animals and inanimate objects: insects, fish, dolphins, whales, or horses but also trees, plants, writing brushes, needles, or kitchen knives. Nakamaki's thesis is that these practices are based on the connection of such objects to the kinds of services and consumption they represent for humans. Concretely, he shows how it is specialized professions – fishermen, tailors or barbers, for instance – that feel the special need to commemorate such flora and fauna and implements. At the same time, however, he is very careful to caution that we should not automatically attribute 'positive' ecological consequences to such activities. Memorials for fish or kitchen knives, to put this point by way of example, do not necessarily serve to control the exploitation of nature. Rather than attributing to them a romantic notion of ecological responsibility we should be aware that they may be implicated in the very processes of capitalism.

Elmer Veldenkamp's paper **Memorializing and Remembering Animals in Japan** deals with the variety of ritual practices through which animals are monumentalized, celebrated and remembered in Japan. In this respect, Veldenkamp focuses on a set of phenomena that seems peculiar to Japan: ceremonies in which people pray for the 'souls' or 'spirits' of dead animals for a safe trip to heaven or a successful rebirth. The two cases through which Veldenkamp explores this issue are contemporary pets and animals that died in the battles fought by Japan. He shows that there are different dynamics at work in these two instances. For pets, the commemoration and establishment of altars in Buddhist temples are centered on individual animals – with their own names and history within families – and the rites are aimed at dealing with the problem of 'pet loss.' For military animals, barring a few cases, the commemoration is done for categories of fauna that served the military apparatus of the Imperial forces. Thus, this kind of commemoration is closely linked to ideas about service to the state.

This paper carries some interesting theoretical implications. Marshall Sahlins (1976) suggests in his essay on the cultural underpinning of American eating habits that the rule in regard to the edibility of different species is related to their nearness to human society. What Veldenkamp's essay suggests is a similar structural logic underlying the ways in which pets and war animals are culturally understood and commemorated in Japan. Thus the nearness to humans predicts whether they will be commemorated as individual animals – pets and some horses – or as categories – draft animals, for example. As for war animals – horses, dogs and pigeons – the idea is that these categories of animals have served in a subordinate position to the humans of the military. Indeed, in many religious sites, such as Yasukuni Shrine, they are located in rather peripheral parts. This contention appears to be strengthened by the fact that one temple Veldenkamp has examined has mortuary rites not only for pets but also for unborn fetuses and dolls: that is, 'beings' that are closer to humans in form and meaning but not 'really' human.

In a curious way, Veldenkamp's essay hints at a wider process that has evolved in Japanese society. In his essay on ancestor worship, Robert Smith (1974) proposes that there has been a transformation in the kinds of attitudes shown to ancestors and their souls. From being threatening entities they have been transformed into beings towards which affection should be shown. This change in attitude, in turn, can be seen in the kinds of services and commemorations held for them. What Veldenkamp's findings suggest, is that we may find a similar kind of shift in regard to attitudes to animals as pets. These seem to have transformed from being threatening entities (Knight) or 'mere' servants of humans to being close companions. In this manner, practices related to commemoration may provide us with fruitful entry points to the analysis of wider cultural processes in contemporary Japan.

Eyal Ben-Ari's article is entitled **Coincident Events of Remembrance, Coexisting Spaces of Memory: The Annual Memorial Rites at Yasukuni Shrine.** It represents an attempt to trace out the complex events that comprise the annual memorial rite for the war dead at this Shinto shrine. Ben-Ari argues that this yearly occasion consists of a host of concurrent actions, practices and behaviors that include official spiritual ceremonies, personal and familial pilgrimages, visits by top politicians, reunions of old soldiers, a Hyde Park like forum for open debate, and a tourist attraction. According to him, the very multiplicity of the events and the open-endedness of the day as a whole permit various groups to further their agendas, implement their goals, through what is going on. But as he cautions, the word 'agenda' here is too political and intentional, for some individuals simply go to Yasukuni to have a good time, to see curiosities or to express their personal connection to the war dead. What does hold the day together is a rough center to right-wing consensus (excluding extremists) based on tolerance for a variety of viewpoints about how to come to terms with the problematic past represented by the Second World War.

The annual rites at Yasukuni are arguably the most central and contested of the commemorations held for the general category of Japan's war dead (as opposed, for instance, to the dead of a specific prefecture, or the victims of the atom bombs). Yet most of the interpretations put forward in order to understand these rites have been principally political in their perspective and have established their contentions on the analysis of historical and contemporary texts and the pronouncements of political elites. As such they tend to see the rites as a move towards the rehabilitation of the Imperial Military and the revival of Japanese nationalism (Harootunian 1999). When examined more closely, however, it seems that after the war millions of soldiers and their families who were left with much personal pain and grief began to search for a meaning to the experience of the war and its losses and privations. Ben-Ari argues that apart from being political moves, the rites at Yasukuni allow this grief to be expressed and provide some meaning to the loss. The pilgrimage to Yasukuni Shrine thus allows many individuals and families to link their personal memories and sentiments to the collective level.

Scot Hislop's chapter is entitled **Summer Grasses: Memory and the Construction of Landscape in** *Oku no Hosomichi*. Hislop contributes tools and questions taken from literary theory to the discussion of memory by interrogating previous interpretations of Bashō's *Oku no Hosomichi*. Through this case he asks a question clearly centered on the cultural assumptions at base of 'our' Western disciplinary notions about memory. Hislop asks whether our forms of memory are universal or are the products of a peculiar historical genealogy that limits as well as opens up ways of talking about remembering. His thesis is not a simplistic one that pre-modern texts provide us with some fulcrum point 'outside' of modernity from which to examine such assumptions. Rather, he appears to argue that because such texts do not conform to our 'modern' notions they may provoke interesting questions.

In this regard he shows how the link between memory and landscape was part of socially shared contexts and communities. He begins by demonstrating that 'our' ideas of memory are usually linked to realist assumptions about people's – and in the literary texts, authors' – 'self' or 'subjectivity.' Through a careful reading of two excerpts from *Oku no Hosomichi*, Hislop reveals that shared memory is more important than personal memory. Shared memory is based on the use of *utamakura*, a category of poetic words that are often place names or the names of features associated with them that are used to cultivate allusion and intertextuality within a tradition. In this case, the shared memory is that of the very small community that Bashō belonged to in the seventeenth century and which required knowledge of the poetic classics of both China and Japan. It is to this community and its imagination that Bashō appealed to in his depictions of landscapes and not to the 'actual' scenery that he witnessed. In Bashō's depictions the eternal and the fleeting are brought together in one depiction. In other words, because Bashō was working with a shared memory landscape to guide him, the scenery is not something we could capture on camera but rather is critically dependent on shared memory.

Takagi Hiroshi's essay is entitled **The Meiji Restoration and the Revival of Ancient Culture**. It deals with the birth of the concept of 'national treasure' during the last decades of the nineteenth century. This concept and the set of practices attendant upon it were aimed at reviving the ancient culture of Japan. Like the institution of such practices in other contexts (Anderson 1983; Abu El-Haj 2001), the idea was to forge a link between the new nation-state and a 'true' and 'authentic' (and therefore legitimate) past. This link with the past was forged by bypassing Japan's middle ages and early modern period and finding old shrines and temples, uncovering monuments and collecting artistic possessions from the 'ancient' period. Like many newly established nation-states, Meiji Japan was the site of ongoing efforts to invent and legitimate 'new' traditions: that is, sets of cultural forms and practices that provide, *inter alia*, storified versions of past events which form bases for present-day legitimation. No less importantly, Takagi shows the primary means through which the administration of cultural assets was carried out through state arms. In other words, these collective actions involved the state's bureaucratization of the past. In fact, at the bottom of these practices was the idea that such cultural assets are not the 'private' ownership of individuals, families or religious institutions but rather belong to the 'state' as representing the collective.

Yet his contribution goes beyond a portrayal of state efforts to create a past. Takagi shows how the past of Japan was systematically internationalized and globalized during this period (see also Christ 2000). Thus, for example, he shows how parts of the state's new collections were shown in the International Exposition in Paris in 1900. The idea behind the consumption of the Japanese past by international audiences was that this culture too had an artistic heritage worthy of the 'family' of civilized societies of the period (Gong 1984). In order to be able to display such elements of the past, Japan had to institute a European sense and idea of time – basically linear and divided into stages beginning with the 'ancient' – so that it could be understood by international audiences. At the same time, however, as Takagi shows, it was difficult for Japan to join the 'first class' nations by simply copying them. Rather Japan has to create its own individuality and unique cultural tradition to present to the West. From the perspective of social memory studies, the implication is thus that one cannot understand the discovery and use of the past without understanding the global situation.

Michele Bambling's contribution **Japan's Living National Treasures Program and the Paradox of Remembering** presents a fascinating case of the memorialization of living individuals. In official bureaucratic parlance these people are deemed 'important intangible cultural properties' – the public term is 'human national treasures' (*ningen kokuhō*) – and designated from such fields as drama, music or the applied arts. In this manner these special designations – of 'traditional' artists and artistry – fit the political agenda of the state in trying to produce and maintain the version of a national cultural identity dealt with in Takagi's essay. But what happens to people once they are thus designated and recognized? Bambling explains that there are two basic paradoxes at the base of such state-mandated designations, paradoxes centered on the administration or bureaucratization of creativity. The first centers on the individuals themselves. According to Bambling many of them feel burdened and stressed by the expectations now placed on them as special 'carriers' of tradition and heritage. Concretely, the special recognition as 'national treasures' actually works toward paralyzing them in artistic terms.

The second paradox centers on innovation. The Ministry of Education insists, as Bambling notes, that the aim of the designation is not to venerate the holders of the title but to ensure that the special skills of these arts are transmitted correctly to future generations. Yet the new technological means – recording and documenting – of the artistic process have created deeply ambivalent attitudes to innovation and the secrets of the art. Since the recorded versions now form standards for constant comparisons and appraisal, a certain 'de-humanization' of the artistic process is effected. Human memory, to put this by way of example, is conceded to the use of sheet music, tape and video recording. In this way, the older stress on innovation as an important link between the past and the future is actually erased. No less importantly, as Bambling contends, because memory is in essence intangible and traceless, it is by nature embodied in human experience and cannot be directly stored in technological means.

Michael Bourdaghs' article **What it Sounds Like to Lose an Empire? Happy End and the Kinks** offers a fascinating comparative analysis of post-imperial memory in the popular, essentially rock, music of the 1960s and 1970s. It compares two socially aware rock groups in Britain and Japan for what their music and lyrics reveal about how the imperial venture of these countries is remembered and handled. Bourdagh analyzes the use of irony in remembering the past when he shows how the British harking for the past is mediated through fantasies produced by American popular culture. The irony, he contends, is that such mediation creates a popular postwar music that leads to a general indifference and forgetfulness of colonial times. In the Japanese context, Bourdaghs explains how the band Happy End was part of a search and discovery of a 'real' Japanese version of rock (and not a mere imitation of the Western variety). As he demonstrates, they sang in Japanese but more importantly were part of a wider search for the 'authentic' Japan which took place through such 1970s genres as folklore or history.

The paper seems to approach and then to distance itself from issues related to nostalgia, to a longing for something. This is most apparent in Bourdaghs' attempt to pin down what it is that members of the Japanese rock group are harking back to. They seem to be in a very different position than the Kinks – and many other artists in Britain – in that the 'Japanese Empire' is not fully accepted in contemporary society as a model of past 'goodness.' If anything, as we previously argued, the core of contemporary Japanese nostalgia centers on notions of '*furusato*'. Thus interestingly, in grappling with the loss of empire, the group Happy End does not appeal to a fantasy of the national folk, the creation of a monumental history, or the developmental narrative of modernization. Rather, they remember the past in an unstable and highly ambiguous present (Ivy 1995) by deliberately inventing an inauthentic, unnatural form of Japanese and singing it.

John Knight's article is called '**Remembering the Wolf: the Wolf Reintroduction Campaign in Japan.**' It deals with attempts to rehabilitate this animal's 'difficult reputation' (Fine 2001) because the key image of wolves is that of a dangerous predator that threatens humans. Concretely, the paper focuses on the work of the Japan Wolf Association and its attempts to reintroduce wolves to Japan. The association is trying to create a more favorable image of the wolf through stressing its contribution to exterminating vermin, wider ecological themes of species preservation, and links to the idyll of the forests of the past in which nature and humans were in a purportedly harmonious relationship. In this manner, the recreation of a good image for the wolf is based on the place of the wolf in Japanese folklore (as helpmate to humans), the existence of wolf shrines and the critique of the excesses of modernization and industrialization.

Knight's essay contains fascinating suggestions about global models of remembering. Take his proposition that the children's fairy tales of Little Red Riding Hood and the Three Little Pigs were imported into Japan – to be told at home, read in school or enacted in children's dramas – but that it is their remembrance that has led to the image of the wolf as predator and as morally wrong. Autobiographical memories and their lingering effects thus remain quite intense along the life course. Moreover, it is not coincidental that the association portrays Meiji wolves as the 'real' wolves just as the Meiji period is often taken to be an icon of the real Japan. But, as he shows, this story has a contemporary twist to it. In trying to reintroduce wolves into Japan, the association has problems with finding suitable candidates. Concretely, the decision has been made to make this reintroduction centered on Mongolian wolves and not animals from the United States. The former are said to be like the now extinct Japanese ones and thus they are not an 'alien' species. This move is an interesting example of how memory of animals is actually based on human ideas of kinship and cultural proximity.

Thang Leng Leng's paper is entitled **Preserving the Memories of Terror: Kōbe Earthquake Survivors as 'Memory Volunteers'**. It deals with the private, state and civic efforts made by survivors of the earthquake that hit Kōbe in 1995 to tell their story. The idea at the base of these efforts was to look at the memory of the disaster as a set of assets that can and should be used to transmit certain messages. Thang's focus is on a group of senior volunteers that are the carriers of these memories. As such it echoes Yoneyama's (1999: ch 3) portrayal of how survivors of the atom bombs actively began to adopt identities as 'witnesses' and 'storytellers.' At the beginning, the primary activity of the Kōbe volunteers was to take visitors on tours of the places where the earthquake occurred and where there are still visible signs of its effects. But with time the stress shifted from telling the story of the frightening instance of the quake and the harshness of living in shelters afterwards to linking the tale to moral messages to the young. As such the paper adds to our volume the element of intergenerational transmission of memory in which such themes as stopping school violence, volunteering, or connections to older generations are emphasized. In this manner, the shift in the story-telling is from memories of victims to those of survivors.

In addition, as Thang shows, the activities of the survivors ironically contributed to a certain process of decontextualization of the quake. In transmitting a variety of educational and moral messages to the children before whom they appeared, these individuals seemed to circumvent the problem of the responsibility for the faulty building of large parts of Kōbe. Remembering the quake thus is part of the depoliticization of questions of responsibility and accountability. This process is facilitated by the shift in the narratives from learning about to learning from the earthquake.

The chapter by Tsu Yun Hui **The Violent and the Benign: How Kōbe Remembers its Rivers** deals with the ways in which the city of Kōbe maintains two concurrent perspectives of rivers: as both threatening and as benevolent. Concretely, it explores the kinds of agents – governmental bodies, schools, civic associations, and private individuals – and practices – homepages, newsletters, and brochures – through which these images are created and recreated. Finally, it deals with how this contradiction is handled within the idea of *machi-zukuri*, or community making. Tsu's argument is that at the same time as the city's fascination with the control of rivers is related to the control of nature and the power of modern tech-niques (based on the flooding disasters in modern history), it is also enthralled with the idealized, nativist view of nature and culture and through that of modernity (which creates an idealized past that probably never existed anywhere). In this dual image of the rivers we see an echo of a wider duality regarding nature in Japanese culture (Kalland and Asquith 1997) which is related to an even deeper ambivalence towards the fruits and excesses of modernity. At bottom of this perspective is the environmentalist view of modernity that combines both pride and anxiety, a harking for the past but in a controlled environment allowed by the very modern techniques being used. Nature is transformed accord-ing to a constructed nostalgic memory: the gentle rivers, sloping hills, friendly community spirit are all created in an artificial manner.

Like the case examined by Bambling there also seems to be a basic paradox here: the attempt to artificially preserve – to bureaucratize and engineer – the natural. As Tsu puts it, the questioning of urban living and a harking for the past take place against the background of palpable phys-ical improvements to the waterways of the Kōbe. Yet the creation of human-friendly rivers, in turn, aggravates the burdens human put on nature. Within this kind of depiction, we would argue, rural localities are seen as a sort of repository of the past, of ideals and of 'tradition'. The portrayal of past or peripheral places thus serves to remind many Kōbe residents, and Japanese more generally, of how things used to be and of how they should be. This Japanese nostalgia 'boom', however, clouds the relationship between the local and the national (see Kelly 1986). It focuses, for instance, on the harmonious relations between people and rivers within particular or specific localities but then decontexualizes them in the service of more general emphases on the significance of these links. To put this somewhat coarsely, for people visiting these sites in Kōbe, it matters less that they go to Kōbe (or any other locality) than that these places represent a more generalized notion of what kind of past they represent.

AND THE STUDY OF JAPAN?

It may now be appropriate to suggest something about the relationship between this volume and what may be termed its specific historical situatedness. Thus, we think it fruitful to offer a number of speculations about the historical moment in which we write and its relation to our scholarly engagement with memory and monuments. As we suggested earlier, the connection between our scholarly focus and present historical circumstances is related to a set of processes – the extended economic crisis, social unease and political instability, to mention only a few – that Japan has been undergoing in the past decades. The onset of these processes has not spelt the disappearance of values and sentiments propagated by many hegemonic groups during the postwar era. What does seem to be happening in Japan is that competing world views and assertions of Japanese identity and peoplehood are finding greater public expression. Yet the development of these critiques in and around Japan cannot be understood apart from changes in the wider (perhaps world-wide) intellectual atmosphere. Michael Jackson (1989) has termed this period one of an anxiety on the part of scholars about the status of anthropological knowledge and methods. It is our suggestion that this crisis or anxiety and the attempts to deal with it, have seeped into the human and social scientific disciplines dealing with issues related to the past, commemoration, and remembering in Japan.

By writing and publishing about the past, memory, monuments and commemoration we are also, of course, participating in the public discussion now taking place about contemporary Japan. Perhaps this is a modest aim, but what we can contribute, we believe, is a certain opening, a questioning of current trends.

REFERENCES

Abu El-Haj, Nadia 2001 *Facts on the Ground: Archeological Practice and Territorial: Self Fashioning in Israeli Society.* Chicago: University of Chicago Press.
Anderson, Benedict 1983 *Imagined Communities: Reflections on the Origin and Spread of Nationalism.* London: New Left Books.

Befu, Harumi and Kazufumi Manabe 1991 'Ninonjinron: The Discursive Manifestation of Cultural Nationalism.' *Kwansei Gakuin University – Annual Studies* 15: 101–15.

Ben-Ari, Eyal 1991 *Changing Japanese Suburbia: A Study of Two Present-Day Localities*. London: Kegan Paul International.

Ben-Ari, Eyal 1992 'Uniqueness, Typicality and Appraisal: A 'Village of the Past' in Contemporary Japan.' *Ethnos* 57(3–4): 201–18.

Ben-Ari, Eyal 1998 'Globalization, 'Folk Models' of the World Order and National Identity: Japanese Business Expatriates in Singapore.' In Ian Reader and Marie Soderberg eds. *Japan in Asia*. London: Curzon Press. Pp. 51–77.

Bestor, Theodore C 1989 *Neighborhood Tokyo*. Stanford: Stanford University Press.

Buruma, Ian 1994 *Wages of Guilt: Memories of War in Germany and Japan*. London: Jonathan Cape.

Chalk, Alan 2002 'Teaching Pearl Harbor Films, American and Japanese.' *Education about Asia* 7(1): 22–8.

Chang, Iris 1998 *The Rape of Nanking: The Forgotten Holocaust of World War II*. New York: Penguin.

Christ, Carol Ann 2000 'The Sole Guardians of the Art Inheritance of Asia: Japan and China at the 1904 St. Louis World's Fair.' *Positions* 8(3): 675–709.

Eley, Geoff 1997 'Foreword.' In Martin Evans and Ken Lunn eds. *War and Memory in the Twentieth Century*. Oxford: Berg. Pp. vii–xiv.

Evans, Martin and Ken Lunn 1997 'Preface.' In Martin Evans and Ken Lunn eds. *War and Memory in the Twentieth Century*. Oxford: Berg. Pp. xv–xx.

Fine, Gary Alan 2001 *Difficult Reputations: Collective Memories of the Evil, Inept, And Controversial*. Chicago: Chicago University Press.

Fujitani, Takashi 1998 *Splendid Monarchy: Power and Pageantry in Modern Japan*. Berkeley: University of California Press.

Giddens, Anthony 1985 *The Nation-State and Violence*. Cambridge: Polity Press.

Gluck, Carol 1993 'The Past in the Present.' In Andrew Gordon, ed., *Postwar Japan as History*. Berkeley: University of California Press. Pp. 64–95.

Gong, Gerrit W 1984 *The Standard of 'Civilization' in International Society*. Oxford: Clarendon.

Gong, Gerrit 2001a 'The Beginning of History: Remembering and Forgetting as Strategic Issues.' *The Washington Quarterly* 24(2): 45–57.

Gong, Gerrit ed. 2001b *Memory and History in East and Southeast Asia*. Washington D.C.: CSIS (Center for Strategic and International Studies) Significant Issues Series.

Harris, Sheldon H 2002 *Factories of Death: Japanese Biological Warfare, 1932–1945 and the American Cover-Up*. New York: Routledge.

Harootunian, Harry 1999 'Memory, Mourning, and National Morality: Yasukuni Shrine and the Reunion of State and Religion in Postwar Japan.'

In Peter van der Veer and Hartmut Lehmann eds. *Nation and Religion: Perspectives on Europe and Asia*. Princeton: Princeton University Press. Pp. 144–60.

Harootunian, Harry 2000 'Japan's Long Postwar: The Trick of Memory and the Ruse of History.' *The South Atlantic Quarterly* 99(4): 715–39.

Hein, Laura and Mark Selden 1997 'Commemoration and Silence: Fifty Years of Remembering the Bomb in America and Japan.' In Laura Hein and Mark Selden eds. *Living with the Bomb: American and Japanese Cultural Conflicts in the Nuclear Age*. Armonk: M.E. Sharpe. Pp. 3–34.

Hein, Laura and Mark Selden (eds) 2000 *Censoring History: Citizenship and Memory in Japan, Germany, and the United States*. Armonk: M.E. Sharpe.

Igrashi, Yoshikuni 2000 *Bodies of Memory: Narratives of War in Postwar Japanese Culture, 1945–1970*. Princeton: Princeton University Press.

Ivy, Marilyn 1995 *Discourses of the Vanishing: Modernity, Phantasm, Japan*. Chicago: Chicago University Press.

Jackson, Michael 1989 *Paths Toward a Clearing: Radical Empiricism and Ethnographic Inquiry*. Bloomington: Indiana University Press.

Kalland, Arne and Pamela J Asquith 1997 'Japanese Perceptions of Nature: Ideals and Illusions.' In Pamela J. Asquith and Arne Kalland eds. *Japanese Images of Nature: Cultural Perspectives*. London: Curzon. Pp. 1–34.

Keller, Nora Okja 1997 *Comfort Women: A Novel*. New York: Penguin.

Kelly, William 1986 'Rationalization and Nostalgia: Cultural Dynamics of New Middle-Class Japan.' *American Ethnologist* 13: 603–14.

Kurimoto, Eisei 2000 'Nation-State, Empire, and Army: The Case of Meiji Japan.' In Tadao Umesao, Takashi Fujitani, and Eisei Kurimoto eds. *Japaneses Civilization in the Modern World, XVI: Nation-State and Empire*. Osaka: National Museum of Ethnology. Pp. 95–110.

Kushner, Tony 1997 '"I Want to Go On Living My Death": The Memory of Anne Frank.' In Martin Evans and Ken Lunn eds. *War and Memory in the Twentieth Century*. Oxford: Berg. Pp. 3–26.

Maclear, Kyo 1999 *Beclouded Visions: Hiroshima-Nagasaki and the Art of Witness*. Albany: State University of New York Press.

Mehl, Margaret 2000 'History and the Nation in Nineteenth Century Japan and Germany.' In Tadao Umesao, Takashi Fujitani, and Eisei Kurimoto eds. *Japanese Civilization in the Modern World, XVI: Nation-State and Empire*. Osaka: National Museum of Ethnology. Pp. 43–60.

Nussbaum, Stephen P 1985 The Residential Community in Modern Japan: An Analysis of a Tokyo Suburban Development. Ph.D. Dissertation. Cornell University.

Ohnuki-Tierney Emiko 1993. *Rice as Self: Japanese Identities through Time*. Princeton: Princeton University Press.

Olick Jeffrey K. and Joyce Robbins 1998. 'Social Memory Studies: From "Collective Memory" to the Historical Sociology of Mnemonic Practices.' *Annual Review of Sociology* 24: 105–40.

Piper, Nicola 2001. War and Memory: Victim Identity and the Struggle for Compensation in Japan. *War and Society* 19(1): 131–48.

Robertson, Jennifer 1992 *Native and Newcomer: Making and Remaking a Japanese City*. Berkeley: University of California Press.

Robertson, Jennifer 1998 *It Takes a Village: Internationalization and Nostalgia in Postwar Japan*. In Stephen Vlastos ed. *Mirror of Modernity: Invented Traditions of Modern Japan*. Berkeley: University of California Press. Pp. 110–29.

Sahlins, Marshall 1976 *Culture and Practical Reason*. Chicago: Chicago University Press.

Schudson, Michael 1995 'Dynamics of Distortion in Collective Memory.' In Daniel L. Schacter ed. *Memory Distortion: How Minds, Brains, and Societies Reconstruct the Past*. Cambridge, Mass.: Harvard University Press.

Seraphim, Franziska 2003 *Participatory Democracy and Public Memory in Postwar Japan*. *Woodrow Wilson International Center for Scholars*. Asia Program Special Reports No. 109. Pp. 13–7.

Smith, Robert 1974 *Ancestor Worship in Contemporary Japan*. Stanford: Stanford University Press.

Tanaka, Stefan 1993 *Japan's Orient: Rendering Pasts in to History*. Berkeley: University of California Press.

Tilly, Charles ed. 1985 *The Formation of National States in Western Europe*. Princeton: Princeton University Press.

Treat, John Whittier 1995 *Writing Ground Zero: Japanese Literature and the Atomic Bomb*. Chicago: Chicago University Press.

Vlastos, Stephen ed. 1998 *Mirror of Modernity: Invented Traditions of Modern Japan*. Berkeley: University of California Press.

Winter, Jay 2000. 'The Generation of Memory: Reflections on the 'Memory Boom' in Contemporary Historical Studies.' *German Historical Institute Bulletin* 27: 1–13.

Yoneyama, Lisa 1997 'Critical Warps: Facticity, Transformative Knowledge, and Postnationalist Criticism in the Smithsonian Controversy.' *Positions* 5(3): 779–809.

Yoneyama, Lisa 1999 *Hiroshima Traces: Time, Space and the Dialectics of Memory*. Berkeley: University of California Press.

Zelizer, Barbie 1995 'Reading the Past Against the Grain: The Shape of Memory Studies.' *Critical Studies in Mass Communication* 12: 214–39.

PART 1

Remembering the Dead

Monuments for the Untimely Dead or the Objectification of Social Memory in Japan[1]

JAN VAN BREMEN

Truly, people live in colloquies with the dead. (SHINTANI TAKANORI)

For between man and man, and woman and woman was the mediating influence of the dead. And between the gulf that separated each of the dead from each other was the mediating influence of the living.
(MALCOLM LOWRY)

INTRODUCTION

On 2 October 1947, the Netherlands Military Mission in Tokyo addressed a memorandum to the Civil Property Custodian in the General Headquarters of the Supreme Commander for the Allied Powers in Japan, regarding a certain Japanese war painting in which the Netherlands Government was interested, painted by Koiso Ryōhei (1903–88) and entitled 'The Meeting in Kalidjati'. It depicts the meeting that began sometime after four o'clock in the afternoon on 8 March 1942 between the Dutch delegation, headed by the Governor-General of the Dutch East Indies and the Commander-in-Chief of the Dutch East Indies Army, and the Japanese delegation, headed by the Commander and the Chief-of-Staff of the Japanese expeditionary forces, to discuss a cease-fire.[2] The result of the negotiation was the unconditional surrender by Governor-General Tjarda van Starkenborgh Stachouwer and Lieutenant-General H. ter Poorten to General K. Imamura, Commander of the 16th Army, effective as of 9 March 1942.

Koiso drew at least three realistic versions of the scene. One is entitled 'Before the Meeting.' It shows the room in the officer's house, with chairs and table arranged, where the delegations are to meet. In this painting only the Japanese delegation is present, on their side of the table, clearly recognizable, waiting for the Dutch to arrive. A second version shows the room with both parties in it, each on their side of the table, the participants clearly recognizable. The third version shows the meeting, now with the Japanese delegation full face, while the Dutch delegation is harder to recognize, being seen only from the back.

The Diplomatic Section in the General Headquarters of the Supreme Commander for the Allied Powers in Japan acknowledged the Dutch request on 18 November. It answered that 'The ultimate disposition of this and other paintings has not been decided by the Supreme Commander, but the Mission may rest assured that the Netherlands' interests will receive due consideration.' What the Dutch concern over Koiso's painting was remains unclear, but I surmise that the Mission's interest was not unrelated to the sort of questions concerning artifacts and social memory that are the subject of this chapter.

In the General Headquarters of the Supreme Commander for the Allied Powers in Japan, two bodies were active with regard to Japanese works of art between 1946 and 1948. One was the Arts and Monuments Division in the Civil Information and Education Section. The other was the Combat Art Section of the Office of Chief Engineer. Chief Engineer, Major General Hugh J. Casey, wrote in a memorandum of 26 February 1946:

> During the war the Japanese government retained the services of approximately 100 artists to cover military and home front activities pertaining to the prosecution of the war. An unknown number of paintings running over several hundreds were prepared, largely on direct order from Japanese War and Navy Departments.

He ended his message with this observation:

> It is believed in any case in connection with the demilitarization of Japan, all such paintings which glorify Japanese war operations should be secured and taken from the Japanese for destruction or such further disposition as higher authority may indicate, assessing their value as directed by Commander-in-Chief (quoted in Hirase 1999: 6–7; 9).

This remark may have appealed to the Netherlands Military Mission and drawn its attention. It attempted to take possession of Koiso's painting, perhaps in order to hide it from public view, perhaps with the aim to destroy it. The canvas immortalizes a scene that the Dutch authorities would rather forget, if not remove from the records of history altogether. At the time the Dutch government did not like to rekindle in the minds of the people it tried to re-colonize with military force the memory of the surrender of the colonial government to the armed forces of Japan in their country. In the course of the Dutch attempt to retake its former possession, which had declared independence on 17 August 1945, many Indonesians lost their lives, along with Dutch soldiers and soldiers of the former Japanese imperial army, who had deserted after the surrender of Japan to join the inexperienced freedom fighters, a phenomenon seen at the time also in other parts of Southeast Asia, swelling the ranks of the untimely dead.

At least two of Koiso's original compositions survive to this day (2002). The oil painting 'Before the meeting' is conserved in the Hyōgo Prefectural Museum of Art. It was displayed in the Himeji Municipal Museum of Art in the exhibition 'Art and War' (*Bijutsu to sensō*) from 26 May to 10 July 2002, in what was perhaps one of the first post-war exhibitions of wartime art in a public museum.[3] Another drawing by Koiso, also displayed during the exhibition, shows the two delegations face to face, two reporters at the open door in the anteroom. Meantime, a photograph of the artist in his study shows part of an unfinished oil painting depicting the Dutch delegation from the back. The Dutch Military Mission tried in vain to erase this material memory trace of the Dutch surrender but left a trace of its attempt. Wartime art, kept by temples and shrines, museums, government agencies, scholarly and private collectors, is a witness and memory container. Social memory is constituted of events experienced, known, heard and invented by groups of people. It is moored in locations and objects, abilities, knowledge and narratives that are forever vanishing, inescapably erased, ignored and lost.

This chapter explores the relations between artifacts and social memory in Japan, where one finds a large number of monuments built for the untimely dead, people who died in accidents, disasters or wars. Thirty thousand mortuary monuments for the military war dead alone are counted in the isles today. What roles do objects play in social memory, its preservation, construction, falsification, recovery and loss? Studying society and culture through artifacts is a tested method, but if the method is not new, the material dealt with in this chapter is. The uncountable number of monuments commemorating the war dead on the level of the household, the local community, corporate bodies and the nation were largely unstudied until the present in Japan.

THE UNTIMELY DEAD OR THE VICTIMS OF ACCIDENTS, DISASTERS, OR WARS

The meaning of the English word 'untimely' is 'ill-timed, mistimed, inconvenient, inopportune, inappropriate, inapt, awkward, unsuitable, infelicitous, premature, early' (*Concise Oxford Thesaurus*) and thus 'happening or done at an unsuitable time; happening too soon or sooner than normal' (*Concise Oxford Dictionary*). It applies to the recipients of funerary monuments and memorials in Japan who died as conscripts in the wars. 'Untimely death' is not defined by bodily age alone. It is a social rather than biological measure. A family of terms is used to express this kind of death. They include haphazard, coincidental, collateral, blind and chance death. One author uses the term 'fatality' (Awazu 2002). Another speaks of 'interrupted life' (Nakamaki in this volume). Yet another chooses 'abnormal death' (*ijōshi*) as the generic name for untimely death (Tanakamaru 2002). The Japanese language also has the word '*henshi*', meaning an unnatural or violent death. These terms point to a common manner of death. They indicate that the deceased did not die in a way that their families or communities would regard as a 'normal death' (*seijōshi*).[4]

Several categories of dead spirits are distinguished in Japan by laymen and scholars. After one hundred days, the newly dead (*shirei*) become the old dead. The old dead, if properly ritually cared for and guided, after what amounts to a posthumous life course of some three decades, can become the settled ancestral dead (*sorei*) and then ancestors (*senzo*), who will benefit and protect their descendants. The dead spirits who have been forgotten, or not properly remembered, remain unsettled. In that state they are a danger to the living, who may be haunted by their ghosts or vengeful spirits. It is widely thought that 'If the dead are honored, known and recognized, they will differentially, and in terms of structural differences, bestow blessings' (Turner 1992: 34).

Whatever the reasons, memorization of the dead has become an ever more conspicuous feature of Japanese society and culture. Complying with folk models, ethnologists distinguish at least five types of spirits of the dead. Table 1 below sums them up.

Table 1: Categorization of the Dead in Contemporary Japan

Type A	ancestral spirits	example: family ancestors
Type B	abandoned spirits	example: wandering spirits
Type C	evil spirits	example: Kitano Tenjin
Type D	revered spirits	example: Meiji Jingu
Type E	heroic spirits	example: Yasukuni Shrine

These five classes of dead spirits fall into two groups:

Group I	AB	become Buddhas
Group II	CDE	become gods

The two groups receive funerary architecture of a different kind:

Group I	receive mortuary monuments
Group II	receive shrines

Finally the two groups receive rites of a different kind:

Group I	receive requiem rites
Group II	receive prayers and petitions

(Source: Shintani 1999: 23)

Overlap may occur as dead spirits may belong to different categories and more than one class. An 'untimely death' is also a 'bad death.' A sudden, violent and often miserable death produces the most unsettled spirits that need to be placated in order to remove their emitting dangerous and deadly retribution (*tatari*). This belief creates an incongruity regarding the spirits of soldiers who died in action. State ideology declares that they instantly turned into gods on account of this fact. Beliefs hold that the effects of a bad death, and of death as such, need to be removed in the course of a ritual process.

MONUMENTS TO BRAVE SPIRITS AND SOLDIER GODS

Monuments were built to the spirits of the conscripts who died in the wars that the Japanese state fought since the introduction of military conscription in 1873.[5] The wars made deep imprints on society. The untimely death of so many young and adult men left great lacunae in society. They can be read from genealogies on both the micro and the macro level.[6]

The definition of the persons who have died an untimely death in war is not always unequivocal (Kawamura 2002). On the level of the state, the Ministry of Health and Welfare (*Kōseishō*) determines who is or is not included in the mass of the war dead. People are included or excluded according to various standards of discernment.

A basic distinction made among the spirits of the dead is one between those who are forgotten and those who are receiving proper ritual care from kinsmen or members of the social body to which the dead belonged (Tanakamaru 2002: 55; Fig.1). Ritual tribute is paid by families, civic associations, organs of the state, business corporations, educational institutions, religious bodies.

From the Meiji period (1868–1912) onwards the name 'heroic spirits' (*eirei*) came in use as a title bestowed upon the military war dead. The rites, state and civil, centered on the heroic spirits involve artifacts connected to them. These include personal belongings, such as letters, articles of clothing, or military equipment, photographs, bodily remains or substitutes as well as statues, monuments and shrines built to them.[7]

The heroic spirits are regarded as living gods. In Japan the notion of living gods has a long history.[8] The number of living gods begins to expand in the early modern period. It reaches an explosive level with the onset of the industrial period. Concerning the deifying of humans, only a handful of cases were found in the ancient and medieval periods. In the Edo period, the numbers increase and even living people were deified. In the Meiji period, building shrines for the dead and worshiping them almost became a fashion. Well-known examples are the Heian Jingū in Kyōto, the Meiji Jingū for Emperor Meiji, Nogi Jinja for General Nogi Maresuke, and Yasukuni Shrine in Tokyo for the heroic spirits (Boot 2000: 144). The most elevated among the heroic spirits are those who received the name of 'soldier god' (*gunshin*) (Motoyasu 2002: 136). Ethnologists have assigned them to a group of beings called 'living gods' (Miyata 1970).

Monuments to soldiers not intentionally erected for the purpose of worship have become a focus for rites and beliefs. Statues of General Nogi Maresuke (1849–1912), a prominent soldier of Meiji Japan, have been the object of a 'Nogi creed' and rites. In this respect, statues of admiral Tōgō Heihachirō (1847–1934), the commander of the Japanese union squadron that destroyed the Russian Baltic Fleet in the Russo-Japanese War, at Yokosuka and other places in the country, may represent the Navy.

State ideology taught that a soldier's spirit (*jinrei*) instantly turned into a heroic spirit and a god (*kami*) by the act of dying for the country. The beautification of the untimely war dead found its adherents, but many people had their doubts: deification regardless of one's nature and station (Tanakamaru 2002: 193)? The first soldier god to appear in the Russo-Japanese War (1904–5) was Hirose Takeo (1868–1904), the commander of the navy vessel *Fukui-maru*, who met his death in action in the early morning of 27 March 1904. The news was relayed to General Headquarters in Tokyo and reported in the newspaper *Asahi shinbun* on 30 March under the headline: 'The death of Soldier God Hirose'. The newspaper continued its reports on the Hirose case: the recovery of some of his remains; their transportation to Tokyo; the funeral at Aoyama Cemetery on 13 April and the epitaph on the tomb, proclaiming Hirose a 'soldier god'. The emblem 'soldier god' was brought into circulation by the civilian sector, not on the instigation of the armed forces. It was spread by the mass media, and objectified in durable monuments and buildings.

In 1910 a consortium of civilians took the initiative to erect a bronze statue to Hirose. In that year, the government, in the person of the Minister of Education, joined in the memorialization. The tale of Hirose was included in a reader for elementary school pupils and a song composed in his memory included in an elementary school song book. But the interest in soldier god Hirose waned and dwindled until 1933, when the initiative was taken to build a shrine to Hirose in his native city of Takeda in Ōita prefecture. At the shrine's dedication in 1935, Hirose received the posthumous promotion to admiral. The interest in soldier gods was rekindled by the war in China (1937–45, Shintani 2000: 158–161). Every soldier killed in action instantly became a heroic spirit. Still only a few, even among those who died a heroic death, became a soldier god. Civilians played an active role in the beautification of the war dead and their memorialization.

Erecting a statue in the likeness of a person who has died is a practice that goes back before the Meiji period. A statue of the Boddhistva Jizō may have a face chiseled in the features of the dead child or adult for whom it was made. Statues in stone made in the likeness of the war dead may stand alone or in a group. A Chūreiden was built in 1954 in the grounds of a temple in Yamanashi prefecture to house the 49 spirit tablets and wooden busts of the war dead from the parish. The busts are said to resemble the soldiers, made by a sculptor from a photograph. More than 50 years after the war memory is fading. The annual rite for the war dead that used to take place in autumn has been moved to coincide with the celebration of *bon* or All Souls. There is also a nomenclatural collapse of such labels as *'eirei,' 'chūrei,' 'junkoku'* (Iwata 2003: 23–32).

The Japanese attack on Pearl Harbor on 7 December 1941 that started the Pacific War created nine new soldier gods. Chief warrant officer Kamita Sadami is one of them. His exemplary last letter to his parents was widely admired and diffused. What the official record does not retain is the fact that his parents were displeased with his death in service to the country. Upon being told the news and congratulated by the local mayor, they gave as their opinion that they would rather have him alive than a soldier god. That sentiment did not go down well at the time. The knowledge of this act would have been lost from social memory with the death of the last surviving witnesses of the scene in Kamita's home town in Hiroshima prefecture but for the work of a historian who took an interest in the case (Shintani 2000: 164–167).

The civilian actions mentioned above are best understood as requiem rites and attempts to arrest memory rather than as outpourings of pure nationalism. Sadami's urn and photograph have retained their place in the Buddhist house altar of his family and receive daily ritual service in addition to the periodic rites. Every year on Sadami's death day his parents had a Buddhist requiem mass read in a nearby temple. The younger brother who heads the Kamita household has continued that practice, his mother's words echoing in his ears and mind: 'Don't ever forget eldest brother . . .' (Shintani 2000: 166).

MEMORY LOCATIONS FOR THE WAR DEAD

Social groups and institutions authenticate what is remembered or forgotten in their architecture, archives, rites (Douglas 1987). In the civil wars of the nineteenth century in Japan the practice arose to built special shrines called *shōkonsha* for the spirits of the war dead, first in the ranks of the rebellious armies in the Chōshū domain, where they numbered 16 by the time of the Meiji Restoration (1867) (Murakami 2001: 13). Ryōzen Gokoku Jinja was established in Kyōto in the founding year of the Meiji period (1867) as a 'nation protection shrine' (*gokoku jinja*). The 52 new prefectures followed suit and each established a nation protection shrine for the veneration of the war dead from its province. The shrines served, not unlike the *kokubunji* of old, to consolidate the new imperial state.

At the end of the Pacific War in 1945 the number of the Japanese war dead memorialized in the shrines for the war dead had risen to over 2,400,000 souls. The national shrine for the war dead, Yasukuni Shrine, gives these figures beginning with the military dead in the Meiji Restoration (Table 2).

Table 2: War Dead in Yasukuni Shrine by Theatre of War (as of 17 October 2001)

Meiji Restoration	7,751	Satsuma Rebellion	6,971
Sino-Japanese War	13,619	Formosan Expedition	1,130
Boxer Uprising	1,256	Russo-Japanese War	88,429
First World War	4,850	Sainan Incident	185
Manchurian Incident	17,175	China Incident	191,220
Pacific War	2,133,778	Total	2,466,364

(Source: http://www.yasukuni.jp/annai.gaiyou.html)

A note needs be appended to this tally. The count does not represent the total number of the war dead. Two groups of the untimely war dead have been left out of this reckoning. One group is the '*gunpu*,' military porters, camp followers and war service laborers. They numbered hundreds of thousands of Japanese and many more Koreans and Chinese. Many were killed at the front, in accidents, or succumbed to wounds or diseases (Harada 2001: 183–201). The other group consists of the unknown soldiers.

A third group consists of non-Japanese victims of Japanese aggression. There are graves for Chinese victims of the Sino-Japanese War (1894–5) in the first military cemetery in Sanadayama, Ōsaka. The latest graves there date from the 50th anniversary of the end of the Second World War

(1995). A group of monuments on Mt Kōya in 1979 commemorates the war dead of the 'Five Peoples of Manchuria.' In the grounds of Ryōzen Gokoku Jinja stands a Memorial Hall for the World's Unknown Soldiers, including the Allied personnel who perished in territories under Japanese control in the Second World War. A file cabinet contains cards, ordered by nations and states, bearing the names of the Allied personnel commemorated at the site.

The spirits of the war dead enshrined in Yasukuni Shrine are those whose remains, usually partial, could be returned to their relatives or relations. The remains of unknown soldiers who died in the wars cannot be handed over to relatives and cannot be enshrined in Yasukuni Shrine.

So the war dead have received differential treatments. The known dead are recognized as '*hotoke*' and over time can be elevated to the status of an ancestor or find salvation. The unrecovered, forgotten and unknown war dead become '*muen botoke*,' spirits without relatives or relations. Lacking ritual attendance, they remain in this miserable state for a long time if not forever: unemancipated, undelivered and a danger to friend and foe.

After the end of the war in 1945 repatriates brought home the remains of many unknown soldiers and civilians killed in the war. In 1950, the Americans returned to Japan the remains of 4,822 unidentified soldiers from the Philippines. Deputies of a host of committees and agencies have visited the former battlefields to recover and repatriate remains, artifacts, pebbles, soil. Memorials have been built at battle sites at home and abroad. They range from simple to monumental and stand on sites ranging from the sober to the highly commercial.[9]

The Ministry of Health and Welfare collected the unknown remains and housed them in governmental offices. In 1953 the All Japan Society for the Establishment of a Communal Crypt for the Unknown War Dead, in concert with associations of bereaved families from all over the country, began to press the government to erect a national tomb to the unknown soldiers and civilians killed in the war, specifically after September 1937.

Chidorigafuchi was designated in 1956 as the location for this in view of its proximity to Yasukuni Shrine and the Imperial Palace. The memorial garden is laid out on a north-south axis.[10] The Self-Defense Forces Facilities School (*Jieitai Shisetsu Gakkō*) leveled the grounds. Artists and architects designed the garden and buildings, which a number of companies constructed. On 28 July 1958, the cornerstone was laid in the name of the Ministry of Health and Welfare. In 1959, the Foundation for the Public Establishment of a Memorial Garden for the War Dead in Chidorigafuchi (*Chidorigafuchi senbotsusha boen hōshikai*) opened the Chidorigafuchi National Memorial Garden much as it stands today (Gotō 1986: 25–29; Shintani 2000: 161–164).

The National Tomb for the Deceased Servicemen is a large porcelain coffin, measuring 200 x 110 x 90 cm and weighting five metric tons, made of pebbles gathered at the major battle fields. It holds a gold-foiled metal urn, donated by the Emperor, containing ashes symbolic of all the unknown soldiers who lost their lives. The unknown soldiers' tomb is placed above ground, in the center of a hexagonal roofed shrine. The remains of the unidentified war dead are stored in thirty coffins placed in the basement. The ossuary is divided into six rooms holding the remains taken from the different theaters of operation. The total number of the dead memorialized here is 2,123,300 (Table 3).[11]

Table 3: Ossuary Chidorigafuchi National Memorial Garden

Ossuary	Theater of war	Unknown remains entombed
Room No. 1	Japan and environs	239,900
Room No. 2	Manchuria	46,700
Room No. 3	China	521,300
Room No. 4	Philippines	498,600
Room No. 5	South East Asia	230,900
Room No. 6	Pacific, Soviet Union	585,900
Total		2,123,300

(Source: Ossuary Chidorigafuchi National Memorial Garden (27 May 2002))

As the materialization of a symbolic classification of the dead, Yasukuni Shrine houses the spirits of the known war dead, raised to the status of heroic spirits and guardian gods. The Chidorigafuchi National Memorial Garden is the resting place for the remains of the unknown victims, military and civilian, of the Fifteen Years War (1931–45), who belong to the class of lost souls. The first group receives petitions, the second, requiem rites.

The French historian Michel de Certeau calls such spaces set aside for commemoration such as Yasukuni Shrine (for the remains and spirits of the known war dead) and Chidorigafuchi National Memorial Garden Communal Crypt (for the remains and spirits of the unknown war dead), including the buildings and monuments and the rites performed there, 'memory locations' (*lieux de mémoire*). Memory locations are places of commemoration, typically monuments, churches, temples, shrines, museums, built to contain memory accounts and narratives. In Japan, memory locations and objects connected to the untimely dead abound.

MILITARY GRAVES AND CEMETERIES

At the turn of the century, a nation-wide survey, including Manchuria, was made of monuments dedicated to the war dead. In two years, it recorded more than twenty-thousand of the estimated thirty-thousand monuments.[12] The new military cemeteries of the Meiji period were built as civic monuments, free of religious elements if not of state ideology. The gravestones were uniform in height and girth, strictly regulated and different for conscripts and low ranking officers. A soldier received an individual headstone. The funerary monuments for officers were free of restrictions (Harada 2001: 216). Military cemeteries may contain graves of civilian suppliers to the military and of allies or enemies.

The government established 91 military cemeteries between 1873 and 1945, 84 Imperial Army and 7 Imperial Navy cemeteries across the country (Harada 2001: 236–241, Table 18). In August 1897, the War Ministry decreed that Army and Navy personnel were to be *buried* (instead of cremated) in military graveyards. The name 'cemeteries for military use' (*gunyō bochi*) was changed to 'cemeteries for interment' (*maisō bochi*). The result of this policy was that the cemeteries came to house mainly the remains of soldiers who had died in peacetime at nearby barracks, military hospitals or prisons. From afar, bodies could not reach the cemetery in time. The interment order was a part of the government's religious reforms and anti-Buddhist campaigns. Soldiers buried in temporary graves near the front during the Sino-Japanese War were later disinterred and permanently buried in military cemeteries in Japan. The ban on the cremation of the bodies of soldiers was lifted when the anti-Buddhist campaigns came to an end.[13]

As casualty figures mounted to high levels during the Russo-Japanese War, individual graves were increasingly consolidated into mass tombs. This practice continued in the war with China (1937–45) and the Pacific War (1941–5). It spelled the end of individual graves and headstones. The mounting casualty and the protraction of the war also caused the discontinuation of the practice to build monuments for victorious survivors. Two different monuments were built to commemorate the Sino-Japanese War and the Russo-Japanese War. One is to those who lost their lives, the other to those who returned victoriously alive. After the outbreak of war with China in 1931, monuments for survivors of wars and military campaigns were no longer built. The monuments for the dead took on monumental proportions.

MEMORIALS AND CELEBRATIONS FOR THE UNTIMELY WAR DEAD

The civic monuments erected for soldiers who died in the wars with China and Russia are inscribed on stones called '*chūkon no hi*' or 'memorial stone for the loyal war dead'.[14] They are all over the country: in corner of a schoolyard, in shaded and secluded spots in public parks, on temple and shrine grounds (Ōhara 1984: 217). Military cemeteries were not used for the celebration of requiem rites before the Fifteen Years War. They were a place to honor servicemen within the confines of the military. During the Fifteen Year War military cemeteries changed from restricted military sites into centers for public mourning, and became incorporated into civic memorial services. In postwar Japan the requiem rites for the civilian and military dead continued. They were coupled to peace manifestations and solidified in new memorials and monuments, noticeably peace monuments, parks and museums.

In 1938, a movement arose to build a new public monument named '*chūreitō*' in every city, township and village in the country and in places overseas to commemorate the spirits of the war dead. The movement was incorporated a year later as the Greater Japan Association to Honor the Loyal Spirits (*Zaidan Hōjin Dai-Nippon Chūrei Kenshō-kai*) under the auspices of six ministries: the War Office, the Admiralty, the Home Ministry, the Foreign Ministry, the Welfare Ministry and the Department of Overseas Affairs (Harada 2001: 250).

The leading figure in the organization was General Hishikari Takashi (1871–1952). The Association aimed to construct over 500 monuments to the loyal war dead throughout Japan and at the major battle sites where the imperial forces had fought. Hishikari presented his idea in a book entitled *Chūreitō monogatari* (*The Tale of the Memorials to the Loyal Spirits*) published in 1942. The memorials to honor the spirits of the loyal war dead differed from earlier monuments in size and spirit. *Chūreitō* honoring the spirits of the loyal war dead were elaborate ossuaries, massive memorials and monumental structures ranging from 10 to 60 meters in height. By mid-1942, the Association had built 104 of them in Japan and abroad. They were costly to construct. Money was raised in a national campaign under the slogan 'Donate a day to a battle dead' asking people to offer a day's wage to the Association. The purpose of the monuments was to serve as sites for memorial rites conducted or attended by representatives of the citizenry, women's associations and educational institutes (Harada 2001: 227–228).

Responsibility for the military cemeteries, following the abolition of the armed forces in the postwar period, fell to the Ministry of Health and Welfare, and other official and private bodies. To memorialize the untimely dead from their midst, associations preserved and rebuilt war memorials. New memorials were also established as a result of official and private efforts. The memorials take their place in a hierarchy of mourning sites. The national Yasukuni Shrine is followed by the prefectural nation protection shrines which are followed by local war memorials. The memorialization includes journeys to collect soldiers' remains overseas, to construct funerary monuments, to hold mortuary rites at former battle sites, and bestowal of posthumous awards of valor by the central government. Supported by the country's postwar economic might, Japanese organizations built memorials and shrines for the war dead on the sites of battle fields in the Ogasawara Archipelago, the Philippines, Saipan, Papua New Guinea, Burma, Malaysia, Indonesia, Russia and Mongolia.

New ossuaries built to house the remains collected after the war at overseas battlefields range from the local and common to the central and prestigious. A Pagoda Ossuary for the War Dead of the Burma Theater was built in 1980 on Mt Kōya, the headquarters of Shingon Buddhism, one of the most prestigious and efficacious places for funerary architecture in Japan. It is located alongside the pilgrim path that leads to the Inner Sanctuary where the monk Kūkai is believed to have been sitting in meditation for one thousand years awaiting the coming of the next Buddha. Its social base is an association of bereaved families, veterans and supporters formed in 1978 for conducting requiem rites for the remains and the souls of the war dead collected in 1956 and 1975 during expeditions to Burma, India and Thailand.

COMMEMORATION AND PEACE MONUMENTS

After the Greater East Asia and Pacific War, requiem sites for the war dead have also become places to express the wish for lasting peace. Monuments small and large have been built and dedicated to this dual purpose around the country. The Spring for the Repose of the Dead (*Chinkon no Izumi*), set in the compound of Miyagi prefecture's Gokoku Jinja in the city of Sendai, is such a monument. It is dedicated to maintaining the postwar peace and prosperity of the country and to lending repose to the souls of the 56,000 soldiers from the prefecture who have lost their lives on foreign battlefields. Running water washes over the monument built with stones and materials taken from the parish shrines where prayers for victory and good luck in battle used to be said, and from the battlefields where men from Miyagi lost their lives: Guadalcanal, Guam, Saipan, China, Burma, the Kurile Islands, etc. The monument was dedicated on 15 August 1995, the 50th anniversary of the end of the war.

New memory locations for the victims of wars and the wish for peace are the postwar peace museums, now found in some 25 locations in Japan. From 1955 to 1980, there were only seven. The three biggest and best-known ones were in Hiroshima, Nagasaki and Okinawa. Four smaller ones were the Mutsu Memorial Museum in Yamaguchi, the War Memorial Museum for Drafted Soldiers in Fukuoka, the Sōka Gakkai Toda Memorial Peace Museum in Yokohama, and the Tokyo Metropolitan Daigo Fukuryū-maru Museum.

The number of peace museums doubled to 15 in the 1980s. In the first half of the 1990s, it rose to 24, and stands at over 100 today (2003). The steep rise came about as a result of the commemoration of the 50th anniversary of the end of the Second World War. Peace Ōsaka, built on the edge of the grounds of Ōsaka Castle and opened in 1991, is a representative example (De Back 2002). Peace museums memorialize the untimely dead at the home front as much as the soldiers who died in battle.

The Shōwa-kan, located near Yasukuni Shrine, the Chidorigafuchi National Memorial Garden and the Imperial Palace in Tokyo, is one of the newest. The museum was established on the initiative of the Japanese Association of Bereaved Families (Nihon Izokukai[15]) with the support of the Ministry of Health and Welfare. Planning began in 1979, and the museum opened on 27 March 1999. It preserves items used during the war to heighten the fighting power of the soldiers, such as 'one thousand stitches belts' that were offered to soldiers as protective amulets. The purpose of the museum is to show life during and after the war for the benefit and edification of the postwar generations.[16]

The 50th anniversary of the end of the Greater East Asia and Pacific War in 1995 was commemorated in a number of special exhibitions organized by prefectural or metropolitan museums in former garrison towns in Japan. The Sendai Museum of History and Folklore organized two exhibitions. 'The Life of the People during the War' was shown from 29 July to 28 October 2001. 'The Life of the People During WWII' was opened from 20 July to 15 September 2002.[17] The Nagoya Municipal Museum held an exhibition on wartime life in Japan. The Ishikawa Prefecture History Museum staged the exhibition 'The People at the Home Front – Life and Prayers' from 29 July to 27 August 1995. The first postwar exhibition of works of art created during the war opened in the Himeji Municipal Museum of Art from 26 May to 10 July 2002. These exhibitions focus on life in the army, at the front, and at the home front. The exhibits are photographs, films, publications, sound recordings, documents, artifacts and works of art from the war periods. The institutions are large memory containers and centers of collection, preservation, and research. In addition to museums and academic collections, war items are kept by religious institutions and in private collections.

Citizens' groups have taken initiatives to preserve local narratives and records of the wars to commemorate those concerned and edify later generations. An example is the set of publications issued by a group formed to record the experiences of wartime life in the city of Odawara based on local testimonies and documents (Iida et al. 2000). Associations of bereaved families have built memorials for the untimely dead from their midst in their care. With the help of the latest technology they constructed a virtual Monument for Those Who Died for Their Country (*Junkoku no Ishibumi*), which is accessible at its website. Material monuments continue to be built. The Association of Bereaved Families of the Itō District in Wakayama prefecture, a district bordering on Nara prefecture and the Ōsaka Metropolitan Area, erected a sober but costly monument in 1997 in the new cemetery on Mt Kōya. It lists – chiseled into the surface of slabs of grey stone – by place of origin and name, the military war dead from the district. The memorial was dedicated as a Foundation Stone for Peace (*Heiwa no Ishizue*). It represents a new class of monuments that link memorialization of the war dead and prayer for life in peace (Yakabi 2002).[18]

The chronicles of the stones: artifacts as memory containers and erasers of history have an interdependent relationship. Generations are ceaselessly facing impermanence in a social world suspended between the past and the present, between presence and absence, located at a point that both is and is not here (Ivy 1995: 20). Social memory consists of acts of memorialization and re-memorialization in objects, accounts and narratives, and the re-enactment of the past in rites or ceremonies important for the constitution of a social group in the present. 'It would be comforting to think of memory as a simple record . . . as fragments of preserved reality, sometimes more and sometimes less complete, but reflecting, as far as they went, a true image of what used to be. Of course, it is nothing of the kind: it is an artifact and a trickster, and an active trickster at that, nor merely a relic of the past, but the past shaped and adapted to the uses of the present – and of the present then as well as the present now.' (R.I. Moore in Fentress and Wickham 1992: viii). The social meaning of memory is little affected by its truth. It is selective, distorted, and inaccurate, and can be exact. The transmission of factual information is only one of the functions that social memory performs.

Social memories are kept in material forms. Funerary architecture and war memorials commemorate events that began in the past and reach into the present. Specific objects can be gathered in collections informally as memorabilia or formally in museums to convey a sense of collective identity. Objects which are specially made for the purpose of social memory receive a special form and location and often bear a text or inscription. They are installed in order that a person, a group, an event, an activity, or a principle be remembered, or even commemorated in the future. These objects serve as 'condensed symbols' and play a role in maintaining and changing social memory. The status of objects as things for remembering is a matter of social definition, framing some artifacts as mementos, others as of historic interest, yet others in such a way that they remain merely functional. It brings into focus the difference between objects as functional parts of the world and as special items by which humans remember.[19]

People collectively constitute and function as integrated memory systems. One aspect of joint recall is the social practice of commemoration to recall and celebrate events and persons that are part of a jointly acknowledged generational and cultural identity and common understanding. Some disasters or accidents that befall people have become an integral part of collective folk memory. In other cases, they have been forgotten. In his book on social memory of 1952, *Les Cadres Sociaux de la Mémoire,* the French sociologist Maurice Halbwachs distinguished between history and memory. Not all scholars hold to this distinction today but at their peril. In popular memory events are often misunderstood and distorted. A good example is the folk myth that the builders and owners of the ill-fated *Titanic* claimed that their ship was unsinkable. This apparently was not true (Coates and Morrision 1991: note 7, p.82).

But if some groups sustain social memory others fail to build it. A nautical disaster that goes unremembered was the *Princess Sophia*, a ship owned by a subsidiary of the Canadian Pacific Railway Company, operated during the First World War (1914–18), carrying passengers and freight on the inside passage route between Vancouver and Skagway, Alaska. In late October 1918, at the height of one of the largest out-migrations from the Yukon River valley since the end of the Klondike gold rush of 1897–8, it left Skagway, ran aground on Vanderbilt Reef in the Lynn Canal about 20 miles north of Juneau, and after 40 hours on the rocks, sank in a driving blizzard. All 353 passengers and crew on board died in what was acknowledged to be the worst maritime disaster in the history of the Pacific Northwest. Eight percent or more of the white population of the Yukon Territory died that October evening. There are no fewer than five memorials to the crew of the *Titanic*, a well-remembered nautical disaster, in Southampton, England, where many of them lived. There are no memorials anywhere to the victims of the *Princess Sophia* except for the tombstones of those whose bodies were recovered. The transient nature of the community in the far northwest meant that the disaster was largely forgotten and its significance lost to the region (Coates and Morrison 1991: 72; 79; 83).

In Japan, people retain instruments of remembrance for their dead: spirit tablets, gravestones, and registers of death days (Yano 1993). What is their value as memory retainers of condensed objects such as these? Artifacts can contain, retain, erase, or falsify memories. A series of poems by the Illinois lawyer and poet Edgar Lee Masters, *Spoon River Anthology,* that gives voice to 214 small-town dead and living characters interlocked by fate, was a *succès de scandale* on account of the fact that personal memory does not always square with public memory. Richard Bone, the stone mason of the town, says of the funerary monuments that he made:

> When I first came to Spoon River
> I did not know whether what they told me
> Was true or false.
> . . .
> And I chiseled for them whatever they wished,
> All in ignorance of its truth.
> But later, as I lived among the people here,
> I knew how near to the life

Were the epitaphs that were ordered for them as they died.
But still I chiseled whatever they paid me to chisel
And made myself party to the false chronicles
Of the stones,
Even as the historian does who writes
Without knowing the truth,
Or because he is influenced to hide it.
(From the *Collier Classics*, 1962 edition, p.189)

The poem warns to approach with care objects of social memory.
A Japanese pioneer who studied the working of social memory along the lines later taken by Pierre Nora (1992) was the architect, folklorist and urban ethnographer Kon Wajirō (1888–1973). When studying the aftermath of the Great Kantō Earthquake of 1923, he created a new discipline in the 1920s and 1930s that he named '*kōgengaku*' or the study of things and life in the present, in contrast to archaeology '*kōkogaku*,' the study of old things and remnants. Kon translated his term as 'modernologio' or 'modernology' (Kon 1986). It speaks against the orientations of the folklorists of the day, who tried to find and conserve surviving traces and residual practices of folk life, which were thought to contain, preserve and transmit timeless custom, as an act of memorialization. Kon described the present, creating a storehouse of memory for the future based on the experience of the present rather than to communicate the memory of the past (Harootunian 2000: 128). Kon sought, observed, recorded and collected data from people who could recall the lived experience at the moment it was occurring. The method is a minute documentation of daily life and its material culture. The social and material bodies construct, maintain, change, loose or destroy social memory anchored in material objects and ritual practices that constitute with narratives, the collective representations born of a social existence interlocked by fate.

REFERENCES

Awazu Kenta, 2001 Kindai Nihon nashonarizumu ni okeru hyōshō no henyō: Saitama ken ni okeru senbotsusha-hi kensetsu katei o tōshite. *Soshiorojika* v. 26, no.1–2: 1–33.

Awazu, Kenta, 2002 War Memorial in Modern Japanese Context: The Transformation of Nationalistic Representation. In Klaus Antoni, et al. (eds), *Religion and National Identity in the Japanese Context*, pp.37–49. Münster: Lit Verlag.

Boot, WJ, 2000 The Death of a Shogun: Deification in Early Modern Japan. In John Breen and Mark Teeuwen (eds), *Shinto in History: Ways of the Kami*, pp.144–166. Surrey: Curzon Press.

Bremen, Jan van, 2002 Bridging the Demographic Divide: Afterlives and Niches for the Dead in Japan. In A. Klein, R. Lützeler, & D. Ölschleger (eds),

Modernization in Progress: Demographic Development and Value Change in Contemporary Europe and East Asia. Japan Archiv, Band 4, pp.309–336. Bonn: Bier'sche Verlagsanstalt.

Brocades Zaalberg, JK, 1991 De foto's van de overgave in Kalidjati. *Mars et Historia* 25(6): 235238.

Coates, KS and WR Morrison, 1991 Towards a Methodology of Disasters: The Case of the *Princess Sophia.* In Ray B. Browne and Pat Browne (Eds), *Digging into Popular Culture: Theories and Methodologies in Archeology, Anthropology and Other Fields,* pp.71–83. Bowling Green, Ohio: Bowling Green State University Popular Press.

De Back, Tycho Thamar, 2002 Het verleden voorgesteld. Een onderzoek naar een modern vredesmuseum in Osaka. Unpublished M.A. thesis. Center for Japanese and Korean Studies. Leiden University.

Douglas, Mary, 1987 *How Institutions Think.* London: Routledge & Kegan Paul.

Endō, Jun, 1998 The Shinto Funeral Movement in Early Modern and Modern Japan. Translated by Norman Havens. *Transactions of the Institute for Japanese Culture and Classics* 82: 312–282.

Fentress, James and Chris Wickham, 1992 *Social memory.* Oxford: Blackwell.

Fujii Tadatoshi and Arai Katsuhiro eds, 2000 *Jinrui ni totte tatakai to wa, 3. Tatakai toe minshū.* Tokyo: Tōyō shorin.

Fukuta Ajio et al. eds, 1999–2000 *Nihon minzoku daijiten.* 2 volumes. Tokyo: Yoshikawa Kōbunkan.

Fujitani, Takashi, Geoffrey M. White, Lisa Yoneyama eds, 2000 *Perilous memories: The Asia-Pacific War(s).* Durham, N.C.: Duke University Press.

Gotō Fumitoshi, 1986 *Yasukuni shinkō to Nihonjin.* Tokyo: Human document sha.

Halbwachs Maurice, 1952 *Les Cadres Sociaux de la Mémoire.* Paris: Presses Uniersitaires de France.

Harada Keiichi, 2001 *Kokumingun no shinwa: Heishi ni naru to iu koto.* Tokyo: Yoshikawa Kōbunkan.

Harada Keiichi, 2002 Dare ga tsuitō dekiru no ka: Yasukuni jinja to senbotsusha tsuitō. *Studies in War Responsibilities* 36: 2–9.

Harootunian, Harry D, 2000 History's Disquiet: Modernity, Cultural practice, and the Question of Everyday Life. *The Wellek Library Lecture Series at the University of California, Irvine.* New York: Columbia University Press.

Hirase Reitai, 1999 *Bulletin of Himeji Municipal Museum of Art* no.3. Himeiji: Himeji Municipal Museum of Art.

Hishikari Takashi, 1942 *Chūreitō monogatari.* Tokyo: Dōwa shunjū sha.

Howell, David L, 2003 Visiting War Memorials in Saipan. *Nichibunken Newsletter* 51: 5–6.

Iida Akiko et al., 2002 *Shimin ga kataru Odawara chihō no sensō.* Odawara: Senjika no Odawara chihō o kiroku suru kai.

Ivy, Marilyn, 1995 *Discourses of the Vanishing: Modernity, Phantasm, Japan.* Chicago: Chicago University Press.

Iwata Shigenori, 2003 *Senshisha reikon no yukue: sensō to minzoku.* Tokyo: Yoshikawa Kōbunkan.

Jūgo no hitobito: inori to kurashi. Ishikawa Prefectural History Museum, 1995.

Kingendai no sensō ni kan suru kinenhi: hibunkenshiryō no kisoteki kenkyū hōkokusho. Kokuritsu rekishi minzoku hakubutsukan, 2003.

Kawamura Kunimitsu, 2002 Senbotsusha to wa dare ka: shinpojiumu 'senbotsusha no yukue' e mukete. *Nihon Gakuhō* 21:1–10.

Kitamura Riko, 1999 *Chōhei: sensō to minshū.* Tokyo: Yoshikawa Kōbunkan.

Kon Wajirō, 1986 Kōgengaku. In *Kon Wajirō shū*, vol. 1, pp.53–108. Tokyo: Domesu.

Lowry, Malcolm, 1969 (1953) Strange Comfort Afforded by the Profession. In *Hear us O Lord from heaven they dwelling place*, pp.99–113. London & New York: Penguin Books.

Lowry, Malcolm, 1972 [1962] *Dark as the Grave Wherein My Friend is Laid.* London & New York: Penguin Books.

Maschio, Thomas, 1994 *To Remember the Faces of the Dead: The Plenitude of Memory in Southwestern New Britain.* Wisconsin: University of Wisconsin Press.

Masters, Edgar Lee, 1955 *Spoon River Anthology.* New York : Macmillan.

Miyata Noboru, 1970. *Ikigami shinkō: hito o kami ni matsuru shūzoku.* Tokyo: Banshobō.

Miyata Noboru, 1996 *Minzoku Shintō ron: minkanshinkō no dainamizumu.* Tokyo: Shunjūsha.

Motoyasu, Hiroshi, 2002 *Gunto no irei kūkan: kokumin tōgō to shisha tachi.* Tokyo: Yoshikawa Kōbunkan.

Murakami Shigeyoshi, 2001[1974] *Irei to shōkon:Yasukuni no shisō.* Tokyo: Iwanami.

Nora, Pierre, 1992 *Realms of Memory: Rethinking the French Past.* New York: Columbia University Press.

Ōhara Yasuo, 1984 *Chūkonhi no kenkyū.* Tokyo: Akatsuki shobō.

Radley, Alan, 1990 Artifacts, Memory and a Sense of the Past. In David Middleton and Derek Edwards (Eds), *Collective Remembering*, pp.46–59. London: Sage.

Satō Masaya, 2001 *Sensō to shomin no kurashi.* Sendai: Sendai Municipal Museum of History and Folklore.

Satō Masaya, 2002 *Sensō to shomin no kurashi 2.* Sendai: Sendai Municipal Museum of History and Folklore.

Shintani Takanori ed., 1999 *Shigo no kankyō: Takai e no junbi to haka.* Kyoto: Shōwadō.

Shintani, Takanori, 2000 Irei to gunshin. In Fujii Tadatoshi and Arai Katsuhiro eds. *Jinrui ni totte tatakai to wa*, vol.3, *Tatakai to minshū*, pp.147–169. Tokyo: Tōyō shorin.

Tanakamaru Katsuhiko, 2000 *Samayoeru eirei tachi: kuni no mitama ie no hotoke.* Tokyo: Kashiwa shobō.

Turner, Victor, 1992 [1975] Death and the dead in the pilgrimage process. In

Edith Turner ed., *Blazing the Trail: Way Marks in the Exploration of Symbols / Victor Witter Turner*. Pp.29–47; 167–173. Tucson and London: University of Arizona Press.

Yakabi, Osamu, 2002 'Foundation Stones for Peace' and Memorials to the War Dead. *Studies in War Responsibilities* 36: 19–27.

Yano Keiichi, 1993 Shisha no kioku sōchi: ihai, haka, kakochō. *Shakai Minzoku kenkyū* 3: 31–67.

Yano Keiichi, 2000 Kioku to senzō kannen. *Nihon Minzokugaku* 223: 1–33.

Yokoyama Atsuo, 2001 *Senjika no shakai: Ōsaka no itosumi kara*. Tokyo: Iwata Shoin.

Zimmermann, Francis, 1989 *Le discours des remèdes au pays des épices : enquête sur la médecine hindoue*. Paris : Payot.

Internet source:
http://www.yasukuni.jp/annai.gaiyou.html

NOTES

[1] Earlier versions of this chapter were read in the conference 'Monuments and Memory Making in Japan' in the Department of Japanese Studies, National University of Singapore, 8–10 July 2002, and in the Institute for Research in Humanities, Kyōto University on 26 July 2002. A visiting researcher from February to July 2002, the author is deeply indebted to the Institute for Research in Humanities, in particular to Dr. Masakazu Tanaka, for the hospitality and help he received. The chapter has benefited greatly from this stay, the advice and help of leading researchers of wartime life and war commemoration in Japan. Everyone is thanked here.

[2] It is not completely clear who the members of the two delegations were. For research on the Dutch delegation see Brocades Zaalberg (1991). I should like to thank dr. J.A. de Moor of the Institute for Military History, Royal Netherlands Army for the generous assistance received.

[3] A reproduction of the picture is seen on the cover of the catalog. A larger image with an explanation appears on p.14 as exhibit no.10.

[4] An enlightening treatment on the merits of polytheistic classification in the context of Hindu medicine was written by Francis Zimmermann (1989: 145–150).

[5] Memorials and rites for people who died an untimely death as a result of a disaster, accident, or illness are the subject of current research and another paper by the author (van Bremen 1998).

[6] Jane Bachnik, 'Remembrances of Wartime Experiences in a Community in Nagano Prefecture, Japan,' seminar given at the Centre for Japanese and Korean Studies, Leiden University, 17 October 2002.

[7] See Miyata's (1996: 209–231 [orig. 1992]) brief exposition on the relationships believed to exist between objects and spirits in Japan.

[8] See Miyata's (1970; 1996:150–176 [orig. 1974]) early treatise on humans worshipped as gods in Japan.

9 A visitor 'was struck by the contrast between the high level of commer-
   cialization in Okinawa and the lack of it in Saipan' (Howell 2003: 6).

10 Yasukuni Shrine is laid out on an East-West axis. What is the significance
   of these different orientations, if any, when seen from the viewpoint of
   directional symbolism? The main pathway of the Cornerstone of Peace
   Heiwa no Ishisue is laid out in the direction of the morning sun on 23 June
   the day when the battle for Okinawa ended.

11 Graves or memorials housing only a tiny part, or even a substitute, of
   remains of a person are commonly found in Japan. A person may have
   several graves or memorial locations, perhaps widely dispersed, in this
   way.

12 The figure was arrived at in a two-year survey (2000/1) published in a
   detailed report, *Kingendai no sensō ni kan suru kinenhi*, by the National
   Museum of Japanese History in March 2003. I should like to thank Awazu
   Kenta for obtaining my copy.

13 Shinto burials can be seen as a product of the Meiji reforms but the movement for Shinto funerals goes back to the early modern period (Endō
   1998).

14 *Kōjien* defines *Chūkon* as the 'spirits of persons who died paying the utmost
   in loyalty' (*chūgi wo tsukushite shinda hito no tamashii*).

15 The Nihon Izokukai was established to lobby the state on behalf of the
   financial interests of the children and family members of soldiers lost in
   the war.

16 I should like to thank Kerry Smith, Department of History, Brown
   University, for a copy of his manuscript: 'The Shōwa Hall: Memorializing
   Japan's War at Home' (23 pp., n.d.).

17 I should like to thank Mr. Masaya Satō, compiler and author, for copies of
   the catalogue.

18 Memorials to the civilian war dead, and victims of other disasters, are
   found throughout Japan. They are the subject of a different paper (van
   Bremen 2002).

19 This paragraph is indebted, much of it verbatim, to Radley (1990).

Memorial Monuments of Interrupted Lives in Modern Japan: From *Ex Post Facto* Treatment to Intensification Devices

HIROCHIKA NAKAMAKI

INTRODUCTION

Some people die of old age and some are killed in traffic accidents. The former die a natural death while the latter have their lives interrupted for some 'unnatural' reasons. Here an 'interrupted life' means death. According to Buddhism, this type of death falls in the category of unnatural death, i.e. 'disaccording with karma' (*higō no shi*). In other words, this category does not include deaths due to one's deeds in previous lives, but refers to cases where life is terminated by unexpected happenings. Interrupted lives include not only death in traffic accidents but also death from sickness, in battle and in a broad sense, by abortion as well. Talacot Parsons et al. (1972) classify premature death into two types: an impersonal occurrence or an intentional deed. Sickness and accidents belong to the former category and violence to the latter. In any case, it is natural that people should have a special feeling toward an interrupted life. The problem is how to express such a special feeling socially – how to behave – and how to adjust to it psychologically. This paper analyzes 'premature deaths' from the viewpoint of devices.

What special devices are made for those whose lives have been interrupted? How are people required to behave toward the dead in this category? Generally, a memorial monument is erected for the repose of the dead person, and memorial service is held regularly and on special occasions. People offer their condolences to the dead who were unable to complete their anticipated course of life. Mourners wish to show sympathy for the bereaved families, and they may thus be able to reduce any feelings of guilt they may have.

The subject of a memorial service or a service for the repose of a soul is not limited to humans. It is a popular custom in Japan to recognize the terminated lives of animals and even inanimate objects and to hold memorial services for them. The Japanese word for 'memorial service' (*kuyō*) is a Chinese word translated from the Sanskrit word *puja* or *pujana*. Originating in ritual conduct based on Buddhist thought, it signifies offerings to Buddhist priests or to the souls of the dead. The Japanese term is sometimes translated as 'spiritual nourishment' in English. Although *kuyō* is of Buddhist origin, in Japan the object of such memorial services is extended to trees, plants, insects and fish, and it becomes very much like animism.

In Japan the idea of a memorial service, which is Buddhist and animistic, is evident in various monuments and pagodas in the street. It is worthy of notice that most of them are related to interrupted lives. The National Museum of Ethnology, Japan, once conducted a two-year nationwide survey regarding various types of memorial monuments. Researchers collected data on their own standard, i.e. there were no restrictions as to the definition of memorial monument. Nor was there any obligation to cover certain topics, regionally or historically. They reported some 550 monuments in the museum's reports on 'cultural materials in Japan' (Kokuritsu 1999, 2001). It was striking that more than half of the monuments concern interrupted lives. Based on these reports, I will describe some of the characteristics of memorial monuments.

MEMORIAL MONUMENTS AS *EX POST FACTO* TREATMENT DEVICES

Looking at memorial monuments from the viewpoint of devices, we can identify their basic characteristics as *ex post facto* treatment devices for death. Especially in the sense of a social *ex post facto* treatment toward interrupted lives, memorial monuments play a role in acknowledging death socially and producing collective memory. In other words, erection of a memorial monument is a method of social cognition, and it functions as a device for the transmission of memories.

The reported cases fall roughly into three categories: (1) memorials for humans; (2) memorials for animals and plants; and (3) memorials for disposed items. There are also cases of memorials for relics, but their relationship with interrupted life is weak.[1] Within the category of memorials for humans, monuments built in memory of the war dead by social groups are the greatest in number. These are followed by monuments built by vocational groups for those who died in service or in the line of duty. Ranked third are those for victims of disasters. In the case of memorials for animals and plants, those for animals outnumber those for plants. Individually, memorials for horses rank first in number, and cattle and dolphins come second and third. Memorial services for disposed items were conventionally conducted for certain vessels and tools (Matsuzaki 1996: 23–32, Tanaka 1987:1–9). From the viewpoint of interrupted life, I use the word 'disposed' to indicate otherwise useful items that were discarded or went into disuse at some point during their normal 'lifespan.' Among disposed items, burial mounds dedicated to writing-brushes are the most common. I will now describe each category of memorials in detail.

1. Varieties of the Memorials for Humans

Remarkable among memorials for humans are those for warriors who have died an unnatural and non-karmic death. Old memorial monuments include Jūsan-zuka ('Thirteen Burial Mounds'), which was erected (date unknown) for the worship of fugitives from the Heike clan who lost a battle against the Genji clan, and Rishō-tō (tower of receiving graces from Buddha), built in 1344, which honors Emperor Godaigo and his fallen soldiers. As for more recent examples, many memorial monuments for the Second World War suicide squads (*tokkōtai*) exist in Chiran Town, Kagoshima Prefecture, including the following:

- Peace *Kannon* (Goddess of Mercy) for the Repose of the Souls of Suicide Squads (1955).
- Memorial Monument for the Repose of the Souls of Young Air Conscripts (1975).
- Mother of a Suicide Attacker and Memorial Monument: Torihama Tome (1986).
- Memorial Monument Inscribed with a Song for the Repose of the Souls of Suicide Attackers (1988).
- Memorial Lantern for the Repose of the Souls of Suicide Attackers (1988).
- *Ari-rang* Memorial Monument (1999, Kagoshima).
- Monument of Wailing and Oath. For 11 suicide attackers who came from the Korean Peninsula, (2000).
- Monument Dedicated to a Firefly. A soldier left a message saying that he would come back as a firefly on *bon* (2002).

Next is a list of major memorial monuments for the war dead since the Meiji period in chronological order:

- Hekiketsu Monument ('Green Blood' Monument) (1975, Hokkaidō). For the war dead of the Tokugawa Shogunate army in the Battle of Hakodate (1868–1869).

- Memorial Monument Dedicated to the Colonial Troops (1878, Hokkaidō). For the colonial soldiers (*tondenhei*) who were killed in the Satsuma Rebellion (1877).
- Boshin Battle Monument (1880, Tochigi Pref.). For the Tokugawa Shogunate soldiers who were killed in the Battle of Boshin (1868).
- Monument Dedicated to Brave Warriors (1906, Toyama Pref.). For the local war dead who were killed in the Russo-Japanese War (1904–5).
- Monument Commemorating the Joint Funeral of the War Dead and Those Who Died from Diseases Contracted at the Front during the Russo-Japanese War in 1904–5 (1907, Kagawa Pref.).
- Tomb for the Joint Funeral of the Officers and Soldiers Killed in the Manchurian Incident (1933, Kagawa Pref.). The Manchurian Incident (1931).
- Tomb of the Dead from the China Incident and World War II (1949, Kagawa Pref.).
- Monument Dedicated to the Dead from the Battle of Boshin (1954, Tochigi Pref.). Battle of Boshin (1868).
- Monument Dedicated to the Spirits of the Heroes Killed in the Battle of Okinawa at the End of the Second World War (1965, Hokkaidō). Erected by the war bereaved.
- Monument Dedicated to the Departed Spirits in Nomonhan (1967, Hokkaidō).
- Tower of Comrades in and around New Guinea (1967, Kōchi Pref.).
- Monument Dedicated to the Heroes who Died for Honor on Attu Island (1968, Hokkaidō).
- Memorial Monument Dedicated to the Three Wrecked Ships and Memorial Monument Dedicated to the War Dead in the Second World War (1968, Hokkaidō).
- Memorial Monument Dedicated to the War Dead in Burma (1977, Nagano Pref.).
- Tower Dedicated to the War Dead and Comrades who Fought in the Philippines (1977, Kōchi Pref.).
- Statue of Mother (1980, Kagawa Pref.): Mother on the home front.
- Memorial Monument Dedicated to the Detainees who Died in Manchuria, Mongolia and Siberia (1985, Kōchi Pref.).
- Monument Dedicated to the Repose of the Imperial Navy Destroyer *Tachibana* (1981, Hokkaidō).

There are also reports of memorials for people who have died in the line of duty:

- Memorial Monument Dedicated to Heroes from Satsuma (1920, Kagoshima Pref.). For the casualties of the flood prevention works of Kiso River.

- Monument Dedicated to Policemen Who Died on Duty in Kochi Prefecture (1927, Kōchi Pref.).
- Monument Dedicated to Communications Workers Who Died on Duty (1930, Hokkaidō). Erected by the Union of Third-Grade Postmasters.
- Monument Dedicated to Postmen, Policemen and Fire Fighters Who Died on Duty (1937, Kagawa Pref.).
- Monument Dedicated to the Settlers Who Died in Manchuria (1956, Kōchi Pref.).
- Memorial Monument (1928, rebuilt in 1958, Hokkaidō). Scaffolding work.
- Memorial Monument Dedicated to Koreans Who Died on Duty (1960, Hokkaidō). For the Korean people who were forced to work at coal mines.
- Ōte *Kannon* (Goddess of Mercy) (1964, Fukui Pref.). For the telephone operators who died on duty in the air raids in 1945.
- Memorial Monument Dedicated to Unknown Settlers in Hokkaidō (1985, Hokkaidō). In Daijōin Yakuōji Temple.

As for disasters, there are many memorials for those who died of hunger in the Edo period. They are especially found in various places in Iwate Prefecture. However, there is no report of such memorials from the Meiji period:

- Memorial Tower Dedicated to Those Who Died of Epidemics and Hunger in the Famine in 1783 and 1784, Regardless of Whether They Left Behind Those to Attend Their Graves (1976, Iwate Pref.).
- Memorial Tower Dedicated to Those Who Died of Hunger and Epidemics (1805, Iwate Pref.).
- Memorial Tower of Famine in the Tenpō era (1844, Fukui Pref.).
- Memorial Tower of Death by Starvation (1855, Iwate Pref.).

Besides, there are memorials for the victims of natural disasters such as *tsunami* (tidal wave), earthquakes, lightning storms, and avalanches:

- Monument of *Tsunami* in the Kanpō Period (1941, Hokkaidō). Caused by the eruption of Ōshima.
- Memorial Monument Dedicated to the School Children (1956, Fukui Pref.) who were Killed: the Fukui Earthquake.
- Stone Buddhist Image in the Form of a Salt Vendor (year unknown, Kagawa Pref.). A salt vendor was killed by lightning.
- Memorial Monument (1936, Fukui Pref.). Dedicated to the repose of the railway workers who died during their snow-removing work in 1936.

As an example of an animal-related disaster, there is a case of bear-hazard.

- Monument in Memory of Bear Attack (1977, Hokkaidō). Bear hazard in Tomamae Town.

As for human-caused disasters, there is the following case of a fire.

- Tower in Memory of Severe Damage Caused by a Major Fire in March, 1934 (1938, Hokkaidō). Fire in Hakodate.

Although memorials for humans cover a wide range, only a few such cases are reported outside of war, death in the line of duty, or natural disaster. This, however, does not necessarily mean that memorial monuments of that sort are small in number. For example, only one memorial for children is reported. A Jizō of Pregnant Women (1855, Toyama Pref.) was built by a wealthy merchant who had lost his daughter and grandchild due to hard labor. But I presume that not a few images of Jizō must have been built to mourn the souls of the children who drowned or died in traffic accidents. The two-volume *Research Reports* contains no description of the erection of Jizō and Kannon statutes and towers in memory of aborted fetuses – a practice that has become popular since the 1970s. This example shows that there is a disparity between reality and the reports.

One interesting thing about the reports is that the cases reveal special characteristics according to time and region. First of all, the following cases are reported as examples of life interrupted by executions in the Edo period.

- Tomb of Tamao, Secretarial Clerk, and Gondayū (1863, Kagawa Pref.). They sued Kongōin for the management of Konpira Shrine, but lost the case and were executed. The tomb was erected 200 years later for fear of a curse by the executed.
- Jizō Images of Nanaine (1858, Ishikawa Pref.). Dedicated to the seven principal architects who were put to death because they led a movement to demand rice in 1848.
- Memorial Monument Dedicated to the Victims of the 'Bagworm Riot' (1936, Fukui Pref.). A peasant uprising.

We should not overlook love-suicides in the Edo period:

- Memorial Tower of Hiyokuzuka (Edo period, Gunma Pref.). The tower was erected for the repose of the lovers who drowned in a flood while eloping.
- Mound of a Lovers' Suicide at Sawatamagawa River (about 1989,

Fukui Pref.). The play 'Suicide at Sonezaki' was modeled after this event.

The examples that reveal special regional characteristics are graves of pilgrims found dead on the road. The oldest case in the report is a tomb of a pilgrim (1828, Kagawa Pref.).

As for monuments connected with murder cases, the following examples are included in the report:

* Monument of Haber's Misfortune (1924, Hokkaidō). Haber, agent of a German consul, was killed by a former retainer of the Akita clan in 1874.
* Monument of Martyrdom in Nikolayevsk (1928, Hokkaidō). The monument was built to remember an incident that occurred in Nikolayevsk, Siberia in 1920.

To remember those who sacrificed their lives for society or the people, the two following examples are included in the report:

* Tomb of a Girl (1967, Kagawa Pref.). Erected at the time of repair work. It was based on a legend of a girl sacrificed to prevent a reservoir from collapsing.
* Tomb of a Woman Diver (year unknown, Kagawa Pref.). The legend says that a woman diver was killed in a battle against a dragon as she fought to get back the treasure that her lover, Fujiwara Fuhito, had obtained from Tang China.

2. Varieties of Memorials for Animals and Plants

Memorials for animals and plants are as popular a custom as memorials for humans. Memorials honoring fish served on the table outnumber those for other animals. Next come horses. The importance of horses is understandable as they played a major role in farming, transportation and military affairs. Memorials for deaths on a mass scale involving those of pests and dolphins constitute a genre of their own. Examples of memorials for plants are few, and those that do exist are related to the art of flower arrangement.

First of all, monuments for fish in general are listed below:

* Memorial Tower Dedicated to Fishing and Hunting (1721, Hokkaidō). It was erected by Matsumae Kumaishi Village.
* Memorial Tower Dedicated to Fishery (1843, Ehime Pref.). It was built in commemoration of a large take of sardine in 1843.
* Memorial Tower Dedicated to Fish (1929, Ehime Pref.). It was built by the founder of the cultivation of young yellowtails to memorialize cultured fish.

- Memorial Tower Dedicated to Sea Creatures (about 1970, Toyama Pref.). Mizubashi Port, Toyama City.
- Memorial Monument Dedicated to Sea Creatures (1985, Tokyo). It was built by Chiyoda Fisheries Co., Ltd.
- Memorial Monument Dedicated to Cultured Fish (1996, Shizuoka Pref.). It was built by the nursery for freshwater fish.

As for monuments for particular types of fish and shellfish, they include herring, salmon, yellowtails, blowfish, bonito, eels and pearl oysters:

- Memorial Tower Dedicated to Herring (1757, Hokkaidō). An overabundance of herring was caught and some buried in the ground.
- Statue of Kannon Dedicated to Yellowtails and Pearl Oysters (1982, Ehime Pref.). It was erected by the Kitanada Fishermen's Association.
- Memorial Monument Dedicated to Blowfish (1965, Tokyo). It was built by the Federation of Blowfish Restaurants in Tokyo.
- Memorial Monument Dedicated to Salmon (1968, Hokkaidō). It was built in commemoration of the 100th anniversary of the foundation of Ishikari City.
- Monument Dedicated to Salmon (1981, Hokkaidō). It was built by the Fishermen's Association.
- Memorial Monument Dedicated to Bonito (1994, Kōchi Pref.). It was built in commemoration of completion of the series *Pole-and-line Fishing in Tosa* by Aoyagi Yūsuke.[2]
- Memorial Monument Dedicated to Eel (1995, Shizuoka Pref.). It was built by the Association of Eel Broilers.
- Statue of the Goddess of Mercy Dedicated to Pearls (1989, Ehime Pref.). It was erected for a memorial service for pearl oysters.

Dolphins and whales are not fish, but burial monuments for them have also been built here and there:

- Memorial Tower Dedicated to Dolphins (1827, Shizuoka Pref.).
- Memorial Tower Dedicated to Dolphins (1882, Shizuoka Pref.). More than 600 dolphins were caught.
- Memorial Tower Dedicated to Dolphins (1949, Shizuoka Pref.).
- Tower Dedicated to Whales (1885, Nagasaki Pref.). It was erected in commemoration of whales which strayed into Isahaya Bay.
- Memorial Tower Dedicated to Whalers (1975, Hokkaidō). It was built by captains and harpooners working for deep-sea fishery companies.

Various memorials for horses have been built since the old days, as seen in Batō-Kannon, an image of Kannon with a human body and the head of a horse. Memorials for military horses deserve special mention (also see Veldkamp in this volume):

- Bato-kannon (year unknown, Gunma Pref.). For a blind horse which fell into a riverbed and died.
- Memorial Monument Dedicated to a Beloved Horse (1925, Shizuoka Pref.).
- Memorial Monument Dedicated to Deceased Loyal Military Horses (1930, Kagawa Pref.). It was built by the 11th Army Division.
- Memorial Tower for Military Horses That Died at the Front (1938, Nagano Pref.). The inscription reads 'Participation in the China Incident. Namu-Amida-butsu'.
- Memorial Monument Dedicated to Military Horses That Died at the Front (1941, Nagano Pref.). It was built by the father of a cavalry soldier.
- Memorial Monument Dedicated to Military Horses (1984, Kagawa Pref.). To console the souls of the 1300 military horses belonging to the 40th Artillery Regiment.

Reported cases of cattle monuments are fewer than those for horses. I suppose the actual situations are the same:

- Memorial Monument Dedicated to Dairy Cattle (1941, Kagawa Pref.). Erected by the Association of Dairy Farmers. The inscription reads 'Breed cattle with love and thanks'.
- Memorial Monument Dedicated to Cattle (1941, Shizuoka Pref.).
- Memorial Monument Dedicated to Cattle Used for Plowing (1986, Kagawa Pref.). A great number of cattle died in an epidemic in 1874.

Memorials related to the raising of horses and cattle are also found:

- Memorial Monument Dedicated to Livestock (1947, Nagano Pref.) built at a slaughterhouse.
- Memorial Monument Dedicated to Livestock (1957, Kagawa Pref.). It was built by the eighth-term students of the department of animal husbandry, Ishida High School.
- Memorial Monument Dedicated to Animals (year unknown, Kagawa Pref.). It was built by the Livestock Industry Public Corporation of Kagawa Pref.

Linked with Taira-no-Sanemori's folklore, *mushi-okuri*, a torch procession for driving away noxious insects from rice fields, used to be carried out in various places. Memorial mounds and towers for insects were also built:

- Sanemori Mound (year unknown, Kagoshima Pref.). Commemorating the offering of dances to expel insects.
- Memorial Mound Dedicated to Insects (1828, Kagawa Pref.). This is a memorial for insects killed in the repair work of the main road.

- Memorial Mound Dedicated to Locusts (1940, Toyama Pref.). People collected the exterminated rice-eating insects and dedicated a memorial for them.
- Memorial Mound Dedicated to Grasshoppers (1968, Hokkaidō). It was built for grasshoppers exterminated in the 1880s.
- Memorial Stone (year unknown, Kagoshima Pref.). This was placed for insects killed during farm work.

There are also memorials for creatures such as dogs, cats, rats, honey bees and silkworms:

- Memorial Mound Dedicated to a Dog (1786, Kagawa Pref.). This was made for a pet dog that barked at a large snake and was bitten in the neck.
- Memorial Mound Dedicated to a Cat (year unknown, Shizuoka Pref.). A pet cat was killed in a fight against a rat.
- Memorial Mound Dedicated to a Rat (year unknown, Shizuoka Pref.). The rat above was truly penitent and pledged to become a guardian for a large catch.
- Memorial Dedicated to Honey Bees (1980, Kagawa Pref.). This was built by the Beekeeping Association in Kagawa Prefecture.
- Memorial Dedicated to Silkworms (1987, Gunma Pref.). A lot of mulberry leaves were damaged by a hailstorm. The silkworms which could not be reared were buried under the ground.

Cases involving plants are restricted to those related to the art of flower arrangement:

- Tower of the Flower Spirit (1937, Nagano Pref.). This was erected by the head family of the Murata sub-section of the Matsumura school.
- Tower of the Goddess of Flowers (1967, Kōchi Pref.). This was erected by the Flower Arrangement Association in Kōchi Prefecture.

3. Varieties of Memorials for Disposed Items

Among types of memorials for discarded items, those for needles and writing-brushes are well-known folk events. The memorial service for needles is a custom in which old and useless needles are thrust into a lump of bean curd or *konnyaku* (devil's tongue) and then thrown into a river or sea, or they may be dedicated at the Awashima Shrine in Wakayama Prefecture. It is popularly known as 'The Eighth Day Event,' as it is carried out on 8 February or 8 December. The memorial service for writing-brushes is an event in which useless brushes are dedicated at a mound of brushes or burnt in a holy fire (*goma*). In both cases, people attend the memorial services wishing for improvement in sewing or writing techniques. There are many reported memorials of this kind:

- Memorial Mound Dedicated to Needles (1972, Kagawa Pref.). The memorial service for needles started with an accident in which a girl student of a dressmaking school swallowed a needle by mistake.
- Statue Dedicated to Needles (1992, Kagawa Pref.). The inscription reads, 'To reward the love of needles'.
- Memorial Mound Dedicated to Writing-Brushes (1876, Toyama Pref.). For the memorial service for writing brushes used at *terakoya* (private elementary school in the Edo period).
- Memorial Mound Dedicated to Writing-Brushes (2001, Kagawa Pref.). This was built to commemorate the 20th anniversary of the restoration of private school Kanzan-juku.

Following are cases relating to barbers and beauty salons.

- Monument Dedicated to the Spirit of Hair (1956, Kagawa Pref.). This is a memorial for hair built by the Trade Association of Barbers and Beauty Parlors Business and Environmental Hygiene.
- Tower Dedicated to Hairdressers (1971, Hokkaidō). The tower was originally built by hairdressers in 1861, and restored by the Association of Barbers and Beauty Parlor Business in Hakodate.
- Kannon Dedicated to Scissors (1981, Tokyo). This was erected in Zōjōji Temple by Yamano Aiko, foundress of a dressmaking school. A memorial service is held on 3 August as it is regarded as the 'Day of Scissors'.

Regarding other discarded tools, there are the following cases:

- Memorial Mound Dedicated to Brushes (1963, Shizuoka Pref.). It was built by the Association of the Paper Hangers in Shimizu City.
- Memorial Mound Dedicated to Brushes (1976, Gunma Pref.). It was built at Haruna Shrine by the Tokyo Brush Fraternity.
- Memorial Mound Dedicated to Kitchen Knives (1972, Hokkaidō). It was made by the Sapporo Guild of Cooks.
- Memorial Mound Dedicated to Bamboo Whisks (year unknown, Kagawa Pref.). It was made by a tea ceremony group.
- Memorial Anchor (year unknown, Kagawa Pref.). It was built by salvaging companies.

The calendar, too, is one of those disposable items:

- Memorial Mound Dedicated to Calendars (1983, Tokyo). It was also built to function as a sundial by the National Council of Fans and Calendars and the National Federation of Calendar Publishers.

Undelivered mail (because it failed to reach its destination and thus to fulfill its intended purpose) is also the subject of burial monuments, though it is not exactly the same as 'disposed items':

- Memorial Tower Dedicated to Undelivered Mail (1971, Nagano Pref.). It was built on the initiative of Ide Ichitarō, then Minister of Posts and Telecommunications.

MEMORIAL MONUMENTS AS INTENSIFICATION DEVICES OF INTERRUPTED LIVES

It is not necessary to belabor the point that memorial monuments serve as memory transmission devices of terminated lives, as monuments for the dead and for dead animals are built with the very purpose of retaining them in memory. Moreover, when an inscription indicating the purpose of erection or a wish appears on a stone monument, it gives clear expression to the wish to pass down a memory forever by means of stone. Rather what I am concerned about is that the phenomenon of interrupted lives might be intensified by erecting memorial monuments or conducting memorial services. This is because there is the risk that memorial monuments and services for animals and disposed items sponsored by certain occupations serve to justify them (e.g., fishery) instead of checking their effects.

Let me discuss some concrete examples. First, in the case of humans, memorial monuments for the war dead or those who died in the line of duty have a deep social and psychological meaning in functioning as an *ex post facto* treatment. However, such memorial monuments also enable incidents of terminated lives to affirm death in battle or death in the line of duty, and by so doing they function as devices of intensifying death. Even so, some of the war memorials have a checking function on war. For example, the Monument of Renunciation of War by the Educational Division of the Suicide Attack Squad (Kagoshima Pref., 1985) has an anti-war resolution inscribed onto it.

On the other hand, the practice of dedicating memorial monuments for animals and disposed objects may encourage the over-exploitation of nature or wasteful use of material resources. Rather than direct encouragement, it may function as an indirect encouragement by failing to exert any check on exploitative or wasteful practices. Furthermore, it might cause people to assume the attitude of passive onlookers, who tolerate such abuses. The Memorial Mound for Kitchen Knives, for example, has been built to memorialize slaughtered chickens and fish as well as kitchen knives. However, it is hard to discern in the practice any critical awareness of problems attendant to the large-scale consumption of chickens and fish. By saying this, I am not opposed to the erection of memorials for kitchen knives, nor am I criticizing the economic system of capitalism. Rather I am pointing out the limitations of memorial monuments.

Approaching memorial monuments as intensification devices, I notice the interesting phenomenon that memorialization used to have the purpose of ensuring the repose of souls or assuaging the fear of curses but is now focused on expressing thanks. In the past, people feared curses from those who died unnatural deaths. Typical examples are the Rishōtō (1344, Kagawa Pref.) built to mourn the souls of Emperor Godaigo and his followers, and the Memorial for the Victims of the Bagworm Uprising (1936, Fukui Pref.) erected for those killed in that peasant riot. Today, however, the intention in building monuments has shifted. For example, the inscription of the Memorial of Milk Cows (1941, Kagawa Pref.) reads, 'Breed cows with thanks and love,' and the inscription of the Memorial of Fish (1985, Tokyo) reads, 'May you offer a prayer of gratitude to fish.' Clearly, the concern in these cases is to offer thanks.

From this sentiment of gratitude, we cannot find any concern for managing over-production and overkill. The traditional concept of extinguishing wrongs and karma (resulted from killing and consumption) fostered by Buddhism is no longer present. It is precisely here where one encounters the limitations of devices of *ex post facto* treatment, for these memorials can hardly function as prevention or counterbalancing measures. This seems to be the most problematic aspect of memorials. Citing my view,[3] Nakamura Ikuo made the following comment (2001: 243):

> The modern practice of memorialization permits the efficient and systematic exploitation of natural resources, whether they are living things or inorganic substances. It therefore functions just like a modern system.

He further elaborates that the custom of holding memorials reveals a culture wherein people confirm *post facto* the wrong of killing animals and try to remove their sense of guilt little by little over time. He concludes that if the feelings of pain and guilt can be regularly nullified by means of memorialization, then we must recognize that the practice of memorializing functions as a psychological and cultural device to legitimize the unlimited exploitation of nature (Nakamura 2001: 244). I am of the same view.

REFERENCES

Kokuritsu minzokugaku hakubutsukan jōhōkanri shisetsu, 1999, 2001
    Kokuritsu minzokugaku hakubutsukan kokunai shiryō chōsa iin hōkushū, 20,
    21. Ōsaka: Kokuritsu minzokugaku hakubutsukan.
Matsuzaki Kenzō, 1996 'Kibūtsu no kuyō kenkyū josetsu: kutsu no kuyō o
    chūshin ni.' *Mingu Kenkyū* 112:23–32.

Nakamaki Hirochika, 1990 *Shūkyō ni nani ga okite iru ka*. Tokyo:Heibonsha.

Nakamura Ikuo, 2001 *Saishi to kugi: Nihonjin no shizenkan, dōbutsukan*. Kyōto: Hōzōkan, p. 243.

Parsons, Talcot, Fox Renée C. and Victor M. Litz, 1972 'The 'Gift of Life' and Its Reciprocation.' In Arien Mack ed. *Death in American Experience*, p.1. New York: Schocken Books.

Tanaka Senichi, 1987 'Mingu no kuyō.' *Mingu Mansurī* 20(5): pp.1–9.

NOTES

[1] For example, the Memorial Dedicated to Shaving Knives contains a shaving knife used at the ceremony that inducted Kūkai (Kōbō Daishi) into the Buddhist priesthood.

[2] A 25-volume comic strip published by Shōgakkan over 16 years and made into a movie in 1980 by Shōchiku.

[3] Nakamaki (1990: 82–88) points out that building memorials as *ex post facto* treatments does not have any preventive function.

4

Memorializing and Remembering Animals in Japan

ELMER VELDKAMP

INTRODUCTION

This chapter discusses ceremonies and rituals that, from their titles and explicit contents, express gratitude or pity, or pray for the safe trip up to heaven or the rebirth of the animal's soul. The aim is to find out what animals are monumentalized, memorialized, and remembered for what reasons and in which ways. I will develop my point by picking up two specific cases of animal memorialization and pointing out in what way they fit into what kind of frame of memory and forgetting, which is the main theme of this volume.

THEORIES OF MEMORIALIZATION

Ceremonies and rituals related to souls of animals, as they have occurred in parts of Japanese society from pre-modern times on, most likely originated in feelings of insecurity towards natural factors influencing people's lives and the limitedness of humans to compete with these factors. Well-known examples are the rituals observed by people whose livelihood depends on mountainous regions either for hunting or for cutting trees, of which Chiba Tokuji describes the former in detail in his series of works on hunting societies in Japan (Chiba 1997). Besides the fact that the mountains pose a threat to humans by steep hills, slippery roads and such, the act of chasing and hunting bears and wild boar was a task not without danger. Whaling in pre-modern times also presented a feat of skill of the whalers, who only started to get the upper hand in the battle as technique progressed to give them bigger boats and stronger guns to harpoon the huge marine mammals. The connection between memorial services for these animals and popular beliefs have been pointed out already (Matsuzaki 1996), but on a more concrete level it will not be hard to imagine that these rites functioned partly as a way to deal with insecurity and only limited competitiveness when facing the vast powers of nature.

Rites and ceremonies held for the souls of dead animals in Japan do not just provide the animal's 'spirit' or 'soul' a safe trip to a heaven or a speedy and lucky rebirth. Many of the monuments and rituals or cere-monies are woven into and constitute a web of memory and forgetting. Care has to be taken in addressing these practices, for overt generaliza-tion by defining one body of 'animal memorialization in Japan' neglects the individual traits per case and the various levels of man–animal rela-tionships that may exist in the different contexts discussed in this chapter. The haunting powers of nature as expressed in *tatari* or spiritual curses as an explanatory model have only limited validity in the context of practices of modern society.

In modern urbanized society, the constant increase of knowledge of techniques and machinery sometimes seems to leave little space for prac-tice that is not aimed at a direct economic goal in the sense of what used to be called some or another form of 'western' rationality (van Bremen 1995). In this chapter I look at practices that do not directly give a famil-iar impression to European or North-American points of view, namely memorial rites or ceremonies that claim to pray (in any sense of the word) for the spiritual remains (likely to be covered by the terms in English of 'spirit' or 'soul') of dead animals. Central to this chapter will be consideration of memories and consciousnesses that are at play in memorialization of pets that died in the safety of the household and of animals (for the most important part horses) that died on the battlefields in the wars Japan fought from the end of the nineteenth century to the first half of the twentieth century.

In recent years, interest in memorial services for animals has gained attention by scholars and various explanatory models are proposed to analyze them. In some of these publications, the Japanese terms *dōbut-sukuyō* or *dōbutsu ireisai* seem to be used as an all-encompassing term for any religious practices involving animals.[1] This chapter hopes to shed light on individual traits which vary per case, thereby bringing some structure into the enormous variety of memorial services that is practiced today.

It needs no discussion that commemoration as a social practice con-sists of the opposite practices of remembering and forgetting, and it is mostly concerned with handling or manipulating those memories. Together these two concepts work to construct a history in which people, objects and events are arranged selectively to form a chronological string. For certain cases of animal memorialization, the question whether they concern remembering or forgetting leaves little doubt. I would say that

for instance military horses are primarily remembered and more importantly maybe, through them the time spent at war is revoked in the
minds of those attending the memorial service. Also, pets that are kept
in a small altar or in a pet grave will be remembered for some time, providing the owner with sweet memories. Nevertheless, the fact that some
of the altars are cleaned up after one or two years because the owner stops
showing up implies that the need to remember a pet fades away for some
people. In such a case, the ritual of enshrining your pet in a temple or
cemetery may work rather as a social process to deal with the loss of a
close living being, and may ease the shock of 'pet loss'.

While in some cases the memory of the animals themselves may take
up a central place in the memorials, in other cases the past which those
animals once shared with the participants (wartime, battlefields might
be an example) becomes the main point of attention. In this light, it
would seem rituals for laboratory test animals as performed by the
medical department of many Japanese universities and other biomedical
research facilities (Asquith 1983), and the numerous monuments, Ueno
Park's Kan'ei-ji for animals and objects for instance, are in fact based on
feelings of a different quality towards those animals (if they are supposed
to be present). The relationship between human and animal in question
there is of a very short period and also by definition one meant to be cut
off (literally) at a premature stage. In any case, sticking to a presumed animistic tendency in Japanese religion and its extension into modern times
would result in incongruence in certain cases, which calls for an alternative approach.

On another note, recently Nakamura Ikuo (2001) has pointed to an
explanation of modern variations of *kuyō* practice as a mechanism to
cover up or justify the unlimited use of natural resources, represented by
the processing of animals into food, or animal experiment in biomedical laboratories. The performance of ritual or ceremony 'in return' for the
animal life taken is mentioned as a mechanism to eradicate feelings of
guilt and to soothe the conscience of those who kill, i.e. the human
beings involved. Nakamaki's paper in this volume also relates the practice of erection of stone markers and conducting memorial services for
animals and objects to consumerism, when he suggests that performing
these rituals may provide a cover for continuing the taking of animal life.
By implying that the taking of life is accompanied by prayer for the well-
being of the released soul, one group of mental factors that could work
as a braking mechanism (concretely, the care or fear for animal spirits,
accompanied with feelings of guilt) is deprived of its power, leaving the
way open to more consumption of animal life.

Another suggestion for the apprehension of the concept of soul or
tamashii and memorial services in contemporary Japan is attempted by
Komatsu Kazuhiko (2000, 2002). He refers to the working of the concept
of *tamashii* (soul, spirit) as an operator of memory (*kiokusōchi*). Pointing

out the upsurge of *ireisai* memorial ceremonies especially after the Second World War, he mentions that the literal meaning of the word *irei*, consoling a soul or spirit, in particular applies to 'people who have come to die from other reasons than the karma (*gō*) from previous lives' (*higō no shi wo togeta hito*, p.44). Next, he writes that 'the people who are left behind imagine the frustration (*kuyashisa*) and feel guilt (*ushirometasa*, a term also mentioned in Asquith (1990)) for the person who died and lead themselves to the act of consoling that spirit' (p.45). In Komatsu's view, *irei* is thus a form of consideration towards the person who died unhappily by remembering him or her. Therefore, the very substance of the individual's soul or spirit is directly linked to the memory of that individual. Concretely speaking, this implies that at the point when the memory of that individual starts to fade out, the existence of that spirit also fades with it.

Although unquestioned application of these arguments to any variation of memorial service for humans and animals would lead only to the generalization this chapter attempts to avoid, for pets and *petto kuyō*, this line of thought may prove to possess some validity. In the pet cemeteries mentioned in this chapter, locker-style altars are both reasonable in price and easily accessible, but they are cleared in case the owner does not come to the temple anymore to take care of it, that is when they stop paying the yearly fee for the right to keep an altar at the temple. To provide a safety net for the spirits of dogs and cats that lose their place of residence, one of the temples established a general *dōbutsu kuyōtō*, a general monument for animal spirits, of which one monk assured me that 'any animal could go in there'. When a customer wishes to give up the individual altar, he or she has the choice to have the pet's remains moved ('reburied', *kaisō*) to the general monument. A similarity may be noted with the practice of reserving a special place on a cemetery for old and uncared-for tombstones, sometimes accompanied by a particular monumental stone.[2]

For people with the financial possibilities, a way to remember their pet (or in many cases, one pet after the other) for a much longer time is created through the establishment of a full size grave with a tombstone.[3] These graves are often accompanied by stacks of *tōba*, indicating services being held regularly for those animals.

Especially pet graves incorporate these two opposite aspects of remembering and forgetting. The so to say 'enthusiasm' with which certain pet owners have an altar or tombstone made for their recently deceased pet is in many cases not as long-lasting as in the case of humans. Takeda (1993) suggests that the limits of the pet owner's grief lie around three years after the animal's death. In Komatsu's terminology, this would be the end of the pet's soul or *tamashii*. On the other hand, some of the small altars at both the cemeteries mentioned in this discussion contain more than one urn, and several of the tombstones at the Jikei-in have

names of a number of pets inscribed on the back or on a *boshi* next to
the tombstone in chronological order. The number of pet owners that
take another pet after some time, despite their reluctance directly after
the death of the current one, seems to be significant. Having the pet cremated, putting the remains in an altar or placing a tombstone creates a
credible way of dealing with the loss of a living being that often comes
to be regarded as 'one of the family'.[4]

When we focus on the concrete situation of the acting subjects, which
are the persons who perform the ceremonies or who have them performed by ritual specialists (the latter is more often the case in modern
Japan), we may ask whether it concerns an individual action or a collective action, and who or what induced it. In other words, the concrete
attributes of the subject deserves due attention. The scale or size of the
subject performing the rites may range from an individual or a family (in
the case of pets) to a group of people in the same trade or occupation to
entire research institutes and other non-persons such as industrial food
processing organizations (as is the case with some of the monuments on
the grounds of the Benten-dō of the Kan'ei-ji in Ueno Park, Tokyo).[5] A
factor that is becoming more and more relevant in recent days may be
the expression of individual or group identity and the creation of a
common experience and history by the subjects (those performing the
ritual) themselves through these animal ceremonies. In addition, the
relationship that existed between man and animal differs per case and
forms the sentiments involved to a great extent. Whatever the scale of
the subject or subjects, in memorializing their respective animals they
act as a social entity, and they will take into consideration their own
background as well as their surroundings, external opinions and so on
when they perform the rites. The memories (both in the meaning of individual remembering as well as the recollection of a group-consciousness)
embedded in or evoked by the performance of these ceremonies may
provide useful clues to understanding the motives that underlie them.

Even though animals and other natural phenomena appear in relation
to religious beliefs frequently, the arguments suggesting a form of
'animism' are arguably less appropriate in the contexts I deal with in this
chapter. Below, I will continue my argument with the introduction of
two varieties of ritual for animal souls that are particularly concerned
with the conservation and procreation of both individual and collective
memories as motives for their existence.

First, let us begin by taking a closer look at places of memorialization
of companion animals or pets.

MEMORIALIZING COMPANION ANIMALS

The rise in the 1960s and 1970s of interest in posthumous care of companion animals by their owners has received extensive coverage in the

Japanese media, and with dogs and cats as the main representatives, pet shops, pet cafés, pet hotels and similar facilities have made lives of pets (and certainly the pet owner's experience of those lives) more comfortable. Where animals used to be seen as standing on a level different from their human owners (either higher or lower varying per case), animals as pets have undergone a promotion to a level approaching that of humans. On top of that, animals as pets often share their living environment with humans, whereas that used to be separated. Attribution of human features to pet animals, especially dogs and cats, has moved them from a subordinate position to a level where in some cases, one can almost speak of the pet animal as constituting a social actor by itself (although acknowledging active participatory action on the side of the animal may be a bit far fetched, the influence of pets on their owners on a mental level are quite obvious, resulting in the establishment of the facilities mentioned above). Directly related to this development, posthumous care has also taken on forms resembling that for humans in a great way, with numerous temples and private cemeteries providing a last place for the pets to rest. Below I introduce two temples who host cremation and memorial services for pets in a Tokyo suburban area.

a. Pet Graves at the Jikei-in Temple (Zen-shū), Fuchū, Tokyo

One example of a center of pet memorialism is the Jikei-in, located near the Tama cemetery in the city of Fuchū, Tokyo. Established in 1921 (Taishō 10), ritual activity in this temple is centered around providing mortuary rites and memorial services to pets, *mizuko* or unborn fetuses, and dolls. Appropriate ritual space for each of these separate categories is rather conveniently localized within the temple complex, with the appropriate stone markers to address prayer and offerings to. While the above-mentioned non-human categories are well catered for, it is remarkable that this particular temple has only a handful of graves for human ancestors. It appears that this particular temple was focused on mortuary rites for animals from the time of establishment, and that the main motivation to start providing services to humans was related to becoming a *shūkyō hōjin* (religious rites for animals in the form of graves and memorial statues outnumbers the tombstones for humans by far).

In one corner of the temple grounds, hundreds of identical small Jizō statues for aborted fetuses or *mizuko* are lined up in front of a prayer hall to hold the concerned memorial service in, forming a compact unit within the larger temple complex. On another part of the grounds, an onion-shaped building with a monument dedicated to the memorialization of dolls can be found.

The amount of space taken up by graves for animals, however, is by far the greatest, being split up into two big plots (the temple grounds are cut in two by a road running through it) and a couple of smaller parts of ground onto which graves of various forms are placed. In the back of the temple grounds there is a large three-story ossuary with locker-style niches to place the urn with ashes from the deceased pet in, and for many people this building is the goal of their visit to the temple, to bring incense and flowers to the remains of their beloved pet. The flowers are mostly bought in a booth twenty meters back from the large building. Next to this body of collected individual graves, the temple has erected a general animal monument (which, according to one of the monks: 'any animal can go into', stressing its wide range of possible uses) to take care of animal souls that are no longer taken care of by their former owners. I believe this runs parallel to the popularity of collective memorials in regular cemeteries for humans. On the side of this general monument, a small-size monument for test animals and a monument for small animals raised in elementary schools, dating from the year 2000, have been placed. The sudden rise of memorial services for animals in the second half of the twentieth century, among which pet cemeteries occupy a significant portion, will need no extensive further explanation. However, there is no reason to believe that we have arrived at a phase of stabilization, because new monuments and new contexts are created as we speak.

When walking through a fairly large complex centered entirely on memories of animals, such as the Jikei-in, the reality of these practices for the performing subjects (the owners) is not difficult to see. There are the numerous appeals to feelings of love and care for the pets when they lived as expressed through tombstones and the moving lamentations addressed to unborn children on the *ema* offered at the *mizuko* hall. On a regular Sunday afternoon, couples or families (the actors in this context) walk to the temple's office to apply for a cremation or a memorial service and some time later are seen carrying either the ashes of their pet to the main hall or a *tōba* to the grave of their long-lost companion. While the highly-efficient three-story locker-style ossuary (*nōkotsudō*) may give the average skeptic European viewer annex anthropologist/researcher still some assertion that it is 'only' animals that are dealt with here, the line between man and beast, between what is and what is not human (if such a separation is to be made), turns into a grey zone when one sees the all-out pet graves with luxurious tombstones, flowers in front of them and large amounts of *tōba* stuck in the stainless rack behind the grave, which provide a silent expression of the repeated visits people make to the temple to act out their experience of 'pet loss'.[6]

This temple, as well as the cemetery of the Jindaiji in the next paragraph, issues a color brochure for potential customers explaining the services that can be provided.

b. Jindaiji Dōbutsureien, Chōfu, Tokyo

Located next to the grounds of the Jindaiji temple (Tendai-shū), in the city of Chōfu and not far from the vast Tama cemetery, the Jindaiji animal cemetery is run by the organization *Sekai Dōbutsu Tomo no Kai* (World Assembly of Animal Friends), whose activities involve animal welfare and care of stray pets as well as the management of the cemetery. Somewhat smaller in scale than the above-mentioned Jikei-in, this cemetery was started in 1962 and initially only provided locker-style altars. The altars are housed in a circular ossuary enabling one to walk through the rows of altars in a circle without once having to leave the single-storied construction. In the central space surrounded by the building which holds the altars, a 30 meter high Banreitō ('Tower of ten thousand spirits') rises high up into the sky. At the foot of the tower, a statue of Jūnishi-Kannon ('Kannon bodhisattva of the Chinese zodiac') is enshrined, providing posthumous well-being and safety of the pets whose remains are laid to rest in the cemetery. Most visitors to the pet cemetery start their visit by performing an initial prayer here before going into the building to take care of their individual pet altars. The spaces inside the circular building are filled almost entirely and very recently, memorial space has been expanded by constructing new *reidan* or spirit altars in the open area in the center of the ossuary where the tower stands. These are of a more durable and permanent character and made of black stone similar to that used for regular tombstones. Here the name of the pet, optionally accompanied by a photographic representation, can be engraved on the door and the urn with ashes can be placed inside. Besides providing a place to keep the remains of the cremated pet, the cemetery provides memorial services for the first 7th day, 35 days, 49 days, 100 days, one year anniversaries and so on.[7]

Both cemeteries hold memorial services on the occasions of *higan* (the summer and winter equinox) and the Japanese All Soul's Festival *Bon*, as well as regular (in many cases monthly) memorial services unrelated to auspicious days.

Pet cemeteries are not a phenomenon restricted to Japan. At present, they are to be found in many European countries and in the United States as well. A note by Takeuchi Itsu in the 1930s suggests that the evolution of cats and in particular dogs to a social status close to that of humans is without doubt a development of this century and most likely mainly a post-war phenomenon. In *'Pari no inu neko bochi'* (the dog and cat cemetery of Paris) in his book *Yokushitsu fūkei* ('Bathroom views') of 1933, he writes of his travel to Paris and notes that Parisians maintain a close relationship with their dogs, dressing them up and walking them in a quiet park. Observing this he says that it is 'a sight not to be seen in Japan'.

The cremation and memorialization of pets in Japan is undeniably linked into a complex structure of discourses about ceremonies for dead animals that have come to be known under the common denominator of *dōbutsu kuyō* or *dōbutsu ireisai* as background or premise for the practice. However, the type of animal involved as well as the relationship in which it stood to man is a decisive factor in the character of the ceremonies.

More than consciousness about animal souls in a spiritual sense, it is the memory of closeness between the human and his or her animal which is epitomized in and prolonged through this memorialization.

If we are to take a hint from Komatsu's thoughts mentioned earlier in this chapter, it seems that people commemorate their pets more in the fashion they would take care of an ancestor than as if it would be a potentially vengeful spirit. The soul of the pet *is* present because of the owner's memory of it, and burial or memorialization creates a way to cope with the loss of a pet. Although the initial intention of the owner may be focused on posthumous care for the deceased pet, this way of 'closing up' one chapter of life eventually creates room again for taking care of a new animal without remaining feelings of guilt (which might be a feeling covered to some extent by the above-mentioned *ushirometasa*).

Keeping in mind the feelings of the pet owner who lived with his pet for a considerable time, let us shift our view to another place where human and animal used to work closely together, sharing life and death: the battlefields Japan participated in this past century.

COMMEMORATION OF ANIMAL WAR HEROES: HORSES, DOGS AND PIGEONS

Picking up the theme of memorialization of animals and memories on a slightly different note, let us turn to what is generally regarded outside Japan as one of the major centers of Japanese nationalistic sentiments and commemoration: Yasukuni Shrine (see Ben-Ari in this volume for an account of major celebrations at this shrine) . On the premises of this shrine for 'hero spirits' (*eirei*), the main attention is drawn to the human heroes and victims of the Second World War enshrined in the main shrine hall, but in one corner of the grounds three monuments focus on another aspect of the war sufferings and sacrifices which are given a voice here: the monuments for military horses (erected in 1958), military dogs (erected in 1992) and pigeons (originally from 1929, moved to Yasukuni in 1956) used by the army at that time. The text on the monuments states that the contributions of these animals to transport and communication in the army organization, as well as the fact that many of them died 'in the harness' have made them eligible for the erection of a monument. The monuments address the horses, dogs and pigeons that died in the war *as a whole* and primarily function as monuments honoring the accomplishments of these *categories* of animals during the war.

Memorials specifically dedicated to animals that died during wartime seem to have emerged in the Meiji period in the aftermath of the Sino-Japanese and the Russo-Japanese Wars. The publication *Senbotsu gunba chinkon kiroku* (1992) mentions 54 locations that were established before the Second World War and 51 after that. Among the post-war monuments, the horse statue on the premises of Yasukuni Shrine is the earliest, dating from 1958, followed by the statues at the Gokoku Jinja in Niigata (1962) and at the Takada Park in Jōetsu (1982).

The horse statue at Yasukuni Shrine was created by the visual artist Itō Kunio (1890–1970), who started out creating and selling small clay figures of military horses which had gained popularity due to the government policy encouraging the breeding of horses during the Russo-Japanese War, but he turned to making trophies for the horse races after the Second World War. The horse figure which he donated to Yasukuni Shrine was made after the Second World War and funded by him privately, but the placement on a pedestal on the premises of Yasukuni Shrine did not take place until 1958, when two-time Olympic champion horseback riding and instructor at the Imperial Palace Horseriding Club Kido Toshizō organized a sponsor commission (*Gunbotsu gunba ireizō hōken kyōsankai*) and finally raised the necessary funds.

The people who were initially involved in the establishment of the monument conducted a yearly service, but due to ageing of the members the organization went temporarily into the hands of the local Horse Association (*Aiba Kyōkai*). When voices rose that the organization should be done by people who have shared life and death with their horses, the memorial service was taken over by the newly created Contact Council for the Memorial Service for Deceased Military Horses (*Gunbotsu gunba ireisai renraku kyōgikai*) in 1985, and until 1998 about 400 to 600 people (with an exceptional 1630+ attendants claimed in 1998) attended the service yearly. Various smaller associations of veterans were brought together in this council and would take turns to prepare the memorial service (including the words of the ceremonial text or *saimon*) every year. Changes in scale and technicalities brought the service under the auspices of Yasukuni Shrine from 1999 and the date, which had been the second Sunday of April until then, is now fixed at 7 April.

The object of this memorial service is not limited to horses that died on the battlefields, but may extend to horses that were left behind during the retreat after the end of the war (*Kaikō*,[8] July 1957 issue). Contrary to the Russo-Japanese War, when the horses used in battle were taken back home, wounded horses and remains of fallen horses were now left behind in strange countries. The number of horses mobilized increased from the end of the nineteenth century on, with 23,000 horses for the Sino-Japanese War and 200,000 for the Russo-Japanese War to an astounding figure of 700,000 horses used in military activity both in Japan and overseas during the period towards and during the Second World War (*Kaikō*, January 1993 issue).

The Japanese army started research into the possibility of utilizing dogs in military activities in 1919 at infantry schools, and training facilities were established at these schools, and among the Japanese army in Manchuria from 1933 (*Chinkonroku* p.70). The idea to memorialize these animals apparently did not arise in congruence with the emotions surrounding horses. In contrast to the fifty or so years of the horse statue at Yasukuni Shrine and other monuments dating back to the late Meiji period, the monument for military dogs at Yasukuni Shrine is very recent. The October 1991 issue of *Kaikō*, a monthly magazine for army veterans, calls for individual donations to finance the establishment of the dog monument, bringing up the argument that, although the killed and wounded horses have received relatively large attention after the war, military dogs have nearly been forgotten. The March 1992 issue announces the unveiling ceremony, to be held on 20 March – which is Animal Protection Day (*Dōbutsu aigo no hi*).

Less is the attention given to the monument for pigeons. The Japanese army used pigeons during wartime for messaging and this monument honors the feats of strength of these birds. This monument, featuring a pedestal with on top of it a pigeon sitting on a globe, does not seem to have its own individual ceremony. Both the dog and the pigeon monuments do not receive the attention the monument for horses does because of the fact that the range of use of the former was quite limited and not many people are left to revive their memories.

Contrary to the human war heroes enshrined at Yasukuni Shrine whose names can still be recollected and whose memory still exists in the minds of family and friends that survived, the monuments there for horses and other animals used in war are of a general and collective (anonymous) character. They address 'horses that died during wartime (*senbotsuba*)' as the memory of a collective experience without special reference to individual cases. On the occasion of the last 'national' ceremony as held by the Contact Council in 1998, individual memories and names of horses were collected from the attendants to the ceremony. The individual experiences of the people attending the ceremonies also receive more attention in the accounts in *Kaikō*, the magazine for graduates of the army school. It seems that the attention given to the 'horse stories' increased in congruence with the developments around the monument as described above.

An identifiable individual case which stands in contrast to the collective of '700.000 horses' mentioned in the ceremonial text at the Yasukuni Shrine horse monument in 1992, on a slope just outside the fence of the Higashiyama Middle School in Meguro-ku, Tokyo, you can find a small stone monument of about eighty centimeters high with the inscription 'Batō Kanzeon', similar to the small monuments for deceased horses that can be seen in farming villages around Japan. Next to it, the Educational Committee of Meguro Ward has placed an explanatory panel. It reads as follows (translation by author):

The Batō Kannon of Higashiyama   Higashiyama 1–24
In earlier days, this entire area was the spot of the former Komazawa military drilling grounds and the place where the First Division Imperial

Cavalry of 5000 soldiers and officers and 1200 military horses exerted themselves day and night in drill exercises. Especially the steep hill exercises on the slopes of Higashiyama were severe drills; a cannon was pulled up and down the hill over and over again by a three span or four span of horses.

This monument for Batō Kannon was erected as a memorial stone for two military horses that died during the drills, by the soldiers of the former Army who loved and cared for these horses. On the front side, the characters of 'Batō Kannon' are inscribed and on the back, the origin [of the memorial] is written: "Tomayoshi-gō', lumbar fracture, died Taishō 11, April 23; 'Fukutomi-gō', acute epidemic anemia, died Taishō 11, May 10; Memorial service held Taishō 11 May 22, Third Company'.

Thanks to the good will of the students of Higashiyama Middle School and the local people a shelter was built and it is preserved carefully.
Heisei 4 [1993], March Educational Committee of Meguro Ward

Although we are dealing here with the same military horses as in the case of Yasukuni Shrine and other Gokoku Jinja around Japan, the individual aspect of this monument will be clear. It is significant that in this case, the horses memorialized in the Batō Kannon monument had a name and the subjects responsible for the erection of the stone monument are identifiable *as a social entity*, i.e. both subject and object in the establishment of this monument are clearly defined. One may say that this particular monument is an example of the individual stories that are smothered somewhat by the great scale of the memorial service held at Yasukuni Shrine.

One might argue that the background of this particular case comes close to posthumous care for pets as it became popular in the second half of the twentieth century. Actions like these most likely were personal (individual) enterprises, with the military company that worked with the horses as the concrete actor, and is nowadays also a memorial marker of a historical place (partly thanks to the explanatory panel placed next to it, a sign of recognition by the local authorities). This puts it into contrast with the monument at Yasukuni where the location is significant as a sacred place as well as the central location for the enshrinement of human war heroes/spirits as well. Besides that, the function of this particular ceremony as a get together for veterans around the country should not be forgotten. Gatherings like these are a main stage for memories to be relived.

The outward aspect of erecting memorials for animals in different contexts displays a similarity that may tempt one to search for a general philosophy behind these practices such as belief in animal spirits or guilt relief in all cases, but in fact the particular attributes and motives of these ceremonies vary per case. The practice of performing an *ireisai* or erecting a memorial for both the heroic dead as well as the unhappy dead, as well as variations concerning animals and even objects have become the expression of a wide scope of contexts some of which are touched upon in this chapter. What is to be the focus of study is the proportion to which the different factors of guilt, gratitude, mental peace, belief and the nature of the relationship between human and animal, which all characterize the individual cases, are mixed. Questions should not just search for what the ceremonies 'do' to those involved, but also what those who are involved in the ceremonies 'do' to and with them.

ANALYSIS

This chapter deals with some examples which are illustrative of Japanese contexts in which animals are memorialized or remembered, but the list of variations is nearly endless.[9] Moving away from the trend in Japanese folklore studies to look for the common aspects and general features of customs in very different parts of society, I would support emphasis on the social subjects themselves and the concrete situations they find themselves in. The memories which are conserved within these monuments and which are expressed each time a memorial ceremony is held are only of importance to the people that are directly involved in the history that motivates the performance. It is through the positioning of such a concrete subject into a concrete context or relationship that the practice or the memory becomes a social event.

This does not mean that I think 'animal beliefs' and memorial services should be cut loose from each other entirely. The ritual climate that was created in Japan by blending Buddhist thought with local people's comprehension of parts of their environment they could not directly influence will most likely have played a significant role in providing a feeding ground for these practices to emerge and expand. Relying on reduction to religious practices only, however, ignores the social aspects of the various situations in which human and animal live together.

I want to add a short note on the terms used in Japanese to describe or name the ceremonies described in this paper. Whereas we see the monument for horses named *gunba ireitō* and the yearly ceremony *gunba ireisai* the terms are practically restricted to *irei*, which consists of the characters for *nagusameru* 'to console, to comfort' and *tamashii* 'soul, spirit'. It appears there are souls to be comforted through this ceremony, in this case the souls of horses that died while contributing their strength to humans during military activities. The posthumous ceremonies held for pets are for the greatest part referred to by the term *petto kuyō*, 'memorial services for pets', where the *kuyō* performed is clearly an application of *senzo kuyō* 'memorial services for ancestors' to the frame of companion animals.

Even though there may not seem to be much difference in the two cases as for the fact that both provide posthumous ritual care for animals, the terms used may give away some of the inferred character of the cer-emonies. Military horses are memorialized at Yasukuni Shrine and the national Gokoku Jinja present in each prefecture, and this location infers similarity to that other group of war casualties: the humans enshrined in the shrine mentioned here. In other words, they become categorized on a similar level to the *eirei*, the honorable souls of human war victims. The term *irei* for the practice involved also gives a clue relating this victimiza-tion: many 'memorial services' for people who died in accidents, disas-ters and such (in the case of Japan, think of earthquakes, plane crashes etc.) are designated *irei* and not *kuyō*.

It seems *kuyō* as a label for these rituals stays closer to the actual event of the death of an entity one was familiar with and the memories thereof. Remembrance as it is expressed through *ireisai* here relies heavily on memories of a certain period in the past, such as service in the army. It must be said however that the terms possess a certain looseness which makes it difficult to pin down the actual nuances between the terms.

A tendency which is pointed out by Nakamaki in this volume is the frequent appearance in recent times of thanksgiving festivals or *kansha-sai*. The stress on gratefulness may also cover up distinctions between public and personal experiences such as they are present in this chapter, or underlying motivations of clearing one's conscience of the harm done to other living creatures.

I hope it will be clear from the examples posed here of memorials for animals that died during wartime and the funerals and memorialization of pets, that the period they were established as well as the route they fol-lowed up to the present may differ from case to case. By submitting these cases to individual scrutiny, I hope to have given more insight into their peculiarities than lumping them together in an all-encompassing body of '*the* animal memorialization in Japan' would have.

CONCLUSION

This chapter has discussed the ways in which memories are preserved or recollected through the memorialization of animals in two different con-texts. I hope to have pointed out that the significance of the memories associated with the practice of memorializing animals is closely con-nected to the relationship that the animal and the concerning persons had during lifetime.

The term *dōbutsukuyō* / *ireisai* as a label for one homogeneous body of practices can not be used as an all-encompassing category unless the specific characteristics of the individual practices are taken into account. On the other hand, the fact that animals have historically been given special care after their death can not be neglected but should be used as a background to which to relate the various modern practices of animal memorialization.

Memorial services for pets are highly individual: these animals have obtained a position as a social entity that entitles them to posthumous care similar to humans. Nevertheless, the clearing of altar niches for pets when the owner stops turning up for periodical care show that the limitations of the animal's soul lie indeed within the boundaries of the recollection of its owner, as Komatsu points out for humans.

Ireisai for animals that died during the war, such as they are held at the premises of Yasukuni Shrine and other war hero related shrines, have a distinctly collective character: they address the category of military horses, military dogs and pigeons as an entire category and are remembered as such. Unlike human ancestors or the respective chronology of pets one family remembers at a cemetery plot, these memorial services deal with the dead horses, dogs and such as an unchanging and static historical entity.

The proper assessment of memorial services for animals will have to take into account a number of important aspects in these services. First of all there is the relationship between human and animal which is of great influence on the motivations for holding these ceremonies. Second, the expression of an individual or group identity consciousness or the revoking of memories *through* the performance of these services is one of these aspects. Finally, as another interesting process I would like to point out the shift from 'memory / memorialization of places' (as in the example of the Higashiyama Kannon), where the memorialization of animals is directly connected to the site where the monument is erected, to the emergence of 'places of memorialization', where one location becomes a crossroad of memories and memorials of various kinds (for instance the Jikei-in).[10]

REFERENCES

Asquith, Pamela, 1983 'The monkey memorial service of Japanese primatologists' in: *Royal Anthropological Society News* 54.

Asquith, Pamela, 1990 'The Japanese Idea of Soul in Animals and Objects as Evidenced by Kuyō Services' in: Daly, Donald J. and Sekine, Tom T. (eds), *Discovering Japan – Issues for Canadians*, Captus University Publications.

Jan van Bremen, 1995 'The myth of the secularization of industrialized Japan', in: van Bremen, J.G. and Martinez, D.P., *Ceremony and Ritual in Japan – Religious Practices in an Industrialized Society*. London: Routledge.

Chiba Tokuji, 1997 *Shuryōdenshōkenkyū – saikōhen*, Kazama Shobō.

Kimura Hiroshi, 1988 '*Dōbutsukuyō no shūzoku*' in: Fujii Masao ed., *Bukkyōminzokutaikei 4: Sosensaishi to sōbo*, Meicho Shuppan.

Komatsu Kazuhiko ed., 2000 *Kioku suru minzokushakai*, Jimbun Shoin.

Komatsu Kazuhiko, 2002 *Kaminaki jidai no minzokugaku*, Serika Shobō.

Matsuzaki Kenzō, 1996 '*Dōshokubutsu no kuyō oboegaki*' in: *Minzokuteki sekai no tankyū*, Keiyūsha.

Nakamura Ikuo, 2001 *Saishi to kugi – nihonjin no shizenkan/dōbutsukan*, Hōzōkan.

Ōsaki Tomoko, 1995 *'Ueno Kan'eiji Bentendō no shohi wo megutte'* in: *Jōminbunka* 18, Seijō Daigaku Jōminbunka Kenkyōkai.

Senbotsu gunba ireisai renraku kyōgikai, 1992 *Senbotsu gunba chinkonroku*, Zaidanhōjin Kaikōsha, Tokyo.

Takeda, Dōshō, 1993 *'Gendai ni okeru petto no kazokuka – aru pettoreien no chōsa kara mita gendai no kazokuzō'*, in: Fujii, Masao / Yoshie, Akio / Kōmoto, Mitsugi, *Kazoku to haka*, Waseda Daigaku Shuppanbu 1993.

Takeuchi Itsu, 1938 *'Pari no inu-nekobochi'* (1933) in: *Yokushitsu Fūkei*, Okakura Shobō.

NOTES

[1] For instance, Kimura (1988) writes of the 'custom of memorial services for animals (*dōbutsukuyō no shūzoku*)' and sums up statues for Batō Kannon, boar and deer in relation to mountain deities, the spiritual attributes of dogs and cats and other animals as one set of customs or rituals. It seems the particularities of the different rituals are sacrificed for the greater goal of reading congruence in different aspects of customs of 'the Japanese'. See also Matsuzaki (1996).

[2] This practice would also a phenomenon that started to occur when the significance of a tombstone became more that of a monument (*kinenhika*) and less a marker for the deceased individual in the process of being promoted to ancestor status.

[3] The relation between economic considerations (the cost of the funeral and ossuary) and the form memorialization of pets takes as for the elaborateness of the ritual and dress-up of the grave may prove food for thought, but to my knowledge, up to now no research has been done and this remains as a task for further inquiries.

[4] Taking into account the apparent relatively quick recovery by pet owners from their 'pet loss', this way of putting things should probably be understood as an expression of the closeness people feel towards their pets, and not as a concrete statement, as I have not heard of people including pets into their will, for instance.

[5] See Ōsaki Tomoko (1995) for a complete list and explanation of the respective monuments for animals and objects at this temple.

[6] 'Pet loss' is a term that is widely used in narratives on dealing with the death of one's pet, and had come to be a standard item in the vocabulary of pet cemeteries and related businesses in Japan too.

[7] In Japanese *shonanoka, sanjūgonichi, shijūkunichi, hyakkanichi, isshūki*. These 'death anniversaries' are very similar to the practice for humans, where the practice is usually limited to a final ceremony at 50 years after death (*gojūshūnenki*).

8   *Kaikō* is a monthly magazine published by Kaikōsha, an organization that
    was originally established in 1877 as an organization for graduates of the
    Japanese army's officer's school. It ceased to exist temporarily at the end
    of the Second World War, but was revived again in 1952 as a friendship
    organization for war veterans.

9   Besides memorial ceremonies and monuments for outstanding citizens in
    various forms (the veneration of virtuous citizens or *gimin kuyō*, the deifi-
    cation of heroic figures as *hitogami*), memorialized animals range from
    horses and cows, whales, dolphins and various species of fish to animals
    used in the food industry, laboratory tests and to animals providing
    humans pleasure such as pets and zoo animals. The idea of old tools
    turning into monstrous creatures such as seen in the *Hyakki Yakō Emaki*
    may have given a push in the right direction for the appearance of mon-
    uments and services for lifeless objects such as tea whisks, fans, needles,
    dolls, paper, and very recently floppy disks and stored information in
    general (the Rinzai-shū Myōshin-ji Daiō-in temple provides this service
    and maintains a web page on the subject).

10 I refer to the fact that monuments for animals in pre-modern Japanese
    society used to be erected on the spot where the animal had died (for
    instance the place in the forest where a bear was shot down, the coast
    where a whale was caught, or the roadside where a horse collapsed during
    labor), whereas later on, these practices have come to center around relig-
    ious spaces such as temples and shrines. Seen from this aspect, the exam-
    ples given in this chapter are very modern, although a background in
    older practices can not be denied.

5

Coincident Events of Remembrance, Coexisting Spaces of Memory: The Annual Memorial Rites at Yasukuni Shrine[*]

EYAL BEN-ARI

INTRODUCTION

This chapter focuses on the annual events that take place at Tokyo's Yasukuni Shrine on the anniversary of the end of the Second World War and Japan's unconditional surrender (15 August). The main part of the day involves groups of people who come to pay their respects to, and commune with, the souls of dead soldiers enshrined there. These groups include the families of the dead soldiers, conservative politicians who see the occasion as a source of public support, and members of the general public. Built just outside of the imperial moat in central Tokyo, Yasukuni Jinja (Shrine for Establishing Peace in the Empire) was established in 1869 to enshrine the dead soldiers of the Imperial Army (Tsubouchi and Yoshida 1999). Later, soldiers who died in the Russo-Japanese and Sino-Japanese Wars were also enshrined there and during the 1930s it became a symbolic and ritual center for the modern Japanese state and a prime site linking Shinto, militarism and nationalism (Fujitani 1998: 121–6; Gardner 1995: 1). As part of their drive to limit militarism after the war, the American forces closed the shrine and

* I would like to thank Edna Lomsky-Feder, Nurit Stadler and Vered Vinitsky-Seroussi for discussions leading to the article and to participants at the international conference on 'Monuments and Memory Making in Japan' held at the National University of Singapore.

turned it into a private religious foundation. With the end of the American Occupation in 1952, the dead soldiers (and some civilians) of the Second World War were enshrined there and two decades later, seven Class A criminals – incriminated in the Tokyo Tribunal – underwent the same process (Ōe 1984). Subsequently, leaders and supporters of the shrine were central in efforts to revive the link between Shinto and the state despite the strict prohibition of the new national constitution. Indeed, probably the most famous attempt at restoring the shrine's political importance came with Prime Minister Nakasone's semi-official visit in 1985 to mark the war's fortieth anniversary.

As such, the shrine was and remains a site of contention and dispute centering on the specter of prewar militaristic nationalism, the link between religion and state, the enshrinement of war criminals, and charges that Japan has not taken responsibility for its perpetration of violence during the war. As Hook (1996: 161) explains, wider concern involving the 'role of Yasukuni Shrine in deifying the war dead has given the shrine a central place in the political attempts made over the years to maintain the spirit of militarism and build up pride in the Japanese state' (Hook 1996: 161). Similarly, Kitagawa (1987: 283) warns, the shrine is often associated with the danger that Shinto 'could provide a ready-made channel for national narcissism, which in turn could be manipulated by vote-hungry politicians' (Kitagawa 1987: 283). It is for these reasons that activities at Yasukuni Shrine have been openly opposed by groups both within and outside of Japan (mainly, but not only the governments and social movements within Asian countries that suffered under the Japanese occupation – Korea, China, Taiwan). Internal opposition has been intensified by the fact that there have always been close ties between Yasukuni Shrine and the conservative Japanese Association for the Welfare of Families of War Casualties (Tanaka 1994).

It is against this background that the annual events at Yasukuni should be seen. As Schudson (1995: 359) suggests, turning something into a monument or memorial changes the past in that very process. A commemorated event is one invested with an extraordinary significance and assigned a qualitatively distinct place in people's conception of the past. It is this very process of distinction that is the core of contestation in and around Yasukuni and the ways in which the shrine's activities represent attempts to link the present and the future to the country's problematic past. Here, however, I argue that attempts to invest the annual activities with special significance cannot be simply understood as political maneuvers. Rather, the plurality of occurrences – simultaneous events that take place in concurrent spaces carried out by a variety of actors in front of a multiplicity of audiences – should be at the core of understanding what the annual events achieve and portray. This public occasion includes elements of rituals, public ceremonies, performances, festivals, political statements, museum outings, media events, military marches, and tourist excursions. It is the coexistence of these varied activities which allows the public event to transmit a variety of messages, and to effect a diversity of experiences centered on various pleas for the normalization of present-day Japan.

Fieldwork for this study was carried out during 1998 and 1999 and involved visits to the shrine and museum, attending lectures at the site, and interviews with a variety of individuals who are directly and indirectly related to Yasukuni. I was greatly aided by help in fieldwork and the insights of Richard Gardner, Elise Edwards and especially Sabine Frühstück. The actual day described and analyzed here took place in 1999.

A PORTRAIT

Despite being centrally located, Yasukuni Shrine is marked off from the surrounding streets by a wall that makes it impossible to see what goes on inside. The main entrance is marked by giant Shinto gates, while further inside are parking areas, shops selling food, drink and religious items, another set of Shinto gates, cherry trees, a Noh stage, a museum presenting various military paraphernalia, sub-shrines, reception halls, and many stalls (some permanent and others set up only on festival days). In addition, on 15 August, a large tent with about 350 chairs and a mounted dais is erected on the main walkway and to its side different organizations set up booths to register visitors, offer tea, sell souvenirs, videos or books or disseminate brochures. The innermost part of the shrine includes an outer gateway where people come to pay their respects, and the inner sanctum where the main ritual activity takes place and where daily food offerings are made to the gods. Behind this sanctum is the building holding the sacred registers on which the names of all of the enshrined gods are inscribed.

It is evident that the police have come out in great numbers: arrayed outside and within the shrine are hundreds of uniformed and plainclothes policemen complemented by two buses and a command jeep belonging to the riot police. Inside the shrine officials and some members of its security firm manage the flow of people and events. Right-wing groups are not allowed to park their trucks or vans inside the shrine and when entering it must do so on foot and in groups of no more than about 20 people. From time to time one can hear the sounds of right-wing vehicles blaring nationalist songs or speeches outside the site but these are usually no more than background noises rather than intrusive sounds (one cannot understand the words of the songs or the speeches from the inside).

The most conspicuous visitors are groups of bereaved families who are brought in by prefectural associations on large tour buses. Invariably dressed in black formal wear they are led by tour leaders with flags bearing the names of their prefectures. Also noticeable are coteries of old-soldiers donning new tailored uniforms of the Imperial Army and Navy. According to our impression, these people are not brought in an organized manner but arrive individually to join their friends at the shrine. Groups of Yakuza in suits and with their distinctive hairstyle occasionally walk up the main pathway with the bosses in the middle and the younger members at their sides. Most common among the general public are older and middle-aged individuals and one comes across only a few younger families. Indeed, there are almost no teenagers, very few people in their twenties or early thirties and very few children. Finally, interspersed among all of these people are a very small number of 'eccentric' younger men who also don the uniforms of soldiers, officers and pilots of the Imperial military. From time to time people with pre- and post-War flags of Japan walk among the crowd.

Many people come sporting cameras. These include amateurs seeking to record their visit, press photographers alone or accompanying journalists, television crews from stations within and outside Japan, and professional photographers taking commemoration photographs of large groups. While the press photographers tend to take pictures of typical scenes and the main ceremonies, the attention of many of the amateur photographers is directed to the older and younger men in Imperial military regalia. Inside the inner shrine is another group of press photographers (with video cameras) photographing the important politicians coming to pay their respects to the dead.

Throughout the day a host of parallel activities are held in sites around the shrine. One of the larger stands erected especially for this day is staffed by representatives of the 'Nippon-Kaigi,' an organization characterizing itself as aimed at protecting the history, culture and tradition of Japan. Among the documents handed out at this booth are copies of a monthly newsletter published by the association entitled 'Japan's Breath'. Its subtitle clarifies the purpose of the journal as an opinion magazine aimed 'at building of a country which has pride'. Enclosed in the newsletter is a postcard for registering with the association. This kind of plea makes clear that the day is seen by the organization as a recruiting occasion among a pool of people broadly sympathetic to its cause. The stand, like others around the shrine, also sells videos of the movie 'Pride' which tells the story of Tōjō the Prime Minister of Japan during the war. Other videos include an explanation of the importance of the national flag and a description of the Tokyo War Trials. Among the CDs sold are copies of 'Songs of Yasukuni Shrine'.

Many conversations are struck up between the visitors to the shrine. One man tells me that he comes here every year in August and another four or five times during the year because 'it calms me (*ochitsuite kuru*)'. He continues to say that there is a need to respect dead people (but does not use the word soldiers) in any country and therefore that the shrine is important. When I asked him about a group standing next to us, he looks sideways to make sure no one is looking at him, and answers that he thinks that they belong to the '*uyoku*' (the right wing) but that 99 per cent of the people who come to the shrine are 'regular people (*ippan no hito*)' and so is he. Two middle-aged couples also declare that they come to respect the dead on this day.

One veteran states that later his friends will come wearing uniforms and that they will take a memorial picture together. Pointing to a book in his hands he refers us to a chapter describing where he was in the war (the air wing of the Navy). Another man says that he has been coming to Yasukuni without fail on this day for thirty years (he seems to be in his late 50s). Then going into a harangue of present day politicians in Japan (with his wife vociferously adding her voice) he tells those surrounding him that they have not supported the Association of Bereaved Families. The reason for this, he declares, is that they have no pride in Japan. He then goes on to call all Tokyo University people 'assholes' and to assert that all they can do is read *manga* and play *pachinko*. In the past, he continues, Tokyo University was fine, but today they are all communists, 'red': They too don't know anything about Japan's history or tradition. Finally, he notes that in Japan one finds left-wing newspapers like the *Asahi* or the *Mainichi* with the only really acceptable ones being the *Yomiuri* to an extent and the best being the *Sankei*.

Nearby a man begins to put up a poster and two flags – the Taiwanese and the post-war Japanese one. The poster is about the great cost of suffering and death during the war and the need not to forget its lessons. A man standing next to him explains that the reason for the Taiwanese flag is that Taiwanese soldiers had fought with the Imperial army and lost their lives. An older police officer in plain clothes and two shrine officials explain to the man that the shrine does not allow the posting of such posters and flags and that he should move away. Many people join this little gathering and interject political comments reminding me of Hyde Park in London. The policeman talks very gently to the man and to the people gathered around them. After about twenty minutes a compromise is reached and the man moves his poster and flags to the side of the main walkway. As this goes on, another man begins to march on the road bisecting the shrine. Dressed in the white clothes of a pilgrim and wearing wooden clogs, he holds a plaque on a metal rod and begins to shout out about Japan's defeat and how it was wronged in the war. Despite the fact that his tirade goes on for hours, the police, and most of the bystanders seem to ignore him. Indeed, these two incidents are indicative of a lack of confrontational attitudes among the police and how fringe characters are ignored and somehow 'shifted' into the corners of the shrine.

In close proximity to these two men someone had hoisted another poster on a metal pole. It is about the 600,000 Russians and 60,000

Japanese who died in Siberia and about the Japanese who had lost their lives in other countries. Calling the present constitution 'unnatural' and damaging, it continues to proclaim that it is causing anxiety about the continuity of the Japanese people through to the next generations. Finally the text ends with a declaration about the equality of all human-kind and the need to increase pride and independence by changing the current constitution so that Japan can defend itself. Universal themes of egalitarianism and the sorrow of war are thus linked to ideas about national pride and dignity.

Crossing the street we encounter ten young men dressed in uniforms of Kokushikan University, one of Japan's two Shinto universities. They have little boards in their hands and are handing out postcards. The latter detail the fact that 29 April is the birthday of the emperor and that their organization is dedicated to emphasizing the importance of the emperor and getting Japanese people to think about their past. According to the text on the card they support the upgrading of the birthday of the previous Shōwa Emperor to a national holiday. The boards carried in their hands include a short text stating this point and asking people for their names and addresses to be included in a petition to the parliament.

Opposite this group and suspended on two sets of ropes are about 70 or 80 pictures. Painted in a naive and simplistic manner (with a few explanatory remarks) they depict 'kitschy' scenes from the war: portraits of soldiers, attacking airplanes, bomb victims, scenes of a Buddhist god carrying off the bodies of dead soldiers, and soldiers standing in front of the pre-war flag (based on a the photograph appearing on one of the videos sold in the precinct, suggesting that many, if not all, of the pictures were painted from photographs). Clearly the messages carried by these pictures center on a nostalgia for the military and the heroism it expresses and a plea for understanding the soldiers of the Imperial military as victims. Immediately next to this exhibition of pictures is a stand selling CDs and tapes of wartime songs of the Navy and Army; books about the war and the Tokyo trials; videos about the emperor and empress's visit to Brazil, the liberation of Asia, the 'Heart of Yasukuni', and the 'Truth about 2,000 years of Japan and Korea'; magazines called *Sokoku to Seinen* (Fatherland and Youth); and many copies of a *manga* book by Kobayashi Yoshinori which can be found at any book store today. The 384–page thick comic book is entitled *New Pride Declaration Special: On War.*

Near the walkway is a permanent exhibition of letters sent by soldiers to their families during the Second World War (the letters are changed every month). About twenty people stand next to a notice-board reading a letter. It is from a student-soldier to his mother in which he mentions a visit to a hot springs resort because he had never seen his mother's face happier than on that day. He apologizes for all the trouble he has caused and asks his mother to continue her life as a 'woman of Japan' (*Nihon no onna toshite*). He also writes that she can visit him in Yasukuni if he dies. Nothing in the letter indicates belief in the emperor or anything immediately related to the war. It is as if he wrote to please his mother and make her think of the happy times they had spent together. It also seems that the soldier knew that he was going to die.

Towards ten in the morning hundreds of people gather before the Noh stage. Here a shrine official holds a short ceremony. Mentioning a few words about peace, he asks everyone to say a collective 'Thank you' as they do every year. When he finishes his short words, tens of doves are liberated into the air and the crowd shouts its thank you. When we questioned another official about this event he explains that it is called 'The voice of Japan, a meeting to thank the spirits of the war dead'.

At the inner chamber a steady stream of prefectural groups are ushered in from the side entrance by the shrine's priests and administrators. They participate in a short 15 minute ceremony for the dead. Just outside another flow of people walk up to the external gate of the chamber. They bow, clap, and throw coins into a box before leaving for other parts of the shrine. Interspersed within these flows are a number of limousines that approach the side entrance to disgorge politicians visiting the shrine. One is Hata Tsutomu a former Prime Minister. The atmosphere here is a bit like a smooth running train station with shrine officials timing the arrival and conveyance of various groups and personages.

At few minutes after eleven different groups begin to march up the central walkway to the gate at the outer edge of the inner shrine. The first group, which is heard before it appears due to its use of trumpets (played not very competently), comprises navy veterans wearing white uniforms. It numbers about 15 men carrying a flag and rifles with bayonets and is marched by an 'officer' at the side. Marching is not done in a very professional manner with some of the men out of step. The younger 'fringe' individuals wearing Imperial uniforms attach themselves to the end of this group and so seem to be straggling behind the group. The crowd reacts with great interest to this group taking many pictures of them. The whole scene of marching to and from the shrine takes only a few short minutes.

Another group of ten younger men wear uniforms reminiscent of American marines although their hair is much longer. Wearing armbands with the group's name – Kikuseidō (made up of the ideographs for chrysanthemum, youth and identical) – they are followed by a group of 8 men and two women led by someone like a sergeant. This group wears uniforms that are similar (but not identical) to those used by the Japanese Self-Defense Forces. The men's hair is cut short and the women's placed in tight bonnets at the back of the head. They have unit tags with the number '32' and Mt Fuji on them and badges on the front of their jackets. The sergeant seems to give professional orders for the march. They are also the only group to march in step (suggesting that they had practiced before).

At midday the ceremony taking place in the large tent set up for the occasion begins. Hundreds of people are sitting inside the tent and many hundreds more are standing outside of it. The ceremony is actually a series of speeches. One speechmaker, for instance, talks about the visit of the emperor to America in 1995 and how he was asked 'rude' questions about the war. He goes on to assert that today the people of Japan must have pride and independence; they must be strengthened. When he finishes, the hundreds of people inside and outside of the tent clap for him. At the end of the ceremony a choir of twenty men and women are invited to the stage. They sing two or three songs and then turn towards the inner shrine. All of the audience stands up and with them sing 'Kimi-ga-Yo,' the informal anthem of Japan.

Once this ceremony is over, a group of eight men wearing brown shirts and pants (reminiscent of Nazi uniforms), armbands and a flag of elongated 'ZZ' march up the central walkway. Their commander shouts the marching orders using the following words: 'SS', 'SA'. In contrast to the reaction to other groups almost none of the Japanese take pictures of them (the reaction seems to be one of acute embarrassment). It is only the media and the anthropologists that take photographs of them. One media photographer even gets in between them and takes a picture of their black boots. In addition, and again in contrast to the other groups, a space is created around them and no one comes up to talk to them or touch their uniforms. They do not walk in perfect order and one member especially walks out of step with the others.

At around one o'clock the area around the vending machines becomes a hub of informal activities: groups of veterans, almost all dressed in civilian clothing, congregate there to say hello, talk, eat, and drink. They sign their names at reception tables and carry small pins denoting their membership in veterans' associations. One man stands up in his place and goes into a sort of set speech that one sees in Japanese movies about the wartime period. Many of the younger eccentrics wearing Imperial military uniforms stand waiting for their pictures to be taken and 'bask' in the attention they are receiving. One forty year old man in a uniform of an Imperial Army officer pontificates that one must beware of foreigners and how nice it is that there are so many young people here this year. When someone asks him why he wears the uniform, he replies that it is to honor and to thank the dead.

Outside the main gate a demonstration of right-wing activists takes place. Perhaps a hundred people congregate on the sidewalk opposite the gate while their leader gives a speech about how those who do not visit the shrine are committing a crime. On the truck parked next to them a poster declares that (Prime Minister) Obuchi will suffer heavenly retribution for not visiting Yasukuni. Suddenly a small light-green van with a placard stating 'Opposition to the public visit to Yasukuni' arrives. The police instruct the driver to leave and he does so.

Throughout the day one finds crews of Taiwanese, Russian, German and American television stations. These are complemented by representatives of Japanese television stations and newspapers and magazines. Along these lines, the importance of the annual rites on 15 August lies not only in the thousands of people who visit the shrine but also in the kinds of reports in the media that one finds in all of the major newspapers. In 1999 all of the evening editions of the major newspapers except for the *Nihon Keizai Shinbun* reported on the front page and most of them printed at least one photograph of visitors to the shrine. While the front page articles tend to be relatively factual, reporting how many people attend and which ministers visited the shrine, newspaper articles often list representatives of organizations who gave speeches, report on the content of the speeches, mention that there were more young people such as children and grandchildren of fallen soldiers visiting than during previous years, and carry numerous op-ed pieces about the meaning of Yasukuni.

INTERPRETATIONS

If one wanders around Yasukuni Shrine on 15 August, the picture is of a constant flow of people into and out of the shrine within which concurrent events go on in a multitude of sites. To be sure, the shrine is normally made up of multiple locations, yet today, a whole array of sites are added either formally – like the central tent for the public ceremony, or the smaller tents and stands – or informally as in the men with the cards regarding the birthday of the Shōwa Emperor or the veterans' gatherings around the vending machines. How then, does one make sense of what goes on here?

Halbwachs contended long ago that the past 'serves' the needs and interests of the present. His stress was on the ways in which the past is utilized by current interests and groups. Barry Schwartz (1982), by contrast, argues that in many cases the past has its own power to define or delimit the kinds of issues dealt with in the present. In the Japanese context various historians, like Igarashi (2000), have contended that the past – specifically, the experience of the Second World War – persists to emerge from within, to fester underneath, various phenomena in postwar Japan. Similarly, the central problem addressed in a recent volume on memories of the Asia-Pacific War (Fujitani et. al. 2001: 2) – aptly titled 'Perilous Memories' – centers on how they 'are recalcitrant and menacing' and 'continue to be unsettling.' Indeed, the very images that have been employed to portray the continued 'presence' of the war in contemporary Japan echo this viewpoint: for example, 'Hiroshima Traces' (Yoneyama 1999) or 'Naming the Unnamable' (Igarashi 2000). At bottom of these scholarly works is the contention that the experiences of the war continue to trouble and distress many people in contemporary Japan. Their interpretations of the ways in which these concerns are understood and acted upon, however, tend to center either on issues related to the evasion of national responsibility or to political maneuvering by elites.

Fujitani and his associates (2001: 7), for instance, contend that in postwar Japan the dominant modes of remembering the war have produced a 'national victimology' with the entire population, including the emperor, equally figured as victims of military misdeeds (Fujitani et.al. 2001: 7; also Yoneyama 1999:11; Bourdaghs in this volume). One strand of thinking has taken this perspective to produce a strongly anti-militaristic ethos with the idea that as victim, Japan has a special world role in propagating world peace and understanding (Berger 1998). One finds numerous echoes of this view in Yasukuni Shrine. Some of the displays in the museum, for example, are devoted to the kamikaze pilots and their youth-hood, sacrifice and commitment to the collective. This theme is echoed in the corner devoted to the sad letters sent home by soldiers. But it is the ceremony of the white doves released near the Noh stage, that explicitly declares that one lesson of the Second World War is that Japan should be a peaceful and peace-loving nation.

Another strand of thinking that derives from the stress on a 'national vicitimology' involves attempts at the national rehabilitation of Japan. In their more milder forms these efforts are found in pleas for 'normalization', for turning the country into a country just like any other (Frühstück and Ben-Ari 2002). It is in this light that the comparison that we heard in private conversations between Yasukuni and Bitburg Burial Ground in Germany or Arlington National Cemetery in the United States is important. Within this perspective, the reference point for Yasukuni is the manner by which other countries honor their war dead. To be sure, it could be argued that there is no normalization without apology or coming to terms with the responsibility of Japan (Piper 2001: 131) but the basic plea at base of such comparisons is for considering Japan to be just like any other country. The shrine's attempts as part of the move to keep Shinto relevant in contemporary Japan should be seen along the same lines (Kitagawa 1987: 283). In fact, Yasukuni often presents itself to the wider public as a 'regular' shrine and the videos it sells and the web site it has set up regularly include pictures of children playing on the ground as they would play in 'any' Shinto shrine.

In its more extreme form the stress on national vicitimhood has been expressed in demands to return to the past glories of the nation-state. It is in this light that the public ceremony held by the Nippon-Kaigi and other efforts at gaining 'pride' should be seen. The singing of the national anthem, the speeches calling for pride and dignity, the recruitment of sympathetic supporters, the movement lobbying for turning the birthday of the emperor into a national holiday all center on the importance of the past as a model for the present and the future. It is also in this light that the marches of small groups to the gate to the inner shrine should be seen. These groups which include veterans and a variety of right-wing groups dressed in uniforms and fatigues also hark back to the past of military camaraderie and the glory of a strong Japan. Similarly, politicians use the past as it is represented at Yasukuni as a resource for their conservative political agenda. They see the annual set of rites as a media event in the sense that it provides them with exposure to a large, if anonymous, audience to be reached via television and newspapers.

It is precisely these kinds of endeavors that have figured most centrally in previous scholarly interpretations of Yasukuni. First, a number of scholars have examined the formal and legal standing of the shrine and its activities (Ōe 1991; Tanaka 1993; Tanaka 2001). The questions dealt with by these people involve the constitutionality of Yasukuni and the ways in which various politicians have tried to circumvent constitutional issues by going to the shrine in private capacities. Second, scholars such as Seraphim (2003) have placed the case of Yasukuni in the context of contests between grassroots movements devoted to specific issues. As she argues the repeated failure in the Diet of the Yasukuni Shrine Bill motivated its proponents to organize popular support movements in the style of left-wing citizens' movements. These movements have argued that the state's failure to nationalize the shrine was a violation of the citizens' rights of ordinary Japanese who longed for the official celebration of the spirits of the war dead. A closely related third thread of thought has concentrated on the ways in which the shrine continues to link politics and religion. Thus Harootunian (1999: 147–8) worries that reinstating the link between the state and a shrine devoted to preserving the spirits of Japan's war dead, means 'returning Japan to a time when people were socialized into performing unhesitant service to the emperor.' He continues (Harootunian 1999: 146):

> For many ordinary Japanese, Yasukuni Shrine has become the place that houses the memory of Japan's wars and the heroic spirits who gladly gave their lives for the nation. At Yasukuni, nobody ever asks why a war was fought or if it was a 'just war,' because all of Japan's wars have been just.

Thus, the activities at Yasukuni, according to Harootunian, represent no more than a blind move to restore the past. Indeed, according to him, the people who have campaigned to persuade the state to assume responsibility for managing the shrine wish to reconcile polity and religion as envisaged by the Meiji state. Gardner's (1995) analysis complements that of such scholars as Harootunian. He shows how the shrine strategically uses various kinds of ambiguities in order to present itself to the public in ways that cover up its move to rehabilitate Japan and to link it back to politics. Indeed, the moves by representatives of Yasukuni to create formal connections with politicians and leaders of the Japanese Association for the Welfare of Families of War Casualties should be seen as part of this kind of strategy (Tanaka 1994).

THE PASTS AND THE PRESENTS

We must be wary, however, of an overly political view of the strategic role of representational practices carried out at the shrine. Most previous interpretations have been based on the analysis of historical and contemporary texts and the pronouncements of political elites. Unsurprisingly they contain a very heavy cognitive bias and a predilection to analyze meanings rather than experiences. Take Yui (1997: 67–8) who sees Yasukuni Shrine and the activities in and around it as part of the 'unfinished relations with the war dead'. Yui's stress on the plural nature of these relations is important because the annual rites at Yasukuni, I propose, form an 'umbrella event' for a host of activities. As Zelizer (1995: 222–3) reminds us, 'commemorative dates or holidays are used to remember more than one event at the same time' (Zelizer 1995: 222–3).

Take the governing logic of the event which is based on the simultaneity of events with elements of spatial fragmentation and relatively free flows that reinforce it. Not only is there no one focal point for everyone visiting the shrine, but there is also no overall governing structure, with rather different arrangements and schedules holding for different events. In addition, there is an easy flow into and out of the different activities: no ticketing and, apart from the public ceremony, no seating. To follow MacAloon (1984: 246), the day partakes of the character of a festival rather than a spectacle because in festivals, the roles of actors and spectators are less distinguishable. Indeed, people may take on a variety of roles during the course of the day: participants, actors, and audience. Indeed, the annual rites differ markedly from navy flotillas, air-force flybys, or army parades which are state mandated and controlled and are aesthetic forms that reflect and magnify the precision, exactness, and systemic control of bureaucratic logic (Handelman 1998: xxxvi–xxxvii).

Indeed, it is the juxtaposition of events and their variety that forms the core strength of the event: it is predicated on multivocality (Turner 1969), including multiple performances, messages, and narratives. To be sure, this multivocality takes place within the broad parameters of a centrist and right-wing consensus. The extreme right, however, is either kept out of the shrine or strictly controlled within it. This multiplicity can be interpreted as blurring or obscuring the central message of the heads of the shrine and which raise the greatest opposition among commentators and external groups: Japan's rehabilitation via a return to the glories and values of the Imperial past.

But again things are more complex. After the Second World War there were tens of millions of soldiers and their families who were left with much personal pain and grief and who began to search for a meaning to the experience of the war and its losses and privations. The rites at Yasukuni allow this grief to be expressed and provide some meaning to the loss. As Gardner (1995) states, there are 'those who lost their friends in the war, make an annual visit to the shrine to visit their friends, and oppose, if not detest, all effort to make political use of the shrine'. The pilgrimage to Yasukuni Jinja thus allows many individuals and families to link their personal memories and sentiments to that collective level: the special space of Yasukuni and the time of the annual memorial rites are occasions where the living may interact with the dead, with those enshrined. But because of the contested nature of the shrine and especially the annual rites, the structure of this 'umbrella' event allows the encompassment of personal pain, the search for meaning, and a national narrative in ways that allow a continuity between that past and the present.

It may be worthwhile to compare the Japanese case to the German one in this respect. The governing sentiments of national guilt and shame in Germany did not allow individuals and families to express their pain and grief for what they had undergone. While many paid a high personal price during the war, they found very few socially sanctioned outlets – formal and informal – for expressing the emotions and meaning attendant upon this price. It is an analogous process, I would contend, that we find in Japan. While the dropping of the atomic bomb did 'contribute' to the development of a national victimology, personal voices of families of the bereaved were often silenced as they were categorized as perpetrators of violence. Indeed, it seems as though many visitors to Yasukuni feel emotions similar to those of British pilgrims to war sites who 'say they go to pay their respects to the ones who have died, to affirm that their death was not in vain, that they are not forgotten' (Walter 1993: 75). For many families whose loved ones died abroad, the actual grounds of Yasukuni provide a concrete place to go to and grieve. While I have no direct data in this regard, I would certainly suggest, following Walter (1993: 76) that visits to the shrine are a way to 'complete' their lives.

In this sense I would argue that Harootunian's (1999: 159) contentions are limited:

> Yasukuni is still the place of national memory, but this time resting on the identification between mourning and bereavement – the expression of national sentiment – and a national morality cemented by the regular performance of public ceremonies – spectacles in this age of electronic reproduction – that are eagerly consumed to reinforce ideological assent.

His view is limited primarily because his focus is on the macro-national level, precisely that level that disregards the private pain and individual search for meanings.

At the same time however, the complexity of the annual rites does not end here. The parades and reunions of veterans of the Imperial Army and Navy, for example, link the past to the present in a different manner. For the older veterans, these marches and congregations imply re-experiencing of the cohesiveness of groups of soldiers (although it is rarely the same actual individuals that they served with that they meet). The public enactment of camaraderie among these individuals can be seen as a plea for recognition as a distinct group with its own identity. On a more personal level, military service is anchored in their own individual experience and is often a source of deep emotions such as pride and self-respect. But we may continue to speculate, following Walter (1993: 75), that like ex-soldiers of other armed forces so they too 'feel a debt of honor to their comrades who have died; often they feel guilty that they have survived, knowing it could so easily have been they who were killed had they been less lucky or brave'.

For the younger people who march, parades are not simply an imitation of the past. This is an important point. Because commemorations such as the one held at Yasukuni do 'not insist on any shared, direct experience for its participants' (Zelizer 1995: 219) they appeal to wide audiences and participants. Anniversaries fill a special need in cases in which the institutionalized memories they embody substitute for lived memories that have faded (Zelizer 1995: 225; Schudson 1995). Much of what we 'remember' we did not experience as individuals. For the young right-wing people who march to the gates of the inner shrine, participation in the commemorative rites thus forms a way to link them personally to the now steadily distancing experiences of world war. This is a kind of 'socio-biographical memory' through which we feel pride, pain, or shame with regard to events that happened to our groups before we joined them (Olick and Robbins 1998: 123; Zerubavel 1996). For these younger men wearing Imperial military uniforms, the march includes elements of simulation, a potential future state of military force and discipline which they are 'playing' with.

Finally, the events at Yasukuni Shrine cannot be understood on their own. On 15 August, memorial ceremonies take place in two other places nearby (all located near the Imperial Palace in central Tokyo). The first is held in the nearby Nippon Budōkan. During the ceremony held there, both the Prime Minister and the Emperor and Empress give speeches to honor both military and civilian dead. Held in front of an audience of thousands of invited guests the ceremony is strictly secular in its content. Guests include politicians and members or the bereaved families. Being based on invitations however, the ceremony is limited in the number and kinds of people that can attend it. The other place where a secular ceremony takes place is Chidori-ga-fuchi National Cemetery which was opened by the government in 1959 in order to mourn unknown soldiers and civilians who died in the Second World War. One fifth the size of Yasukuni, it houses a rather austere concrete structure at the center of which is an urn housing the ashes of unknown soldiers. Throughout the day opposition groups, some individuals, government officials and representatives of the media can be seen at the site. But the limits of this place, following John Gillis' (1994: 11) insight about tombs for the unknown soldier is that they offer a way to remember everyone by remembering no one in particular.

Consequently, to follow Vinitzky-Seroussi (in this volume), a wider view reveals that the commemoration of the Second World War is both multivocal and fragmented. Wagner-Pacifici and Schwartz (1991) suggest the idea of multi-vocal commemoration is about a shared space, a shared time, or a shared text (like the Vietnam Veterans Memorial in Washington DC) that carries diverse meanings and can thus be peopled by groups with different interpretations of the same past. Vinitzky-Seroussi (in this volume) suggest that there is a complementary mode of commemoration: a fragmented commemoration includes multiple commemorations in various spaces and times where diverse discourses of the past are voiced and aimed at disparate collectives. What is significant from our point of view is that Yasukuni provides things not provided for in other sites: a series of events that is open to 'anyone' and within which both acutely personal and blandly collective themes can be expressed. Along these lines, officials of Yasukuni were among the groups opposing the establishment of a war museum in Tokyo out of a fear that it would compete with the shrine in terms of commemorating military casualties and offer apologies for Japan's wartime conduct (Hammond 1997: 113–4).

CONCLUSION

As I have argued, the annual commemoration at Yasukuni is comprised of a host of concurrent activities. The very open-endedness of the events and the relative tolerance (within its boundaries) allows a diverse set of participants and audiences to deal with present issues through coming to terms with the past. Indeed, this has been Gardner's (1995) insight. What he calls the ambiguities of the shrine, I would term its multivocality, the multivocality that allows many people to participate out of many motives and understandings. Hence, as I have shown, a political interpretation of these events is too limited. Perhaps the multivocality of the occasion is an outcome of the fact that the state is not directly related or implicated in what goes on there.

REFERENCES

Berger, Thomas U. 1998 *Cultures of Antimilitarism: National Security in Germany and Japan*. Baltimore: Johns Hopkins University Press.

Frühstück, Sabine and Eyal Ben-Ari 2002 '"Now We Show It All!" Normalization and the Management of Violence in Japan's Armed Forces'. *Journal of Japanese Studies* 28(1): 1–39.

Fujitani, T. 1998 *Splendid Monarchy: Power and Pageantry in Modern Japan*. Berkeley: University of California Press.

Fujitani, T., Geoffrey M. White and Lisa Yoneyama 2001 'Introduction'. In T. Fujitani, Geoffrey M. White and Lisa Yoneyama (eds): *Perilous Memories: The Asia-Pacific War(s)*. Durham: Duke University Press. pp. 1–29.

Gardner, Richard 1995 Yasukuni Shrine: Ritual, Memory, Politics and the Personal. Paper presented at a conference on 'Ritual and the State in Asia.' Paris, 26–30 June.

Gillis, John 1994 *Commemorations: The Politics of National Identity*. Princeton: Princeton University Press.

Halbwachs, Maurice 1992 *On Collective Memory*. Chicago: University of Chicago Press.

Hammond, Ellen H. 1997: 'Commemoration Controversies: The War, the Peace, and Democracy in Japan'. In Laura Hein and Mark Selden (eds) *Living with the Bomb: American and Japanese Cultural Conflicts in the Nuclear Age*. Armonk: M.E. Sharpe. pp. 100–21.

Handelman, Don 1998 *Models and Mirrors: Towards and Anthropology of Public Events*. Oxford: Berghahn Books.

Harootunian, Harry 1999 'Memory, Mourning, and National Morality: Yasukuni Shrine and the Reunion of State and Religion in Postwar Japan'. In Peter van der Veer and Hartmut Lehmann (eds): *Nation and Religion: Perspectives on Europe and Asia*. Princeton: Princeton University Press. pp. 144–60.

Hook, Glenn D. 1996 *Militarization and Demilitarization in Contemporary Japan*. London: Routledge.

Igarashi, Yoshikuni 2000 *Bodies of Memory: Narratives of War in Postwar Japanese Culture, 1945–1970*. Princeton: Princeton University Press.

Kitagawa, Joseph M. 1987 *On Understanding Japanese Religion*. Princeton: Princeton University Press.

MacAloon, John J. 1984b 'Olympic Games and the Theory of Spectacle in Modern Societies'. In *Rite, Drama, Festival, Spectacle: Rehearsals Toward a Theory of Cultural Performance*. John J. MacAloon, ed., pp. 241–80. Philadelphia: Institute for the Study of Human Issues.

Ōe Shinobu 1984 *Yasukuni Jinja mondai* Tokyo: Iwanami Shoten.

Ōe Shinobu 1991 *Yasukuni iken soshō*. Tokyo: Iwanami Shoten.

Olick Jeffrey K. and Joyce Robbins 1998 'Social Memory Studies: From 'Collective Memory' to the Historical Sociology of Mnemonic Practices'. *Annual Review of Sociology* 24: 105–40.

Piper, Nicola 2001 'War and Memory: Victim Identity and the Struggle for Compensation in Japan'. *War and Society* 19(1): 131–48.

Schudson, Michael 1995 'Dynamics of Distortion in Collective Memory'. In Daniel L. Schacter (ed): *Memory Distortion: How Minds, Brains, and Societies Reconstruct the Past*. Cambridge, Mass.: Harvard University Press.

Schwartz, Barry 1982 'The Social Context of Commemoration: A Study of Collective Memory'. *Social Forces* 61: 374–402.

Seraphim, Franziska 2003 'Participatory Democracy and Public Memory in Postwar Japan. Woodrow Wilson International Center for Scholars'. *Asia Program Special Reports No.* 109. Pp. 13–7.

Tanaka, Nobumasa 1994 *Nihon izoku-kai no gojūnen. Sekai* Sept pp. 34–52.

Tanaka, Nobumasa 2001 What is the Yasukuni Problem? Japan in the World. http://www.iwaniami.co.jp/jpworld/text/yasukuni01.html

Tanaka, K. Peter 1993 'The Revitalization of Japanese Civil Religion'. In Mark R. Mullins, Susumu Shimazono and Paul L. Swanso (eds): *Religion and Society in Modern Japan*. Berkeley: Asian Humanities Press. pp. 105–20.

Tsubouchi, Yuzo and Tsukasa Yoshida 1999 'Yasukuni Shrine as a Symbol of Japan's Modernization'. *Japan Echo* 26(3): 1–6.

Turner, Victor, 1969 *The ritual process: Structure and anti-structure*. Chicago: Aldine.

Walter, Tony 1993 'War Grave Pilgrimage'. In Ian Reader and Tony Walter (eds) *Pilgrimage in Popular Culture*. London: Macmillan. pp. 63–91.

Wagner-Pacifici, Robin and Barry Schwartz. 1991 'The Vietnam Veterans Memorial: commemorating a difficult past'. *American Journal of Sociology* 97: 376–420.

Yoneyama, Lisa 1999 *Hiroshima Traces: Time, Space and the Dialectics of Memory*. Berkeley: University of California Press.

Yui, Daizaburo 1997 'Between Pearl Harbor and Hiroshima/Nagasaki: Nationalism and Memory in Japan and the United States'. In Laura Hein and Mark Selden (eds) *Living with the Bomb: American and Japanese Cultural Conflicts in the Nuclear Age*. Armonk: M.E. Sharpe. pp. 52–71.

Zelizer, Barbie 1995 'Reading the Past Against the Grain: The Shape of Memory Studies'. *Critical Studies in Mass Communication* 12: 214–39.

Zerubavel, Eviatar 1996 'Social Memories: Steps to a Sociology of the Past'. *Qualitative Sociology* 19(3): 283–300.

PART 2

Art of Memory

6

Summer Grasses: Memory and the Construction of Landscape in *Oku no Hosomichi*

SCOT HISLOP

INTRODUCTION

Of course there are memories which can not be communicated with another. Oka Mari discusses the memory of a 'comfort woman' (a woman forced into sexual slavery by the Japanese military during the Pacific War) who could not eat grilled meat because she had been forced to witness Japanese soldiers burning another 'comfort woman' to death for attempting to escape (Oka 2000: 6). Although we, the readers of Oka's account of the 'comfort woman's' account may be able to understand this 'memory' in some conceptual form, it is clear that at some level we do not understand the woman's memory itself (or we, too, would no longer be able to eat grilled meat). The woman's memory is, at least partially, a 'bodily' memory constructed of traces across the senses. And these traces are difficult if not impossible to communicate in words, no matter how skillful a raconteuse one might be.

There are a further set of problems with this kind of memory, though. The 'comfort women,' through a particularly insidious conjunction of power and knowledge were, for much of their post-war lives, not 'permitted' to relate their memories. Furthermore it is ironic – perhaps even tragic given its relative powerlessness – that the 'discovery' of 'comfort women' was carried out by academics and it has largely been within the academy that their stories have been related. I have to wonder whether other forms of empowerment – forms of narrative with more strategic power – might not have served the 'comfort women' better.

Given that even this kind of 'personal memory' is narrated only within the power/knowledge structures of academic, political and economic discourses and that it is only through these kinds of power/knowledge structures that they can become part of 'social memory,' it seems particularly apt that we begin to question our own construction of memory itself. Are our forms of memory universal or do they have a genealogy? The common sense[1] solution to these kinds of questions would be to turn to psychology or the 'hard' sciences for answers. But here, again, one is confronted with fundamental questions. Might not psychology or even the 'hard' sciences be structurally imbricated in 'common sense' constructions of memory? Could it be that these disciplines only find what they postulated was there from the very beginning? It is academically fashionable to argue thus in some quarters.

So perhaps a better way to find answers to some of these questions is to look at the construction of memory in pre-modern texts. Of course I am aware that it is not possible to overcome the modern or the post-modern and that the traces of memory I find in pre-modern texts will, in some way be modern (or post-modern) because of my own blindness to other forms. Pre-modern texts will not provide us a place to stand outside of modernity and view it. But precisely because of their difficulty and their refusal to conform to our structures of power/knowledge – to our common sense – pre-modern texts may trouble our own categories and provoke further questioning of them. What I propose to provide, then, is not a set of final answers to my questions, but rather to suggest that we must not think of our forms of memory as 'universal'. They are 'constructed' and as such have a history. I hope to suggest that there must be other ways in which the experiences like those of the 'comfort women' might have been transmitted, ways that may have different ethical and political values and potentials.

MEMORY AND LITERATURE

Scholars of literature usually study 'personal' memory. Oka Mari, for instance, in *Kioku/Monogatari* concentrates on the difficulties of communicating one's personal experiences in words (Oka 2000). This emphasis on personal memory should not be surprising since, as Karatani Kōjin pointed out in the afterword to the English edition of *Origins of Modern Japanese Literature*, '. . . [A]s long as a work is seen as the "expression" of the "self" of an "author," that work is already located within the apparatus of modern literature, no matter how antimodern and anti-Western it may be'. (Karatani 1993: 192) Literary readings are predicated on seeing texts as the expression of a self, so memory, in literary studies, is always tied back to the 'self' of the author. Thus, memory is taken to be 'personal memory.' For modern readers this is common-sensical enough that it is rarely, if ever, questioned.

This emphasis on 'personal memory' that is seen as the expression of the 'self' of an author, though, raises a great number of problems which can not be dealt with from within the field of literary studies. Karatani argues that modern writers like Mishima Yukio and Kawabata Yasunari both resisted modernity and the West but when their works are read as the expressions of a 'self' they are being read as literature (Karatani 1993: 192). And, although literature is a relatively recent creation in both Japan and the West, pre-modern, pre-literary texts are also read as the expression of the self of an author, in other words, as literature.[2] Some pre-modern texts are remarkably amenable to being read within the apparatus of modern literature. These are, usually, the texts that form modern canons of national literatures. In Japan, texts like *Genji Monogatari* and *Makura no Sōshi* are relatively simple to read as the expressions of the 'self' of their 'authors' and not surprisingly, they are also foundational texts in the modern canon of Japanese literature.[3]

Today I would like to discuss Matsuo Bashō's[4] *Oku no Hosomichi*, a text that also has a central place in the modern canon of Japanese literature. It is widely read as the expression of Bashō's self, as the personal memory of the journey he describes in the text. It is recognized that some of the events in the text are 'fictionalized'[5] but by and large the text is taken to be a 'non-fiction' account. Even the fictionalized events are, in literary readings, somehow related back to the 'self' of Bashō. By reading the text as literature, the field of Kokubungaku has produced many fine readings of *Oku no Hosomichi*. But *Oku no Hosomichi* was not and could not have been written to be literature. Bashō had no concept of 'literature' (nor, of course, of '*bungaku*' in the sense that the word has been used since the 1890's). To read the text as 'literature' or '*bungaku*' is, at some level, to misread it. Literary misreadings have many implications, but today I will concentrate solely on how they obscure the intimate connections between memory and landscape in the text. It is in this conjunction that a radically different construction of memory becomes 'visible'.

To do this I must begin by questioning the kind of memory that is used to write *Oku no Hosomichi*. Rather than being constructed from the 'personal memory' which literary scholars are so fond of exploring, it is primarily constructed from 'shared memory'. Of course I do not deny that 'personal memory' in fact plays a role in the text. Had Bashō not undertaken the journey that *Oku no Hosomichi* describes, the text would not have been written, or if it had, it would be markedly different than the text we read today.[6] But I will argue that 'shared memory' is much more important than personal memory in the construction of the text.

The community that shared this memory with Bashō was extremely small in the late seventeenth century. It required knowledge of the poetic classics of both Japan and China as well as of various prose texts. Bashō acquired this 'shared memory' through the study and production of poetic texts and he clearly expected the audience for *Oku no Hosomichi* to have a similar set of memories.[7] *Oku no Hosomichi* was not written to be a mass-produced best-seller in the way that *kibyōshi* and *yomihon* would be a century later.[8] Bashō was not trying to address a general audience.

A second, related, and in some ways much deeper, problem with literary readings is that they are predicated on the 'self'. It is commonsensical to assume that while each 'self' is in some way different from every other 'self', there is, at the same time, an unchanging essence of the 'self' that is valid across time and geography. But as Ishihara Chiaki points out, 'It is fair to say that the self (*jiga*) is a product of its times. There have been many different senses of the self that have left their mark up until now. The modern self (*kindaiteki jiga*)[9] is not an exception.' Ishihara further goes on to point out that the basis of the 'modern self' lies in the mind-body dualism of Descartes (Ishihara 1991: 30). It is also this '*kindai-teki jiga*' (or when read in English translation, the 'modern self') upon which literary readings are predicated.

The construction of the *kindai-teki jiga* is carefully pursued in Karatani Kōjin's masterful *Kindai Nihon Bungaku no Kigen* (and the equally masterful translation of this text *Origins of Modern Japanese Literature*). Karatani argues that the Cartesian cogito emerges is, not surprisingly, modern, linear, Cartesian space (Karatani 1993: 140):

> Descartes's conception of 'extension' by which he referred to the object of thought, conceived of the 'landscape as alienated from the human'. Extension for Descartes was unrelated to the medieval conception of figurative space which was assigned meaning in qualitative terms. Descartes's *cogito* belonged solely to the realm of extension. Thus the discovery of interiority must be differentiated from a concept of simple self-consciousness or consciousness of 'existence' (Karatani 1993: 62).

It is only within the Descartian chronotope that interiority and the modern can be constituted. Other chronotopes should give rise to other 'selves'. Along with these other selves, might not other forms of 'memory' also arise?

It does not require great mental gymnastics to realize that Bashō never heard of Descartes or Cartesian dualism. The historical Bashō who wrote *Oku no Hosomichi* did not have and could not have had a 'modern self'. This much is easy to figure out. The way in which the self of the historical Bashō and the textual Bashō of *Oku no Hosomichi* was constructed is a much more difficult problem, one to which I do not have a ready answer. But I think we can begin to approach the problem by looking briefly at some aspects of the construction of self in Buddhism. I am not claiming that this leads us to the 'self' of Bashō (either historical or textual) but I think there is evidence in the passages of *Oku no Hosomichi* that I will discuss that points toward a 'self' that is similar to the Buddhist construction of self, even if it is not completely identical to it.

As far as this chapter is concerned, the most important element in the Buddhist construction of 'self' is the lack of mind-body dualism. This is clearly shown by the fact that in addition to the five senses that we modern subjects recognize – sight, hearing, touch, taste, and smell – Buddhism adds a sixth – something that might best be translated as mind.[10] I do not wish to make too much of this. After all, this kind of construction of the 'body/mind' was a topic of great debate among Buddhist sects. And there is no reason why 'Bashō' (textual or otherwise) was necessarily constructed along these lines. But Bashō's 'mind', in the guise of memory, is every bit as important as his other five 'senses' in the perception and the construction of the landscape that is presented in *Oku no Hosomichi*. These memories from which Bashō constructs the landscape are not 'personal memories' but rather 'shared memories'. And the chronotope within which it takes place is clearly not the chronotope of Descartes. Already we have come a long way from literary readings of *Oku no Hosomichi*.

OKU NO HOSOMICHI: THE JOURNEY AND THE TEXT

In 1689 Bashō and his travelling companion Kawai Sora[11] travelled from Edo through the northern provinces of Honshū and in the years that followed Bashō wrote *Oku no Hosomichi*. The text consists of 49 prose passages (of which I will translate and discuss all of one and part of a second) and a large number of *hokku* (the pre-literary name for '*haiku*'). The prose style is terse and dense; the *hokku* are among the finest Bashō produced. The textual history of *Oku no Hosomichi* is fairly complex and I will not rehearse it here. The reader who is interested in a succinct account should see the explanation in *Matsuo Bashō-shū 2* (Imoto and others 1997: 585–587) which includes a great deal of information about the recently discovered text that is directly from the brush of Bashō and the relation of Bashō's text to the other early texts which are extant.

The two sections I will discuss today are adjacent to each other. In the first section, Bashō and Sora get lost along the way from Matsushima to Hiraizumi. Being lost is not merely wandering along the wrong path. It is also being without memory of place. And because the textual Bashō has no 'shared memory' of the places through which he and Sora wander, there is no landscape for him to describe, only chaos. In the second section the two travellers have made it to Hiraizumi. Here the textual Bashō has memory again and he is able to describe the landscape that surrounds them in rich detail. The comparison between these two sections will provide some leverage on the intersection of self, memory, and landscape in *Oku no Hosomichi*.

CHAOS: THE ROAD FROM MATSUSHIMA TO HIRAIZUMI

I will begin with a translation of the section in which Bashō and Sora get lost:

> The twelfth.
>
> We set out for Hiraizumi.[12] We heard of '*Aneha no Matsu*'[13] and '*Odae no Hashi*.'[14] Then the traces of human beings became rare and only pheasants, rabbits, reapers, and woodcutters crossed our path.[15] We could not figure out the route and ended up getting on the wrong road,[16] finally arriving in the port town of Ishinomaki.[17] Out across the sea we could see Mt. Kinka about which was composed the 'blooming flowers of gold' poem.[18] There were hundreds of boats in the inlet. The houses were packed in tightly and the smoke from their hearths rose without cease.[19] We had accidentally come to this kind of place and started to look for lodgings but no one would take us in. We ended up spending the night in a hovel and when the morning had dawned, we set out on the unknown road, wandering astray from time to time. We glanced at '*Sode no Watari*',[20] '*Obuchi no Maki*',[21] and '*Mano no Kayahara*'[22] as we made our way along an almost endless embankment. We passed by a long and gloomy marsh, spent a night at Toima, and then arrived in Hiraizumi. The route between Matsushima and Hiraizumi was about 20 or so '*ri*'.[23]

Bashō and Sora set out from Matsushima which, amazingly enough, is still considered one of the three most beautiful places in Japan. Indeed it may once have been very beautiful since the bay of Matsushima is dotted with pine covered islands which would be most charming were it not for the preponderance of picture takers, tour guides with loud megaphones, tour boats blaring out sappy music, omnipresent vending machines – in short without all the dross of modern Japanese tourist traps. Unlike the excessively noisy modern Matsushima, Bashō honored the beauty of the bay with silence: he did not compose a *hokku* about it.

Bashō and Sora begin their day well. They hear from others about two *utamakura*, *Aneha no Matsu* and *Odae no Hashi*. *Utamakura* provide Bashō with key components of his landscape. They exist within his shared memory, like they do for all people who have the proper training in classical poetry. These two *utamakura* form part of Bashō's cognitive map of the journey they are undertaking so, as long as Bashō and Sora are near them, they are not completely lost. However these places are not seen, only heard about, so things are not going as well as they might.

Then the traces of people become rare. This, of course, is not good when you are travelling, unless you are specifically trying to get away from it all. Finally Bashō, in a panic, does what any good scholar would in a similar situation – he turns to Mencius. The traces of people have not only become rare, they are now also on a path that is used by pheasants, rabbits, hunters, and reapers. There is the beginning of a sense of panic in the text since it is clear that the travellers are getting more and more lost. In fact, they manage to get on the wrong path altogether and end up in the port town of Ishinomaki.

Ishinomaki today is a town full of permanently shuttered shops, not at all the thriving port that it was in Bashō's day. Not surprisingly, the town, like most others along Bashō's route, tried to cash in on the *Oku no Hosomichi*/Bashō boom in the late 80's (in honor of the 300th anniversary of Bashō's trip). There is a nice statue of Bashō standing in the central park, the pedestal of which quotes *Oku no Hosomichi*. The quote, not surprisingly, is full of ellipses and relates only that Bashō arrived in Ishinomaki. It does not help your image as a tourist destination to advertise how cranky a great poet was to have ended up in your town by accident. The apparatus of modern literature is not alone in the need to suppress texts and contexts.

Even though the Ishinomaki that Bashō wandered into by accident was a major port town, it is of no interest to him. In fact it does not really exist in his cognitive map – his memory. Bashō is only able to conjure up several clichéd tropes to describe the town. The houses are packed in so tightly that it seems they are jostling each other and the smoke from their ovens never ceases to rise into the air. These are symbols of prosperity: extremely standard, extremely clichéd tropes. Bashō does not try to describe the city in less clichéd terms because he has no interest in it aside from his one reference to an *utamakura*. Gazing out across the water, he claims to have spied Mt Kinka, an *utamakura* based on a poem ascribed to Ōtomo no Yakamochi (716–785), one of the representative poets of the late Manyōshū period and considered by tradition to be one of its compilers:[24]

> My lord's reign flourishes and in the eastern province of Michinoku the mountains blossom with gold.

The poem was written to celebrate the discovery of the gold used by the Shōmu Emperor to gild the Great Buddha at Nara. Bashō, however, could not have sighted Mt Kinka while looking out across the water because the mountain is simply not visible from Ishinomaki. Bashō is so lost that he no longer knows what he is looking at. His landscape now is constructed of mis-sightings/mis-citings. When memory fails, the landscape becomes chaotic, if it can even be described at all. Memory is intimately related to the perception of landscape and even to its misperception.

Things turn from bad to worse. Bashō and Sora have trouble finding lodging. The educated reader has seen this coming from the very moment Bashō started to use his clichéd tropes to describe the town: people in places that are prospering are, according to the classical tradition, cold and heartless. Textually, at least, Bashō and Sora find lodgings in a pitiful hut and spend a miserable night. In actual fact they probably spent the night more comfortably. According to Sora's diary, as they were passing along the street, no one would even give them a cup of boiled water to drink. A passerby who seemed to be a samurai saw their predicament and introduced them to some lodgings. Clearly, though, the textual Bashō did not have fond memories of Ishinomaki. It is a chaotic wasteland to him, a place where the hearts of the people are as cold as stone because of their prosperity and love of money. Perhaps the pursuit of wealth is not all that it's cracked up to be.

The next day they set out again. The road itself is miserable. Bashō and Sora pass by several *utamakura* but rather than look at them carefully like they usually do, they merely cast sidelong glances. They walk along a 'gloomy' marsh and are forced to spend another night in a small town, of which there is no description probably because Bashō's memory contains nothing with which to describe it. Finally, the next day, they make it to Hiraizumi. Bashō states that it took them twenty *ri* to cover the distance between Matsushima and Hiraizumi. The word '*ri*' is both a unit of distance and, informally, a unit of time of travel. It is equal to 3.92 kilometers and is about equal to an hour's worth of walking at a pace that one can sustain all day, day in and day out. So Bashō and Sora take about twenty hours of walking to make it to Hiraizumi and it appears from the text, anyway, that it was a cheerless journey.

In this section Bashō describes very little of the landscape that they pass. This will become clearer when I compare this section with the next one. What little description there is comes from Mencius and from clichéd tropes, with the single exception of the 'gloomy marsh'.[25] The one time Bashō gazes upon an *utamakura* it is actually a mis-sighting/mis-citing. When without his cognitive map of the world – without the all-important shared memory to guide him – Bashō has to resort to tired clichés and mis-citation to construct his text. His perception, in other words, is as dependent on the sense of 'mind' as the other five senses. Without 'memory' of a place, it is a chaotic wasteland. This will become clearer when the horrors of the road between Matsushima and Hiraizumi are replaced by the pleasures of being back in a landscape that can be sensed and perceived.

ORDER RESTORED: HIRAIZUMI

Again, I will begin with a translation of the section of *Oku no Hosomichi* I wish to discuss:[26]

The splendor of the three rulers[27] was but a dream within a wink of sleep.[28] The remains of the Great Outer Gate are a couple of miles[29] in this direction. The remains of Hidehira's[30] palace have become fields and only Mt Kinkei[31] retains its form of old. We began by climbing the hill where Yoshitsune[32] had had his mansion and saw the Kitakami, a great river flowing from the domain of Nanbu.[33] The Koromo River flows around the Izumi Castle[34] and into the Kitakami River at the base of the hill that Yoshitsune's mansion[35] stood on. The remains of Yasuhira's[36] palace lie on the other side of the Barrier of Koromo[37] which firmly closed off the exits from the Nanbu domain – seemingly protecting us from the northern barbarians (Ezo). Still, the loyal retainers (of Yoshitsune) chose to hold this palace. Their great exploits have, in the passing of time, become a field of grasses. 'The country in defeat: mountains and rivers remain; in the city: the grasses and trees of spring grow rank . . .'[38] Speaking these lines, I set my hat aside and wept until the hour struck.

summer grasses
the remains of the dreams of mighty warriors

Once in Hiraizumi, Bashō is found again. His cognitive map of the world is useful and thus he is able to describe the landscape around him. And the tone of irritation and fear is replaced with a Bashō who is filled with a nostalgia for the past and able to express the nostalgia in elegant language.

Hiraizumi was a regional capital during most of the twelfth century, ruled by three generations of the Ōshū Fujiwara clan until they were wiped out by Minamoto no Yoritomo, at least in part for harboring Yoritomo's younger brother Yoshitsune. In addition to seeing the temples that remained from the glory days of Hiraizumi,[39] Bashō also wanted to view the sites that dealt with Yoshitsune. Even now the town is a major tourist destination in the Tōhoku region and I am sure there is also at least one statue of Bashō. Without doubt the quotations from *Oku no Hosomichi* on the statue do not elide long sections of the text.

In order to understand the 'realism' of this description – a realism that modern readers will quickly recognize as very different than their own – it is necessary to introduce two concepts. The first is that of a present in which the historical/nostalgic connotations of the past of a place are more important than the denotations of the place itself. The present is and can be constructed only through its relation to the past. This is one important aspect of memory and landscape in *Oku no Hosomichi*, since clearly, if there is nothing to remember about a place, it is a wasteland, much like the space that Bashō and Sora passed through on their way from Matsushima to Hiraizumi. In Hiraizumi, on the other hand, Bashō's memory and his other five senses interact to create the landscape that he is then able to relate in his text. This is not the landscape we see today but not because the town of Hiraizumi has changed in the past 300 years. Were we able to view a photograph of Bashō's Hiraizumi, it would bear little relation to the landscape that Bashō presents because photographs can not capture the kind of historical/nostalgic denotations from which Bashō's landscape is constructed. Bashō's landscape is in no way modeled on the photographic forms of representation that underlie our sense of the 'real' today. It is clearly not a homogenous chronotope in which the modern self exists. It is not 'smooth' in all directions. However we must not be so full of intellectual hubris as to consider Bashō's form of 'reality' any less 'real' than our own. In fact, it is in many ways a far richer version of reality.

The second important concept is intricately intertwined with the first but it is useful to consider it by itself. It is a concept invented by the Japanese scholar Ogata Tsutomu who called it *'za no bungaku'* which might be literally translated as 'literature of the gathering' where gathering refers to a group of people gathered together for a specific purpose. Although Ogata's concept specifically uses the term *'bungaku'*, I think the concept of *'za no bungaku'* actually points away from literary readings despite Ogata's constant efforts to recoup his readings for *bungaku*.[40] Ogata posits three axes of *za* in relation to texts. The first is largely the same as the normal usage of *za* to describe *haikai no renga* or *jun renga* gatherings: it refers to a group of poets who have gathered together in the same time and place to compose a text.[41] This is not terribly difficult to understand but it is also not very important for interpreting the passages of *Oku no Hosomichi* that I am discussing here. The second axis of *za* is among people who are separated spatially. Ogata's examples show how certain concepts, styles, and themes spread among Bashō's disciples in different parts of Japan through Bashō's teaching efforts in person, through exchanges of letters, and through the reading of each other's *hokku* in anthologies. This is also not too hard to understand and although it is intimately related to the construction of 'shared memory' I will not spend too much time on it except to note that the historical Bashō did not compose the text in a vacuum; not only did other poets make use of Bashō's texts, Bashō also made liberal use of the texts of other poets.

The third axis of Ogata's *za no bungaku* takes place across time (and usually across space too).[42] An excellent example of this is Bashō's citation of Du Fu's *shi* that takes place at the end of the section that I have translated and I will have more to say about the third axis of *za* when we get to that section of the text. It is also intricately related to the remembering of the past that allows Bashō to construct the landscape his six senses perceive.

'Za no bungaku' obviates the need to talk about vectors of influence. Influence is, of course, an extremely problematic concept which is usually assumed to travel in a single direction (Bashō influencing his disciples, Bashō being influenced by Tang dynasty poets) but 'influence' clearly travels in two directions along the first axis of *za*. Furthermore, the use of the past in the third axis of *za* is creative. A simple example of

this is Bashō's citation of the *shi of* Du Fu. He does not merely cite it; he uses it creatively within the text to create reverberations with his own *hokku*. This kind of usage is somewhat akin to the rhetorical strategies of *haikai no renga* (and *jun renga*) in which creative change is valued over any form – thematic or otherwise – of 'unity' in the text. *Jun renga* and *haikai no renga* require poets to compose in such a way that each link forms an independent 'poetic world' with the link immediately preceding it but at the same time pushes off from the 'poetic world' created by the previous link and the link immediately before it. Poets trained in this kind of textual form are also capable of using the 'past' in an extremely creative fashion. Far from merely being influenced by Du Fu, Bashō uses Du Fu's texts creatively.

Bashō begins by clearly locating himself and Sora within the geography of Hiraizumi by giving their location in relation to the old gate. This also serves to give some kind of sense of the size and grandeur of Hiraizumi since, when the passage opens, the travellers are standing near Hidehira's mansion which had been overgrown by plains and fields. All that is left at the mansion that is as it was is the model of Mt Fuji that Hidehira had had constructed for his garden. From the beginning Bashō is constructing a text based on both what remains and what has vanished but notice that it is the memory of the vanished that makes it possible to describe what remains: the model of Mt Fuji would be just another pile of dirt were it not where Hidehira's mansion had once stood. The memory of the vanished historical/nostalgic past is what allows the present to be created. This is a landscape that is perceived with six senses, not just five, in a space that is not homogenous.

From Hidehira's mansion, Bashō and Sora head to and climb the hill on which Yoshitsune's mansion had been. Like the remains of Hidehira's mansion, the remains of Yoshitsune's mansion are part of Bashō's memory map of Hiraizumi and thus the area can be described. From the hill on which Yoshitsune's mansion is located the travellers are able to look out across a wide swath of the area around Hiraizumi. Bashō names rivers including the Kitakami River, which he probably also saw in and around Ishinomaki since it cuts across the areas through which Bashō and Sora wandered while lost and the 'old Kitakami River' flows into the sea at Ishinomaki itself. But the Kitakami River is not worth mentioning until its historical/nostalgic connotations overwhelm whatever quotidian denotations it might have had for Bashō. Bashō also mentions the Koromo River which is an *utamakura*. Here it seems that he actually gazes upon it, rather than casting a sideways glance at is as he and Sora did when they were lost. He notes that it encircles the palace of one of the children of the last of the three generations of rulers of Hiraizumi and then flows into the great river (presumably the Kitakami River) at the base of the hill that they are sitting on. While this may be a description of what the river actually does, the description is possible because of the

relation of poetic and historical memory. Rivers flow into rivers every-
where in the world but here, it is the river that is an *utamakura* that flows
into the river that is associated with the death of Yoshitsune. Not only
do Bashō's eyes perceive the river, so to does his mind.

The historical/nostalgic connotations of the present are nowhere
more clear than in the next descriptions: Bashō works in the *utamakura*
Koromo-ga-seki, its relationship to the mansion of one of the sons of the
last of the three rulers and notes that Koromo-ga-seki looks like it is
keeping the 'Ezo' (barbarians) out. Probably it had not had to do this for
centuries. I am not sure if the gate even existed when Bashō visited
Hiraizumi. It may have just been a ruin. But it certainly no longer was
used to keep the 'Ezo' out. The gate exists as part of the landscape for
Bashō because of its past, not because of its present, in much the same
way that the fields that now stand where Hidehira's mansion had been.
It is still the gate keeping out the 'Ezo' whatever its 'objective state' in
Bashō's present might have been because it is constructed from the intersection of Bashō's gaze and Bashō's mind. Without the perception of
memory, the gate would not exist in Bashō's landscape even if it had been
freshly rebuilt. With the perception of memory, the mansion can exist as
part of the landscape even if it has been reduced to fields and plains and
the gate can still be keeping the barbarians out. Since memory/mind is
also a sense for perceiving the world and since Bashō is not a subject
formed from Cartesian dualism, not a *kindai-teki jiga*, we can not expect
his 'reality' to correspond to ours in any meaningful way. But Bashō's
landscape is far richer than our own.

The text begins to reach its climax with Bashō's citation of Du Fu's
famous *shi, Chun Wang*:

> Gazing at the Spring
> The country in defeat: mountains and rivers remain;
> in the city: the grasses and trees of spring grow rank.
> Thinking of the times, I weep to see flowers in bloom;
> lamenting being apart, birds startle my thought.
> The fires of war have burned for three months;
> a letter from home would be worth a pile of gold.
> I have scratched my white hairs shorter still;
> and they no longer hold my hairpin in place.

Bashō only cites the first line of Du Fu's *shi*[43] but Du Fu's text becomes a
part of Bashō's third axis of za and the mood and tone of the whole *shi*
come into play in Bashō's *hokku*. This method of *za*-based citation is critical to the construction of many good *hokku* and without the knowledge
of the cited texts, it is impossible to fully feel the mood of the *hokku*. In
Du Fu's *shi*, the capital city is full of grasses and trees growing rank and
the poet in the text laments the great changes that have come over the

country. The textual Bashō, however, is expressing sadness at the transience of aspirations through the citation of Du Fu's *shi* and the flourishing summer grasses that remain when all the aspirations have been extinguished. By using Du Fu's *shi* in a '*za*' based way, rather than citing it as 'authority' or in order to make up for some lack in his own language Bashō is making creative use of the shi1 that lends depth through reverberation between Du Fu and Bashō. Du Fu's *shi* plays a role akin to the *maeku* of a *haikai no renga* sequence.

Bashō's *hokku* is one of his greatest. The *hokku* achieves its affect by juxtaposing the summer grasses (singled out as one 'unit' by the *kireji* [cutting word]) '*ya*' which is 'translated' as a line break) which return year after year – theoretically forever – with the remains of the dreams of mighty warriors which will never come back. The eternal and the fleeting are brought together to remind the reader of the transience and the folly of aspirations and the reverberations of this take place within the textual moment. The eternal, the past, and the present are all brought into play.

It is, of course, possible to read this *hokku* as if Bashō were a *kindai-teki jiga* and this is the work of scholars laboring under the apparatus of literature. In this kind of reading, Bashō sees the summer grasses, is reminded of Du Fu's *shi* and thence composes his own *hokku* in order to express his feelings about the transience of the dreams of Yoshitsune. Mind and body are separated. But clearly, from the evidence that I have presented so far, this is not the case. Bashō's eyes can not perceive a landscape that is not also perceived by his memory/mind. And the landscape that his eyes can perceive exists because it intersects with 'memory' of poetic texts like Du Fu's *shi* or with historical/nostalgic memories – it is not the homogenous space of Descartes. Of course Bashō and Sora 'saw' summer grasses when they were lost. But those summer grasses were not privileged with a *hokku*.[44] They had no relationship to the poetic memory of the Bashō of *Oku no Hosomichi* and perhaps not to the historical Bashō either. Maybe I can even go so far as to say that Bashō and Sora were unable to 'see' the summer grasses while they were lost in the wilderness because these summer grasses had no relation to the historical or poetic memories that Bashō carried in his head and with which he constructed the 'landscape' that his six senses could perceive. It is not until he 'perceives' summer grasses growing rankly on the hill where Yoshitsune's brave guards made their last stand and not until there is an intersection between the historical memory of Yoshitsune and the poetic memory of the *shi* of Du Fu that Bashō is able to describe the summer grasses as part of the landscape. Without memory – and here the memory is clearly not personal – there is no landscape to be described. The landscape that Bashō perceives exists only in the intersection of visual and the mind senses. Memory is a sense that is activated in much the same way vision or smell is. Until we are able to understand this, we can only rehearse literary readings of *Oku no Hosomichi* over and over.

CONCLUSIONS: MEMORY, BODY, LANDSCAPE

Oku no Hosomichi has usually been read as an expression of the self of Bashō, at least since the creation of the apparatus of literature. The 'self' that is posited is the *kindai-teki jiga*, a 'self' that is based on the concepts of Cartesian dualism. The five senses recognized by English speaking cultures are separated from mind and it is mind that is the ultimate ground of being. The construction of the *kindai-teki jiga* is parallel to this and it recognizes only five senses. Although there have been strong challenges mounted against this kind of 'self' ever since Descartes and even though these challenges have become increasingly impressive in the past 150 years, the *kindai-teki jiga*, or at least some version of it is still alive and well in literary studies. And the field of literary studies sustains itself by reading texts like *Oku no Hosomichi* as an expression of the self of the author. This kind of reading, though, requires a great many occlusions.

But the textual Bashō of *Oku no Hosomichi* is clearly not constructed as a *kindai-teki jiga* and to read this textual construct as such requires erasing the crucial role of memory in the construction of the landscape in the text. The landscape that the textual Bashō is capable of describing is constructed from 'shared memories' (or at least memories that are not personal). Without the third axis of *za*, for instance, Bashō might still have been able to write a *hokku* about summer grasses and the faded aspirations of warriors, but it would not have reverberated as deeply for the educated reader of the text. Bashō and Sora assuredly saw summer grasses growing all along their route but the summer grass growing on the hill where Yoshitsune's mansion stood is clearly privileged. It is privileged because the historical/nostalgic connotations it has in Bashō's memory are more important than its denotations in the present. The other summer grasses had the misfortune to be growing in places where their denotations were more important than their connotations. Only when the historical/nostalgic connotations exceed the denotations can the mind of the textual Bashō perceive an object in the landscape. Bashō might have 'seen' other summer grasses but he did not 'mind' them.

Thus a literary reading of *Oku no Hosomichi* strikes me as gravely impoverished. The text was not, of course, written to be read as literature, even if it has proven amenable to literary readings. Bashō's journey, as represented in this text, is reconstructed as one of memory but not as one of personal memory that is the 'expression' of the 'self' of 'Bashō'. It is, rather, a personal remembering of an already written cultural memory. The author of the text, the historical Bashō, could assume that his readers would share this cultural memory and thus be able to participate in it, even if they had not visited Hiraizumi themselves. The reader who does not have the knowledge to read the text while sharing in this memory will perceive nothing more than a kind of textual chaos that can only be cleared up by chasing the memory traces through dictionaries, encyclopedias, compendia of Chinese poetry, etc. We, the poorly educated modern readers are about as lost as Bashō and Sora were when they were wandering between Matsushima and Hiraizumi. However, educated Edo era readers thoroughly enjoyed the text and, in fact, part of the education required to become a *haikai* master involved retracing Bashō's path in *Oku no Hosomichi*.[45]

But by emphasizing the 'shared' nature of this memory, I am not trying to fit *Oku no Hosomichi* into some kind of structural paradigm in which everything is neatly explained. The text is, of course, constructed by a 'self' even if that 'self' is difficult for us to perceive. Therefore *Oku no Hosomichi* is in no way constructed merely by lining up clichéd tropes and linking them together in a clever fashion, any more so than Natsume Sōseki's *Kokoro* is. *Kokoro*, of course, relies on a certain kind of shared memory in order to be read and we modern readers probably have more of the memory necessary to read *Kokoro* than we do to read *Oku no Hosomichi*, even if we need to be reminded of some things like who General Nogi was. But the chronotope of *Kokoro* is also closer to our own chronotope, the space and time are much smoother (for us anyway) than Bashō's space and time.

I have not denied the possibility of a literary reading of *Oku no Hosomichi* in this chapter although I think literary readings of the text are extremely problematic. First we must ask what kind of 'self' the Bashō in the text has. From my argument above, it is clear that this 'self' is not constructed along the lines of mind-body dualism of the *kindai-teki jiga*. Bashō does not merely organize the things perceived by the five senses with his 'mind' but rather mind is one of the senses that allows perception of things in the first place. In order to perceive the landscape around him, mind/memory must be able to perceive the outer world as much as the eyes and ears do. When the mind/memory can not perceive the outer world, there is no way to organize it textually and there is chaos.

So even if we want to read the text as the expression of the self of Bashō – as literature – we must begin by questioning the construction of that 'self'. It is clearly not constructed in the same way that modern subjects are. There are no traces of Cartesian dualism in the text. Memory is as much a sense for interacting with the world as the five senses we impoverished modern subjects generally recognize. Without memory, there is no landscape and Bashō is lost (and cranky). Where memory fails to perceive, there is only wilderness and wasteland, chaos and heartlessness. Attempts at citing/sighting are only mis-citings/mis-sightings. But when Bashō and Sora arrive in Hiraizumi, the landscape is again perceivable. Only when memory works in tandem with the other five senses can the landscape be described. Bashō's tears in Hiraizumi are the result of sound, sight, and smell coming together with the sense of memory. For if there were no memory of Yoshitsune and the glories of Hiraizumi, there would be no tears, no pathos, and the landscape there too would also be wilderness. It is a landscape that exists only when perceived through six senses.

It is important to note, though, that memory is not limited by the 'geographic' boundaries that modernity has imposed on Japan and on 'Japanese texts'. It is common knowledge that texts that we would now label as 'Chinese' were an extremely important part of the canons and the education of people during the Edo era. Bashō's *za* also clearly includes 'Tang' poets like Du Fu. These poets were not separated from Bashō by boundaries in the same way that they are in the modern canon of Japanese literature. As part of the third order '*za*' for Bashō, the poetry of Du Fu is not an 'influence' but a creative part of 'memory' that allows Bashō to perceive summer grasses and to understand the landscape that spreads out in front of him. Du Fu's lamentations reverberate with Bashō's. In this third order *za* sense, Du Fu stands in the same category as Bashō's favorite 'Japanese' poets, poets like Saigyō, Sōgi, and Chōshōshi.[46]

I can now say something about what landscape is in this text. It is not what we would see had Bashō had a camera to take a picture of the Hiraizumi around him and we were somehow able to view his photograph. Rather it is a textual construct that is critically dependent on memory. Those things in the real world whose historical/nostalgic connotations exceed their denotations are the things which Bashō could perceive and write about. Those things whose historical/nostalgic connotations do not exceed their denotations could not be perceived or written about. Without memory, there is no landscape, only chaos.

Because the construction of this form of memory is clearly different than the construction of modern memory, it seems likely that there is no universal construction of memory. Rather the construction of memory is always historically contingent. I am certainly not offering a construction of memory like Bashō's as a form in which the memories of 'comfort women' and others might be better expressed. However the fact that construction of memory is historically contingent and is imbricated in power/knowledge apparatuses means that the narratives of 'comfort women' might be expressed in other, more powerful ways. Or perhaps the former comfort women have expressed their memories in other ways and, blinded by our own constructions of memory and narrative, we have failed to hear them.

REFERENCES

Haga Yaichi. (1890) 1968 'Kokubungaku Tokuhon Shoron,' *In Ochiai Naobumi, Ueda Kazutoshi, Haga Yaichi, Fujioka Sakutarō*. Hisamatsu Senichi, editor and annotator. Pp. 197–205. Tokyo: Chikuma Shoin Shobō.

Imoto Nōichi, Hisatomi Tetsuo, Muramatsu Tomotsugu, and Horikiri Minoru, editors and annotators. 1997 *Matsuo Bashō-shū 2*. Tokyo: Shōgakukan.

Ishihara Chiaki. 1991 'Kindai-teki Jiga.' *In Yomu tame no Riron: Bungaku, Shisō, Hihyō*. Ishihara Chiaki and others, ed. pp. 30–35. Yokohama: Seori Shobō.

Karatani, Kōjin. 1993 *Origins of Modern Japanese Literature*. Translation edited by Brett de Bary. Durham: Duke University Press.

Mekada, Makoto. 1975 *Tōshi Sanbyaku-shu, volume 2*. Tokyo: Heibonsha.

Oka, Mari. 2000 *Kioku/Monogatari*. Tokyo: Iwanami Shoten.

Qiu Xieyou, editor and annotator. 1998 *Tang Shi San bai shou*. Taipei: San min Shu ju.

Toyama, Susumu, editor and annotator. 1978 *Bashō Bunshū*. Tokyo: Shinchūsha.

Ueno Yōzō and Sakurai Takejirō, ed. 1997 *Bashō Jihitsu Oku no Hosomichi*. Tokyo: Iwanami Shoten.

NOTES

[1] I use the words 'common sense' here as something akin to 'ideology' or 'ideologically correct'. It is both radically and profoundly conservative by nature.

[2] Karatani notes (without giving the source of his citation) that Foucault wrote that literature was established in the West only in the late nineteenth century (Karatani 1993: 195). Haga Yaichi could write in the forward to *Kokubungaku Tokuhon* that the word '*bungaku*' was extremely familiar even if it might be difficult for people to define (Haga 1890: 197). Even though Haga's definition is different than the one that we might give today, it is clear that he is using the word in its modern sense, a sense quite different than the word had had during the Edo era.

[3] It is noteworthy, though, that *Makura no Sōshi*'s canonical status is relatively recent. Although the text was not unknown during the Edo era, it never had the status of a text like *Tsurezure-gusa* or *Tosa Nikki*. Its high status within the canon probably started sometime in the early twentieth century. It is, after all, a text highly amenable to being read as an 'expression' of the 'self' of 'Sei Shōnagon'.

[4] Matsuo Bashō (1644–94) is widely considered the greatest *haikai* poet. He produced a great number of famous *hokku* and *haibun*.

[5] I do not like to apply the 'fiction/non-fiction' binary to Edo era texts since it is clearly anachronistic to do so but will use the terms here rather than go into a lengthy detour explaining '*aru ga mama*'.

[6] It was not necessary in the classical poetic tradition to have actually seen an *utamakura* in order to write about it; it was enough to know the traditional poetic associations. It was enough to know the poetic associations it entered into. So it is possible that Bashō could have written a text about 'travelling' to the north without actually having left his hut. That this

would have been a very different text than the one we read today shows
that 'personal memory' has a role in the construction of *Oku no Hosomichi*.
But I will argue throughout the rest of this paper that this role is secondary to the role of shared memory.

    Utamakura are places with famous poetic associations. Bashō and Sora,
at least within the text of *Oku no Hosomichi*, view a great number of *utamakura* throughout their trip. And *utamakura* play a significant role in the
construction of landscape throughout *Oku no Hosomichi*. I will have more
to say about this below.

7 Since most readers today do not have the requisite memories, the most
widely circulated versions of *Oku no Hosomichi* come replete with annota-
tions.

8 *Kibyōshi* or 'yellow cover books' were prose and picture texts aimed at
adults but did not require a great deal of education to read (that they now
require a great deal of annotation for modern readers shows just how
uneducated the modern reader is, at least in the Edo sense). *Yomihon* are a
kind of prose-fiction text that was popular from the mid- to late-Edo era.
They probably required more education to read but were generally printed
with *furigana* alongside all of the difficult *kanji*.

9 I will henceforth call it the '*kindai-teki jiga*' since it is important not to con-
flate the *kindai-teki jiga* with the senses of self in other cultures

10 I am aware that 'sense' is an impoverished translation of *kon* (which might
be literally translated as 'root'). Furthermore, the construction of body is
much more complex than I have laid it out here. The *rokkon*, for instance,
are intimately related to the *rokushiki*, a relationship that I have ignored
entirely. And the 'senses' are seen as roots of 'delusion' that keep one from
attaining enlightenment. My purpose in bringing the *rokkon* up here is
merely to illustrate another 'construction of self' which may also be more
closely related to the construction of 'self' in *Oku no Hosomichi*.

11 Kawai Sōryō (1649–1710), born in Shinano, also accompanied Bashō on
the trip recorded in *Kashima Kikō*.

12 City in northern Japan from which the three generations of the Ōshū
Fujiwara ruled. See next section for more information.

13 *Utamakura*.

14 *Utamakura*.

15 Attributed to Mencius.

16 Citation of the *tanka* translated below.

17 City in Miyagi Prefecture, current population about 120,000. An important port on the Pacific Ocean side of Japan during the Edo era.

18 In fact, they could not see the mountain from Ishinomaki. See below for
the *tanka* that Bashō cites.

19 These are clichéd tropes for a prosperous town.

20 *Utamakura*.

21 *Utamakura*.

22 *Utamakura*.

23 About 140 kilometers. Looking at the map on page 623 of Imoto Nōichi and others, *Matsuo Bashō-shū 2* I estimate that the direct route would have been about 20 percent shorter.

24 He also has more poems in the collection than anyone else.

25 I am not an expert on 'marshes' in pre-modern Japanese and Chinese texts. Perhaps they are always gloomy and this is also a clichéd trope?

26 For the sake of brevity I have omitted two *hokku* and a prose passage that follow this section I have translated.

27 The three referred to here are Fujiwara no Kiyohira (1056–1128), Fujiwara no Motohira (dates of birth and death unknown), and Fujiwara no Hidehira (see below). These three were members of the Ōshū Fujiwara family and ruled northern Japan from Hiraizumi.

28 This is a citation of the *Kantan* story where the phrase is 炊 but Bashō, like many people during the Edo era uses the homophonous phrase 睡 so I have translated it as 'a dream within a wink of sleep'.

29 *Ichiri.*

30 ?-1187. The third of Hiraizumi's great rulers. He opposed Yoritomo and protected Yoshitsune.

31 Mt Kinkei was a model of Mt Fuji constructed for Hidehira's garden.

32 1159–89. A son of Minamoto no Yoshitomo (1123–60), he hid from the Taira in various places, including Hiraizumi (receiving protection from Hidehira). When his elder brother Yoritomo (1147–99) raised arms against the Taira in 1180, Yoshitsune joined forces with him and helped him defeat them. However, in the years following their victory, Yoritomo and Yoshitsune had a falling out and Yoshistune again sought the protection of Hidehira. When Hidehira died, his son, Yasuhira, attacked Yoshitsune's mansion and Yoshitsune committed suicide.

33 One of the large domains of northern Japan with its seat of power at Morioka.

34 The palace of Izumi Saburō Tadahira, the younger brother of Fujiwara no Yasuhira.

35 Yoshitsune's mansion is known by several names: Takadachi, Hōgan-dachi, and Koromogawa no Tate.

36 ?-1189. Son of Hidehira. He began his rule by protecting Yoshitsune as he had promised his father to do but under pressure from Yoritomo, he eventually attacked Yoshitsune's mansion and after Yoshitsune was dead, was attacked and destroyed in turn by Yoritomo.

37 Also called Koromogawa no seki and Koromo no seki. *Utamakura.*

38 A citation from a *shi by* Du Fu. See below.

39 Related in the section following this passage which I have not translated.

40 At the very least, Ogata's concept of '*za no bungaku*' points away from reading texts as the 'expression' of the 'self' of an 'author'.

41 Of course in this case the word '*za*' usually refers to people gathered together to compose a *haikai no renga* or a *jun renga* sequence. But Ogata extends the concept to other textual forms as well.

42 Although Bashō's citations of *utamakura* and historical sites often take place when he is in close spatial proximity to them. It will become clear, however, that spatial proximity is not essential to the construction of the third order *za* since Bashō also cites Du Fu's *shi* in order to construct the landscape even though the separation in homogenous (Descartian) space between Hiraizumi and Xian is immense.

43 The first two lines of my translation.

44 Had those same summer grasses been seen by a '*haiku*' poet like Masaoka Shiki, though, it is entirely possible that a *haiku* might have been written about them. This is due, in part, to the homogenous space of *haiku*.

45 I do not know whether the aspirants actually went to Ishinomaki or instead took the more direct route to Hiraizumi from Matsushima. The reception of *Oku no Hosomichi* in the mid- to late-Edo era needs more research.

46 Saigyō (1118–90), one of the greatest *tanka* poets, has more *tanka* in the *Shin Kokinshū* than any other poet. Sōgi (1421–1502), one of the greatest *renga* poets. Kinoshita Chōshōshi (1569–1649), an important *tanka* poet in the late-Muromachi and early-Edo eras.

7

What it Sounds Like to Lose an Empire: Happy End and the Kinks

MICHAEL BOURDAGHS

Our being this crazy about music from overseas' countries happens because we feel we are living under the same conditions. So there is certainly something of a sympathetic chord in [our response], one that transcends tradition or cultural background. But that alone is not enough. The problem is, how to make it our own, how to deepen it into a form of subjective consciousness-raising. In doing this, we can't simply belittle tradition or cultural background.

MATSUMOTO TAKASHI, DRUMMER FOR HAPPY END (MATSUMOTO 1971)

The space that Happy End created was unique, even in global terms. It was warped in a fourth-dimensional kind of way, and in conflict with the spaces around it. I'm still caught up in that double helix structure. I catch on immediately to any music that produces this sort of space.

HOSONO HARUOMI, BASSIST FOR HAPPY END (HAGIWARA 1983:104)

What does it sound like to lose an empire? The island nations of Japan and England came out of the 1940s stripped of most of their overseas colonies and struggling to find positions within the new US neo-colonial empire that stretched across both Pacific and Atlantic. Moreover, in both nations, the trauma of lost empire was temporarily salved by promises of a utopian, democratic, and class-free future, but by the 1960s it seemed painfully clear that those promises were not going to be kept. Homi K. Bhabha writes that postcolonial remembering is 'never a quiet act of introspection or retrospection', but rather 'a painful re-membering, a putting together of the dismembered past to make sense of the trauma of the present' (Bhabha 1994: 63). In a somewhat similar vein, this chapter will attempt to make some sense of the complexity of postimperial memory in 1960s and 1970s in Japan and the UK. I will look in particular at popular music, which provided an outlet for expressing the desires, angers, and sorrows that this memory entailed. As the discussion of the relation between 'tradition' and 'rock' in a 1971 Japanese music magazine noted, while rock music in the US carried on the traditions of American folk music, the question was 'in England and Japan, which bear different traditions, how does rock relate to tradition?' ('*Bokura ni totte no dentō no mondai*' 1971). The answer, it turns out, is quite complicated.

The Kinks and Happy End are two of the most influential, if not always commercially successful, rock bands of the period. Each is remembered in particular for retaining a local identity to its music, even as each participated enthusiastically in the increasing globalization of rock music. The Kinks were celebrated for preserving a specifically 'English' quality to their music, especially in their brilliant albums from the late-1960s and early-1970s. Likewise, Happy End is remembered (incorrectly) as the first Japanese rock band to sing its lyrics in Japanese, rather than English. These gestures can be read as a form of resistance to US cultural hegemony – and yet this resistance was couched in the genre of rock music, a genre generally identified as arising out of American cultural traditions. Moreover, both bands struggled to break into the American market, which served as the ultimate arbiter of canonicity in the new genre. The tensions inherent in this irony rose to the surface as these musicians negotiated the 'trauma of the present', subservience to American hegemony, a hegemony that was inscribed in the material bodies of postwar Japanese (Igarashi 2000). As one Japanese critic wrote in 1971, rock music in Japan amounted to a kind of 'colonial culture', in which the very acts of snapping fingers and swaying in time to the music amounted to a colonizing of Japanese bodies.[1]

Both the Kinks and Happy End responded to the traumatic present, as well as to memories of loss, not by engaging in a monumental history, nor by appealing to an ahistorical fantasy of the national folk, nor by appealing to a developmental narrative of modernization. As I will explore below, they responded instead by performing an ironic remembering of the past through song, one that situated the origins of identity in the unstable and heterogeneous present rather than in the distant past. Unlike many of the other genres for remembering discussed in this volume, music, with its inherent reliance on 'noise' – 'an aggression against the code-structuring messages' – prophesies by its very nature the end of the current order and the rise of something different, even as it claims to bring order to the world. 'Listening to music is to receive a message. Nevertheless, music cannot be equated with a language' because 'unlike the words of a language – which refer to a signified – music, though it has a precise operationality, never has a stable reference to a code of the linguistic type' (Attali 1985:27 and 25). It was this very instability and illegibility that both bands would pursue in their acts of remembrance.

*

A celebratory mourning of empire and a fierce anger at the betrayal of postwar promises for a class-free society: these leitmotifs color the music of the Kinks throughout their career.[2] The band, led by brothers Ray and Dave Davies, first burst to the top of world pop charts in 1964 with the song 'You Really Got Me', a single that (along with its follow-up, 'All Day and All of the Night') is often credited with inspiring the hard rock and heavy metal sounds that would appear within a few years. But by 1965, with singles like 'Well Respected Man' and 'Dedicated Follower of Fashion', the band began to stress satirical social criticism in its songs. By the time of the 1966 single, 'Sunny Afternoon', the Kinks were recognized as being among the most astute social commentators in the pop music world.

In particular, the band continues to enjoy high critical esteem today based mainly on the string of six brilliant studio albums it released from the mid-1960s to the early-1970s: *Face to Face* (1966), *Something Else by the Kinks* (1967), *The Kinks are the Village Green Preservation Society* (1968), *Arthur; or the Decline and Fall of the British Empire* (1969); *Part One: Lola Versus Powerman and the Moneygoround* (1970); and *Muswell Hillbillies* (1971). In song after brilliant song, the Davies brothers explored the melancholic traces of Britain's postwar past, often relying on memories of their own roots in North London working class culture to challenge hegemonic narratives of national history.

In particular, the 1969 album, *Arthur; or the Decline and Fall of the British Empire* mapped the Davies brothers' familial past onto the broader narrative of imperial history. Its opening track, 'Victoria', is a remarkable musical hybrid of 'Rule Britannia!' and Chuck Berry-style rock 'n' roll. Its lyrics ironically celebrate the myths of empire and their enjoyment by working-class families, who worshipped the royal family even down to sartorial details, as the song 'She's Bought a Hat Like Princess Marina' demonstrated (even as its musical arrangement switched back and forth between apparently sincere nostalgia and vicious parody). The song 'Mr. Churchill Says' looked back on England's finest hour, when the nation united in mutual sacrifice to save the British Empire. The track 'Some Mother's Son' also remembers the war – this time, however, to savage the cynicism of the ruling elite toward the great sacrifices made by the working class for the sake of the nation.

The three centerpiece songs to the concept album drove the point home. 'Brainwashed', built around an angry guitar riff, denigrated postwar culture, in which the promises of liberation and of a class-free community had given way to consumerism and conformism. 'Shangri-La' continued the devastating parody: it attacked the destruction of local culture in the name of consumerism, even as the song's gorgeous vocal harmonies acknowledged the urgency of the desires that drove postwar culture. Looking at the new housing built in the postwar, Ray (the band's primary songwriter) would sneer 'And all the houses on the street have got a name, 'cos all the houses in the street they look the same'. Finally, the song 'Australia' returned explicitly to the traces of Britain's empire. Based on the actual experiences of the Davies' brother-in-law, the eponymous Arthur, whose emigration down under in the early-1960s remained a traumatic memory of family life, the song celebrated the waning seductions of empire. Australia, it turned out, was where the fantasy of a class-free society had relocated, where equal opportunity was available to all. Musically, the song gave away the source of this new ideological fantasy: by quoting Beach Boys-style harmony as it declared that in Australia, 'We'll surf like they do in the USA'. Such gestures revealed that in postwar Britain, even the fantasies of colonial desire were under the sway of American hegemony.

Together with the irony that marks these songs from *Arthur* – as well as many others from this period – a sharp anger flashes through. Working-class culture and family traditions, all grounded in the pride of empire, had been betrayed and discarded, and the promised utopian community that was to take their place in the postimperial, postwar period never arrived. What arose instead was the new faceless world of bureaucracy and consumption that Davies attacked fiercely in songs such as '20th Century Man' (from *Muswell Hillbillies*) and 'God's Children' (from the 1971 soundtrack album *Percy*). In the meanwhile, Davies celebrated memories of urban working class culture in songs like 'Welcome to Sleazy Town' (from the 1986 album *Think Visual*) or the hit, 'Come Dancing' (from *State of Confusion*, 1983) with its lamentation over the Dance Palace that had been replaced by a parking lot.

Yet Davies also repeatedly foregrounded the ironies of nostalgia: the working class culture that he laments, he acknowledges, was itself largely an illusion, the product of active re-membering of the past in the present. He seems to acknowledge, that is, that the past that nostalgia seeks 'has never existed except as narrative,' so that it is 'a past which has only ideological reality' (Stewart 1993:23). The album *Muswell Hillbillies*, for example, was a loosely organized concept album, lamenting the destruction of London neighborhoods carried out in the name of urban renewal. In it, the band performs music in the country-rock and folk-rock styles most closely associated with American musical traditions. Moreover, songs such as 'Oklahoma USA' reveal that the English identity being mourned was never stable or pure, but always mediated by fantasies produced through American popular culture. In the song 'Muswell Hillbilly', Davies sings a protest against what was lost when his old neighborhood, Muswell Hill, was subjected to urban renewal. In singing of the now vanished culture, one centered ironically on American country-and-western music, the singer demands to be taken back home – home to the Black Hills of Tennessee, which, he acknowledges, he has never actually seen.

At the same time that the Kinks were recording their ironic hybrid form of American country music, on the other side of the globe, the members of Happy End were likewise turning to American popular music, especially the West Coast folk-rock sound, in their attempt to perform a new position for Japanese rock. Given the hierarchies of geo-politics, it is almost certain that the members of Happy End at the time knew the Kinks' music – and, in fact, the two bands were occasionally compared in the Japanese music press (e.g. Kitanaka 1973). It is also nearly certain that the Kinks, like virtually all rock fans outside of Japan, could hardly have known of Happy End's music (though the band did achieve some presence in the US near the end of its career). Japanese rock, after all, was perceived to be an inferior carbon copy of Western music – precisely the mindset that Happy End set out to challenge.

*

The four musicians who would form Happy End originally got to know one another in music circles at Tokyo universities in the late-1960s.[3] Two of the members – bassist Hosono Haruomi and drummer Matsumoto Takashi – had been members of the blues-rock band Apryl Fool, whose 1969 debut album attracted favorable press attention: one review declared that Apryl Fool had the potential to become a truly Japanese rock band, one that transcended mere imitation of the West ('K.T.' 1969; Hagiwara 1983:24–36). Most of Apryl Fool's songs were original numbers, but had English-language lyrics, as was ordinarily the case for 1960s Japanese rock. When Apryl Fool disbanded, Hosono and Matsumoto formed a new band that included rhythm guitarist Ōtaki Eiichi and lead guitarist Suzuki Shigeru. From the start, the new group planned to pursue the folk-rock sound, especially that of the band Buffalo Springfield, but to sing its lyrics in Japanese. The new group began appearing live under the name Valentine Blue in late 1969. Early in 1970, they changed their name to Happy End (Happii Endo, written in *hiragana* script rather than *katana*), and began recording their first album, *Happii Endo*, which was released in August of that year. They would release two more studio albums: *Kazemachi roman*, released in 1971, and then *HAPPY END*, recorded in Los Angeles and released in early 1973. All of the songs on the three albums were original numbers, and all were sung in Japanese.

Although Happy End was not a huge success commercially, they quickly became critical favorites. The first album got favorable, if not overwhelmingly positive, reviews, and was named *New Music Magazine*'s Japanese rock album of the year. Whatever reservations critics had were swept away with the second album, *Kazemachi roman*, which was instantly acclaimed a masterpiece. Many critics still regard it as the great-est Japanese rock album ever recorded.

Critics praised the band because it seemed to have realized the long-held dream of a Japanese form of rock that was original and authentic, and not a mere imitation of Western rock. In this sense, Happy End can

be understood in the context of the return to 'Japan' that the 'ambivalent moderns' of Japan's New Left had been carrying out in many different forms since the early-1960s (Olson 1992). This 'return' repeated an
earlier 'return to Japan' from the 1930s, and not surprisingly central
figures of that earlier rediscovery became intellectual touchstones once
again in the 1960s. Such thinkers as philosopher Kuki Shūzō, folklorist
Yanagita Kunio, and ethicist Watsuji Tetsurō, representatives of various
strains of the 1930s' return to Japan, were rediscovered in the 1960s and
became heroes to a new generation of anti-establishment youths who
rejected the versions of tradition offered up by both the conservative
Japanese state and the establishment Left represented by the Japan
Communist Party. This was also the era that gave birth to *minshūshi*
(people's history), for example, where historians such as Irokawa
Daikichi and Hirota Masaki attempted to counter Orientalist and mod-
ernization-theory versions of Japan's history by recovering the traces of
a non-elite past that had been written out of official histories of both the
Left and Right (Fujitani 1998; Gluck 1978).

It was in the midst of this widespread attempt to remember a specifically Japanese past that Happy End appeared with its hybrid form of
Japanese folk-rock. The band's music contained references to Japanese
folklore (though the folk culture it cited tended to be more urban than
rural – the band's 1973 best-of album was even titled 'CITY'), and the
imagery on its album covers echoed the sorts of folkloric images popular
in late-1960s *manga* such as *Garo* that were widely read by student activists. The second album, *Kazemachi roman*, was intended in particular as
a concept album, elegizing the parts of Tokyo that had vanished in
various waves of postwar urban renewal, mostly notably in the years
leading up to the 1964 Tokyo Olympics. More than anything, though,
what appealed to a generation that hoped to recover an authentic and
subversive stratum of folk culture was the band's insistence on singing in
Japanese. Besides the band's skillful use of studio recording techniques
and its mastery of the folk-rock music style, what attracted most attention to Happy End – as we will see again below – were its skillful lyrics,
mostly written by Matsumoto Takashi, and the odd way in which the
band sung those lyrics in order to merge the rhythms of spoken Japanese
with those of rock music.

As many have noted, the Japanese New Left tended to perceive
Japanese folk culture as existing in opposition to the West, especially the
US. In this East/West binary, authentic Japanese culture was situated on
the side of the East, alongside the other victims of Western colonialism
and neo-colonialism in Asia, as this generation attempted to address the
present-day trauma of American hegemony in East and South East Asia.
But this perception of the Japanese as being the victim of imperialism
also had the effect of erasing the history of Japan's own prewar and
wartime empire. Murai Osamu has demonstrated the complicity of the

1920s and 1930s' discourse of Japanese folklore studies in legitimating Japan's own expanding empire, and a similar case could be made for the 1960s' rediscovery of the folk (Murai 1995). In focusing exclusively on the East/West divide, the postwar 'return to Japan' constructed a version of history that erased heterogeneity and hierarchies of power existing within Asia, with the result that 'Japan's colonial past had been excised from the popular consciousness' (Igarashi 2000:166). This was a period in which the 'myth of the homogeneous nation' increasingly held sway, replacing earlier versions of national identity that had stressed heterogeneity and foregrounded Japan's interrelationships with other nations in East Asia (Oguma 2002). That is to say, the radical new forms of historical memory that arose in the 1960s and 1970s were at the same time an evasion of history.

In that sense, it is hardly surprising that Happy End's music, unlike that of the Kinks, for example, contains no direct references to the loss of empire, though Hosono Haruomi would address issues of Orientalism and Japanese exoticization of both its own and other Asian cultures in a number of solo projects released after the break-up of Happy End (Hagiwara 1983:96–109 and Hosokawa 1999). This absence situates the band's music within what Lisa Yoneyama has called 'the remarkable indifference about Japan's prewar and wartime legacy of colonialism, military aggression, and other imperial practices' that characterizes much (though not all) Japanese historical imagination in the decades following 1945 (Yoneyama 1999:5).

While not dismissing the importance or relevance of this problematic, I would like to argue here somewhat differently. It seems more useful to explore ways in which Happy End's music attempted to remember the past in a different manner, outside the frameworks that led much of Japanese culture, both elite and popular, to erase the memories of empire. The band's music, in other words, did not provide the sort of tidy coming to terms with the past that characterized official narratives of Japanese history, which attempted to restore a 'healthy' national identity in the present, one that supposedly arose through linear progressive development out of the premodern past. Nor did the band's music perform a 'working through' or 'mourning' of the past, such as would characterize a Freudian approach to restore the grieving subject to health (Santner 1993; Ivy 1995:13–15; and Yoneyama 1999:26–33). Instead, Happy End tried to break through existing forms of history and memory by stressing the present moment and the possibility it provided for actively rearranging one's relations with both past and future. What was crucial was the present moment as a space of possibility for a different kind of practice, a performative practice that was perverse and warped. Their music was literally revolutionary – not so much in terms of a Marxist revolution or of a revolution of national liberation (Happy End's members expressed doubts over both), but rather of a Copernican revolution, one that insisted that the problem of history revolved neither around past nor future, but around the present.

This required, of course, a rejection of many of the models through which the past was memorialized in 1960s' Japan. For example, Yoshikuni Igarashi has shown how much postwar Japanese popular culture worked through the traumatic memories of the wartime through a variety of melodramatic narratives and imagery, whether it be the sight of wrestler Rikidōzan triumphing against much larger American opponents, or romantic narratives that attempted to achieve reconciliation through heterosexual romance and domestic bliss. But starting with its very name, Happy End performed a parodic rejection of melodrama as a mode for self-understanding (Anderson 2002).[4] The band, in fact, recorded almost no conventional love songs – its lyrics were intellectual expressions of urban angst and alienation. Likewise, the band expressed discomfort with explicitly politicized forms of music – such as the songs of Okabayashi Nobuyasu, the protest folk singer for whom the band provided backing early in its career. Rather than treat music as a secondary medium, one important only in so far as it conveyed the primary message contained in the lyrics, Happy End insisted on the importance of musicality to any notion of Japanese rock.

What sort of musical remembering, then, did the band practice? Poised at the lip of a trap that seemed to offer only two choices – Japan or the West – Happy End sought a way out through the deliberate use of ambiguity and irony, as well as through foregrounding the materiality of language itself. Even as they built their lyrics around distinctly Japanese imagery and language, they repeatedly acknowledged that a true and transparent return to Japan was impossible. They sought to 'uncover the fragmenting processes of modern westernization itself' without surrendering to the logic of fetishism, to 'the wish for an unmediated return to origins, for the identity of difference, and for culture as unity (for which the voice becomes the medium)' (Ivy 1995:20). The form in which their 'return to Japan' took place involved a deliberate deconstruction of Japan, one that ended up undermining the identities of both America and Japan, East and West. Moreover, although this remains more implicit than explicit in Happy End's music, this destabilizing of identities undermined the possibility of nostalgia for the colonial period as well: the notion of a pan-Asian solidarity that underwrote both 1930s and 1960s anti-modern political radicalism depended on stable notions of Japanese and Asian identities – the very identities that Happy End's music rendered unstable.

This is most clearly seen when we examine the 'rock in Japanese' debate that broke out in 1970 and 1971, largely in response to Happy End's first two albums. As I have already noted, prior to Happy End's emergence, the vast majority of Japanese rock songs were sung in English – even original songs. In contrast, the folk music genre – the other half of the musical soundtrack to Japan's 1960s' student movement – used predominantly Japanese-language songs, so that even cover versions of songs by such American artists as Bob Dylan and Joan Baez tended to be translated into Japanese when sung by Japanese folk singers. This was in part because, as folk music increasingly became dominated by protest songs (a characteristic of folk from the Kansai region, in particular), the primary goal of the music was to transmit the political message of the lyrics to listeners. In folk music, it was believed, voice had to act as a transparent medium of communication, and so the lyrics had to be in Japanese, the native language of the listeners.

By contrast, it was widely believed that rock had to be sung in English to be authentic. Japanese rock bands in the early 1970s were confronted with the same sort of doubts about the 'authenticity' of their music as had troubled Japanese jazz musicians since before the war (Atkins 2001). Rock music was rooted in American and English culture, and so the closer Japanese bands could approach the original models, the more authentic they were thought to be. In an article published at the height of the debate, Hayashi Hikaru would argue that the music of every local culture was born out of the characteristic rhythms of its spoken language. It would be impossible, he implied, to fit Japanese lyrics to musical forms that had originated with speakers of non-Japanese languages (Hayashi 1971).[5] Likewise, Fukamachi Jun, while expressing sympathy for the experiment Happy End was carrying out, in the end declared, 'I just don't believe that the Japanese language can fit rock' and called for Japanese youth to produce their own original form of music that was 'neither classical, nor jazz, nor rock, nor pop' (Fukamachi 1971). On top of such concerns, singing rock in Japanese was perceived as a mark of selling out: those who sung rock in Japanese, such as Group Sounds bands, were producing utterly commodified forms of music, designed not so much for aesthetic integrity as for market success. Finally, Japanese rock bands perceived themselves as participating in a global movement, a participation that seemed to depend on their singing lyrics in a language that was intelligible to audiences beyond the boundaries of Japan. Bands like the Spiders, Flowers, and the Sadistic Mika Band were in fact touring in North America and Europe in the 1960s and 1970s.[6]

The assertion by Happy End that rock could be sung successfully in Japanese challenged this common sense and provoked a sharp and sometimes negative response. Skeptics point out that the 'rock in Japanese' position was self-contradictory. As one critic noted, 'If you're going to say, sing it in Japanese because we're Japanese, then why don't you just go the whole way and come out in favor of *enka* sung in *naniwabushi* style and reject rock? Neither rock in Japanese nor folk in Japanese can lay claim to any traditional lineage . . .' (Nakamura 1971:20). But Happy End sung in Japanese not to lay claim to an authentic tradition: they explicitly denied that any authentic tradition was available to them. Rather, they chose to sing in a form that no reference to the past could authenticate, precisely so as to create a new authenticity in the present.

In later years, Matsumoto Takashi, who wrote the lyrics for nearly all of Happy End's songs, would claim to have been a disinterested observer of the 'Rock in Japanese' debate. The debate broke out largely in response to the first Happy End album but, Matsumoto writes, 'I wasn't in the least concerned with it. I was happy simply to have our songs understood by those people who understood them; I didn't have the slightest desire to engage in some sort of resistance or protest' (Matsumoto 1993). It is clear that at the time, though, Happy End were identified as the main proponents for 'Rock in Japanese'. A 1970 review of their first album declared:

> All of the songs are their own originals, and all are sung in Japanese. According to them, the ones who say Japanese and rock don't go together, that it is foolish, are the ones who are wrong, and that it is meaningless if it's not in Japanese. They don't want rock to end up being a simple import from abroad. (K.T. 1970)

In 1970, Ōtaki Eiichi would declare, 'I'm not doing it in Japanese as any kind of protest.' If one wanted to participate in a global rock scene, he continued, that was fine, but in every country where rock was being performed, it 'had sunk in to become a part of everyday life', and to achieve such an effect in Japan required singing in a language listeners could understand. 'Don't misunderstand me, though – my saying "Japan", "Japan", doesn't mean I'm some kind of nationalist [*kokusuishugisha*]' (Quoted in Take 1999:134).

Writing in 1971, Matsumoto directly addressed the issue of what was 'Japanese' about the music that Happy End played. His generation were stuck, he wrote, between a 'pseudo-West' (*Seiyō-magai*) and a 'sham-Japan' (*Nihon-modoki*), in which neither West nor Japan could provide a stable sense of identity. 'The only means left to us is *to seek out our own Japan*. For me, "Happy End" is a gamble on this, an attempt at a new kind of Japaneseness.' Japanese rock lacks any venerable tradition, he continues. 'The crucial point is that what we do from now on will become a new tradition.' He concludes by directly addressing the reader/listener:

> There is a wind blowing that transcends history. Only to that extent we can call this wind 'tradition'. And if that's the case, then it isn't so hard to hear a new Japaneseness from *Kazemachi roman*. This takes place when the wind that Happy End has refined is taken up inside your own head. It's quite strange: you and I are both called 'Japanese', but our country doesn't seem like our country.
> It's time to take a trip.
> To find Japan. (Matsumoto 1971)

This involved neither a blind yearning for America, nor a nostalgic return to Japan. As Matsumoto wrote in another article from the period, 'insofar as we are a "happy end", the downfall of America and the decline of Japan are both our starting point and our perverse destination'. In a consumerist society in which youth rebellion, including rock music, was quickly commodified, the band would seek out the gaps and forgotten spaces of contemporary Tokyo, seeking to stop up the social machinery with a 'no' (*iie*) that was embedded materially in the name of the band itself. 'This is not because we are Japanese or because we are in Japan. Just as Japan has from our perspective become a *trompe l'oeil* [*kakushie*], the framework of rock itself becomes a Copernican revolution of place – like singing out in a distorted mother tongue [*yugamerareta bokokugo*]' (Matsumoto 1970). As Hosokawa Shuhei has argued, Matsumoto's stance differs from that of late 1960s' folk singers in Japan 'who argued that they sang in Japanese because they *were* Japanese'. Matsumoto did not assume a ' "natural" tie between his language and nationality'; nor did he believe that singing in English could 'resolve the inauthenticity of Japanese as a rock language' (Hosokawa 1999). For Matsumoto, the Japanese language was above all a source of raw material for use in experimentation.

What sort of lyrics resulted from this experiment? '*Haru yo koi*' (Spring, Come Ye Hence; lyrics by Matsumoto Takashi, music by Ōtaki Eiichi) was the first song on the first Happy End album, and the second song ever written by the band. The lyrics were largely adapted from dialogue in the experimental manga *Haru* (Spring) by Nagashima Shinji, who is thanked in the album credits (Shida 2000). The focus of the song lyrics lies not on revolutionary politics nor on romance, but rather on ordinary daily life in the city. Specifically, it takes up the boredom of one who faces the New Year holiday alone, sitting by himself at his *kotatsu*, after having abandoned his family home in an attempt to make it in the big city. Like many Happy End songs, the lyrics are written in 'desu/masu' style. On paper, the lyrics read as a fairly conventional, perhaps existentialist account of urban alienation: many commented when the album was released on how successfully the band had used very ordinary, conversational Japanese in its lyrics.

The lyrics, then, seem unremarkable when you read them, but something strange happens when they are sung. The song demonstrates how Happy End would resolve the supposed contradiction between the rhythms of spoken Japanese and rock music: the Japanese language they sang would be 'warped' and 'perverted'. As Uchida Yūya, leader of the band Flowers and one of the fiercest opponents of rock-in-Japanese, would complain about the song in a 1971 roundtable discussion (in which members of Happy End also participated), 'if you don't play close attention when you listen, you can't understand what they're saying. If you're going to take the trouble to sing in your mother tongue, it should come out much clearer.' (Uchida, Matsumoto, Ōtaki et al. 1971).

But for Happy End, the Japanese language functioned not as a reposi-tory of tradition or identity, but rather as an alienated and alienating tongue – a source of noise. This singing style fits the narrative presented in the lyric: of a young person who has left home and family behind to gamble everything on a new life. The song, that is, rejects the nostalgic discourse of *furusato*, or 'rural hometown', that was so central to postwar Japanese myths of national homogeneity (Robertson 1998). In tandem with this, the language of the lyrics functions not as a transparent medium that bonds the national community, but rather as a form of materiality to be worked over: accents are misplaced, pronunciations are bent, relatively meaningless syllables are extended to remarkable length (e.g. the '*ma*' in a verb-final conjugation '*-mashita*', or the '*no*' in '*mono desu*', or the '*i*' in '*nai hazu*'). In sum, the band invented an inauthentic, unnatural form of Japanese, what Bhabha would call an 'unhomely' form of the mother tongue.

Such experimentation with language – the use of wordplay, of non-standard *kanji*, of *hiragana* to render words normally written in *katakana* – would characterize Matsumoto's lyrics throughout the band's career. The last song from the second album, '*Ai ue wo*' (Starved for Love; lyrics by Matsumoto Takashi, music by Ōtaki Eiichi), for example, similarly foregrounds the materiality of language and may perhaps be the band's closing argument in the 'Rock in Japanese' debate. The song's title, written in *kanji*, seems to communicate a message, one that is repeated in the first line of the lyrics. But as the song progresses, it quickly becomes apparent that nothing is being communicated: the title turns out to be a pun on the opening line of the standard Japanese syllabary, and the remaining lyrics simply recite the remainder of the syllabary (*a i u e o, ka ki ku ke ko . . .*), a string of meaningless sounds – an effect similar to singing the alphabet in English.

When we recall the frequent invocations of the Japanese language as the naturalized ('mother tongue') and transparent bearer of cultural iden-tity, we begin to see the implications of this language play. In Happy End, we hear echoes of Bhabha's description of Frantz Fanon's attempt at a postcolonial form of re-membering, except that of course here the histor-ical problematic is one of postimperialism, rather than postcolonialism. Like Fanon, Happy End 'speaks most effectively from the uncertain inter-stices of historical change' in a voice 'most clearly heard in the subver-sive turn of a familiar phrase, in the silence of a sudden rupture'. In foregrounding the strange materiality of familiar language, in perform-ing on the unstable margins of American music and Japanese lyrics, the conventional alignments of historical memory – self/other, East/West, America/Japan – are shaken up. Occupying neither the position of 'the colonialist Self or the colonized Other, but the disturbing distance in-between', the band foregrounds the present moment and the site from which it launches into song. 'This may be no place to end', as Bhabha notes, 'but it may be a place to begin' (Bhabha 1994:40, 45 and 65). Or, as Matsumoto Takashi put it in the song 'Happy End' from the first album:

> happiness isn't a matter of how things end
> it's about how things begin.

*

There was, then, a moment of optimism, a moment of belief in the present as a beginning, a beginning in which one could bring into existence a new Japanese body through the performance of a new kind of music. This new body would be that not only of children who did not know war,[7] but also of children who had escaped the capitalist culture industry: the song 'Happy End' contained direct swipes at those who defined happiness in terms of material consumption. The band's first two albums were distributed on the URC Record label – the 'underground record club', an independent label that eschewed traditional business practices of the popular music industry. At first, its releases were available by subscription only (though by the time Happy End's albums were released, the company had shifted to more conventional distribution channels), and its performers often refused to appear on television or engage in other acts that were perceived as commercializing. They declined, that is, to participate in 'the ways in which the materiality of diverse voices becomes spectacularized', in which 'nonstandard Japanese practices of the voice have become spectacularized as the singularly representative voice of the nation-culture', a practice repeatedly seen in the Japanese culture industry (Ivy 1995:16–17).

This moment of resistance against the market was brief: even before Happy End broke up, it found itself attacked for its participation in the commodification of rock music – most notably at the August 1971 'All Japan Folk Jamboree', when the band was prevented from performing by a group of audience members who occupied the stage to protest the commercialized management of the festival. Likewise, the subsequent careers of the band members after Happy End's break up in 1973 show them dominating the popular music industry in Japan during the 1970s and 1980s. Three of the band members formed the production group Tin Pan Alley (also known as Caramel Mama), which not only released its own albums but also produced and provided studio backing for a number of up-and-coming superstars, most notably Arai (later Matsutoya) Yumi. Matsumoto Takashi went on to write lyrics for dozens of hit songs by such popular artists as Agnes Chan, Tulip, and Matsuda Seiko. Ōtaki Eiichi enjoyed an enormously successful solo career, including the 1981 album *A Long Vacation*, which won the Japan Record Award as the best-selling album of the year. And Hosono Haruomi went on to play bass in Yellow Magic Orchestra, the most successful Japanese rock band of the late-1970s and early-1980s – and another band that experimented with ironic uses of 'Oriental' and 'Japanese' tradition (Currid 1996 and Hosokawa 1999).

Yet despite the subsequent commercial success of its members, Happy End is ultimately best remembered for being one of the first bands to demonstrate that Japanese rock could espouse values other than those of the market. In the Kinks, too, we find gestures of discomfort with the market. Although the band never rejected the major labels, the band's music was infamous for its non-commercial quality in the late-1960s. At a time when rock music was moving toward a heavier sound, the Kinks moved in the opposite direction, with the result that its 1968 master-piece, *The Kinks are the Village Green Preservation Society*, failed even to crack the top 100 album charts in the US. The Kinks would subsequently again see chart success, but it became something of a boast for them to note that their music was too quirky to achieve the sort of market dom-inance enjoyed by their contemporaries, the Beatles or the Rolling Stones.

Looking back on this music now, and on the fleeting resistance it seemed to offer to the hegemonies of both 'History' and the market, should at the very least bring us to question our own relation to this past. How should we remember Happy End and the Kinks in our present? William Haver argues that the discipline of history often works through a Freudian process of mourning, whereby the abjected corpse of the past is transformed into a manageable object through an act of narration. To wit, 'the work of mourning *historicizes* the dead, and in historicizing the dead restores the wounded ego to its integral propriety'. The past achieves a sort of 'redemption' or 'salvation' by being integrated into the communal subject of history – but at a price. 'And that price is always death, the death of the particular *in* its particularity. And that death is a *sacrifice*. The community of the totality is achieved in the voluntary sac-rifice of individuality' (Haver 1996:57 and 41–42). The noise of the past, that is, is reworked into the codes of narrative. In place of this sort of ideological historicization, Haver proposes the ethical and erotic perfor-mance of a 'sociality' that, without claiming to account for the past in all its otherness, at least acknowledges the existence of limits to knowledge and the necessary heterogeneity those limits impose on any identity in the present. Haver proposes we ground our practice in the ironic form of an impossible yet necessary relationship, the relationship that is non-relation with the Other that is the past.

Happy End and the Kinks both faced the prospect of integration into historical narratives – in fact, into two competing narratives. On the one hand, their music could be narrated as marking the triumph of globaliz-ing American culture and the process of modernization; on the other hand, it could be narrated as marking a 'traditional' and local resistance to American culture. Each, however, responded to the trauma of the present, and to the loss of empire, by performing music in ways that, ambivalently and partially, avoided integration into either narrative. The title track of the 1968 album, *Village Green Preservation Society*, proclaimed the Kinks as the defenders of a whole laundry list of symbols of traditional English culture, including of course the village green. Ironically, the list also included Donald Duck. What other past could a self-proclaimed hillbilly raised in North London claim?

Likewise, Happy End occupied the unstable and ironic space of colonial mimicry, performing there to undermine the stable identities of being either Japanese or American. While this practice did not immediately restore the memories of Japan's own imperial past, it did tend to disrupt the forms of historical imagination through which that past was forgotten (the discourses of *furusato* and of a homogenous national culture marked by transparent linguistic communication). The title of Happy End's final single (also the final track on their final studio LP) spelled out the band's position perfectly: '*Sayonara Amerika, Sayonara Nippon*' (So long, America, so long Japan, 1973). The song, written and sung in Japanese and Japanicized English, was recorded in the United States, with an American producer (Van Dyke Parks) and American studio musicians. Matsumoto Takashi would recall later that the song expressed the disenchantment the band experienced when it realized the dream of recording in America, only to encounter hostility from musicians in Los Angeles. 'We had already long ago given up on Japan, and with [that song], we were saying bye-bye to America, too – we weren't going to belong to any place' (Matsumoto 1993). The lyrics, which consist of repetition of the song's title, followed by the phrase 'Bye bye,' seemed to announce a break with both Japan and the US. Yet the song goes on repeating this refrain of farewell (with the vocals deliberately distorted through a phase filter) for more than four minutes, with an extended fade out at the end, as if the point were not so much the break itself, but rather the repeated performance of the act of breaking with the past. As Hosokawa writes, the song demonstrated that 'it was neither American music, nor its Japanese simulacra, which provided their model. It was only the difference between the cultures that interested them' (Hosokawa 1999:120). The band seemed to understand that 'in order to critique the West in relation to Japan, one has necessarily to begin with a critique of Japan. Likewise, the critique of Japan necessarily entails the radical critique of the West' (Sakai 1989:113–114).

Katō Norihiro and others have recently looked at Japan's postwar historical memory as a misshapen, literally 'twisted' (*nejire*) form, and sought ways by which the historical trauma of war, defeat, and loss of empire could be confronted and thereby worked through to restore psychic health to the Japanese nation (Kato 1997 and Igarashi 2000:207–210). But it strikes me that both Happy End and the Kinks were suspicious of the model of health that underwrites this vision. Such a vision insists that the performative in the present be placed in service of recovering the continuity of the pedagogical: the vision refuses to countenance the possibility of 'a future that would be something other than a continuity with, or maintenance of, the present' (Haver 1996:27). Both bands acknowledged the strong desires evoked through memories of loss, and yet both used irony and the materiality of language strategically to avoid the 'social disease of nostalgia' in which 'the present is denied and the past takes on an authenticity of being, an authenticity which, ironically, it can only achieve through narrative' (Stewart 1993:23). Both bands cast their lot, rather, with the 'twisted' present as a source of possibility, and both undermined the very processes of historicization – be it via melodrama, nostalgia for empire, or *furusato* discourse – by mobilizing forms of ironic performance in the present.

Still, as the title of the most complete study of Happy End acknowledges (Hagiwara 1983), the band itself now functions as a sort of legend (*densetsu*). And even more ironically, the music of the two bands now stands as a kind of monument to a lost moment that evokes desire in our own present day moment. How can we help being stirred by memories of a now past moment when a Copernican revolution by way of music seemed not only possible, but imminent? Today, perhaps we can best remember this past by remaining attentive to the desires it produces in us today, as well as to the lessons it offers us about how postcolonial and postimperial forms of remembering can be articulated to one another to create new possibilities in and of the present, our present.

NOTES

1   Muro (1971:25). All translations from Japanese language materials are mine. Japanese personal names are given in their original order (that is, family name first, given name second), except in references to English-language sources in which the order has been reversed.

2   I have relied primarily on the following sources regarding the Kinks: Bailey (1994); Hinman (1994); Komatsuzaki (1999); Martin and Hudson (1998); Mendelsson (1984); Rogan (1984); and Savage (1984).

3   The most comprehensive source on Happy End is Hagiwara (1983). See also the following special issues of music magazines devoted to the band: *Happii na hibi: Happii Endo no kaze ga fuita jidai* (2000) and *20 seiki saigo no Happii Endo tokushū* (2000a and 2000b). In English, I have relied on Anderson (2002) and Hosokawa (1999). I would like to thank Mark Anderson for introducing me to Happy End's music in the first place.

4   On melodrama in postwar popular culture in Japan, see Igarashi (2000) and Bourdaghs (1998).

5   Hayashi (1971) also argues, however, that contemporary Japanese popular culture is a 'dual language empire' (*nijū gengo teikoku*), in which a native Japanese strain coexists with a *katakana* strain, which provides a kind of

buffer zone that eases the shock when Japanese encounter foreign cultural productions. This, he suggests, may in the future lead to new forms of music arising from this double structure.

6 These bands received some attention in the Western media during their overseas' tours, but the only Japanese singer in this period to break successfully into the Western pop charts was Sakamoto Kyū, whose '*Sukiyaki*' (original Japanese title: '*Ue wo muite arukō*') was a worldwide hit in 1962 and 1963. Sakamoto began his career singing Elvis Presley covers in English at American bases in Japan, but ironically could only break through internationally when he sang in Japanese (Bourdaghs 2002).

7 On the wildly popular late 1960s folk song, '*Sensō o shiranai kodomotachi*' (Children who don't know war), see Igarashi (2000:197–198).

REFERENCES

Anderson, Mark 2002 'Happy Endo.' In *Encyclopedia of Contemporary Japanese Culture*. Sandra Buckley, ed. p. 185. London: Routledge.

Atkins, E. Taylor 2001 *Blue Nippon: Authenticating Jazz in Japan*. Durham: Duke University Press.

Attali, Jacques 1985 *Noise: The Political Economy of Music*. Brian Massumi, trans. Minneapolis: University of Minnesota Press.

Bailey, Rebecca, ed. 1994 *The Kinks: Reflections on Thirty Years of Music*. Kentucky: Trillium Publications.

Bhabha, Homi K. 1994 *The Location of Culture*. London: Routledge.

'*Bokura ni totte no dentō no mondai*.' *New Music Magazine* 3:12 (Dec. 1971):16.

Bourdaghs, Michael 1998 The Japan That Can 'Say Yes': Bubblegum Music in a Post-Bubble Economy. *Literature and Psychology*, 44:4 (1998):61–86.

Bourdaghs, Michael 2002 Mystery Plane: Sakamoto Kyū and the Translations of Rockabilly. *Proceedings of the Association for Japanese Literary Studies* 3:1–13.

Currid, Brian. 1996 'Finally, I Reach to Africa': Ryuichi Sakamoto and Sounding Japan(ese). In *Contemporary Japan and Popular Culture*. John Whittier Treat, ed. pp. 69–102. Honolulu: University of Hawaii Press.

Fujitani, Takashi 1998 *Minshūshi* as Critique of Orientalist Knowledges. *positions* 6:2 (1998): 303–322.

Fukamachi Jun 1971 *Bokutachi jishin no Nihongo no uta wo tsukurō*. *New Music Magazine* 3:11 (Nov. 1971):30–34.

Gluck, Carol. 1978 The People in History: Recent Trends in Japanese Historiography. *Journal of Asian Studies* 38:1 (Nov. 1978):25–50.

Hagiwara Kenta 1983 *Happii Endo no densetsu*. Tokyo: Hachiyōsha.

Happii nahibi: Happii Endo no kaze ga fuita jidai. Special issue of *Rekōdo korekutāzu* 19:10 (Aug. 2000)

Haver, William 1996 *The Body of This Death: Historicity and Sociality in the Time of AIDS*. Stanford: Stanford University Press.

Hayashi Hikaru 1971 *Katakana · kotoba no uta sekai: Watashitachi no nijū gengo teikoku*. *New Music Magazine* 3:11 (Nov. 1971):18–22.

Hinman, Doug 1994. *You Really Got Me: An Illustrated World Discography of the Kinks, 1964–1993*. Rumford, Rhode Island: D. Hinman.

Hosokawa, Shuhei 1999 'Soy Sauce Music: Haruomi Hosono and Japanese Self-Orientalism.' In *Widening the Horizon: Exoticism in Post-War Popular Music*. Philip Hayward, ed. pp. 114–144. London: John Libbey.

Igarashi, Yoshikuni 2000 *Bodies of Memory: Narratives of Postwar Japanese Culture, 1945–1970*. Princeton: Princeton University Press.

Ivy, Marilyn 1995 *Discourses of the Vanishing: Modernity Phantasm Japan*. Chicago: University of Chicago Press.

K.T. 1969 *Nyū gurūpu: Eipuriru fūru* [April Fool]. *Music Life* 19:11 (Sept. 1969):162–163.

K.T. 1970 Review of album *Happy End*. Reprinted in 1995 *Rūtsu obu Japaniizu poppsu 1955–1970: rokabirii kara gurūpu saunzu made*. Kurosawa Susumu, ed. p. 387. Tokyo: Shinkō Music.

Katō Norihiro 1997 *Haisengo ron*. Tokyo: Kōdansha.

Kitanaka Masakazu 1973 Review of The Kinks, *Everybody's in Show Biz*. Reprinted in *Music Magazine* 26:14 (Dec. 1994):252–253.

Komatsuzaki Kenrō, ed. 1999 *Za Kinkii fairu*. Tokyo: Shinkō Music.

Martin, Neville and Jeffrey Hudson 1998 *The Kinks: Well-Respected Men*. London: Music Sales Corporation.

Matsumoto Takashi 1970 *Gendai no rokku wa hōrō kara umareru*. *Music Life* 20:9 (Aug. 1970):150–151.

Matsumoto Takashi 1971 *Bokura no 'Nihon' o mitsukeyō*. *New Music Magazine* 3:12 (Dec. 1971): 33.

Matsumoto Takashi 1993 *Happi Endo no kinjitō 'Kazemachi roman'*. In *Bessatsu Taiyō: Nihon no rokku 50's-90's*. Takahashi Yōji, ed. p. 82. Tokyo: Heibonsha.

Mendelsson, John *1984 The Kinks Kronikles*. New York: William Morrow, 1984.

Murai Osamu 1995 *Nantō ideorogii no hassei*. Rev. ed. Tokyo: Ōta Shuppan.

Muro Kenji 1971 *Nakatsugawa de kanjita watashi no fuman*. *New Music Magazine* 3:10 (Oct. 1971):24–27.

Nakamura Tōyō 1971 *Wareware ni 'naniwabushi' wa sonzai suru ka*. *New Music Magazine* 3:12 (Dec. 1971):18–23.

20 seiki saigo no Happii Endo tokushū 2000a. Special issue of *Rokku gahō* 1 (June 2000).

20 seiki saigo no Happii Endo tokushū 2000b. Special issue of *Rokku gahō* 2 (Oct. 2000).

Oguma, Eiji 2002 *A Genealogy of 'Japanese' Self-images*. Trans. David Askew. Melbourne: Trans Pacific Press.

Olsen, Lawrence 1992 *Ambivalent Moderns: Portraits of Japanese Cultural Identity*. Savage, Maryland: Rowman & Littlefield.

Robertson, Jennifer 1998 It Takes a Village: Internationalization and Nostalgia in Postwar Japan. In *Mirror of Modernity: Invented Traditions of Modern Japan*. Stephen Vlastos, ed. pp. 110–129. Berkeley: University of California Press, 1998.

Rogan, Johnny 1984 *The Kinks: A Mental Institution*. London: Proteus Books.

Sakai, Naoki 1989 Modernity and its Critique: The Problem of Universalism and Particularism. In *Postmodernism and Japan*. Masao Miyoshi and H.D. Harootunian, eds. pp. 93–122. Durham: Duke University Press.

Santner, Eric L. 1993 *Stranded Objects: Mourning, Memory, and Film in Postwar Germany*. Ithaca, New York: Cornell University Press.

Savage, Jon 1984 *The Kinks: The Official Biography*. London: Faber and Faber.

Shida Ayumu 2000 *Haru yo koi*. *Rekōdo korekutāzu* 19:10 (August 2000):101–117.

Stewart, Susan 1993 *On Longing: Narratives of the Miniature, the Gigantic, the Souvenir, the Collection*. Durham: Duke University Press.

Take Hideki 1999 *Yomu J-POP: 1945–1999 shiteki zenshi*. Tokyo: Tokuma Shoten.

Uchida Yūya, Matsumoto Takashi, Ōtaki Eiichi, et al. 1971 Cross talk: *Nihon no rokku jōkyō wa doko made kita ka*. Reprinted in *Music Magazine* 26:14 (Dec. 1994):123–125.

Yoneyama, Lisa 1999 *Hiroshima Traces: Time, Space, and the Dialectics of Memory*. Berkeley: University of California Press.

8

The Meiji Restoration and the Revival of Ancient Culture

TAKAGI HIROSHI[1]

INTRODUCTION

What is it that makes the 'ancient' important for the modern period? Yanagihara Sakimitsu, the Japanese envoy to Russia in the 1880s, once argued that the 'international community' in the late nineteenth century did not possess a unitary 'European culture'. Rather, it was an arena of conflict where the great powers, each with its own history as nation-state, competed for the supremacy of their cultural 'traditions'. Hence, Austria promoted its 'Austrian-ness' to the world just as Russia did its 'Russian-ness.' In this way, the creation of a unique cultural tradition in modern Japan took the form of a revival of a primeval Japanese culture. This creation of ancient cultural tradition was pursued as a strategy for young Meiji Japan to become a 'first-class nation' in the community of nations.

Okakura Tenshin (Kakuzō, 1862–1913) was a central figure in this effort. He gave a beginning to 'Japanese art' by creating a history of ancient Japanese art. He did this in accordance with the discourse of European art history at the time, and his aim was to emphasize that a classical ancient period that rivals that of Greece and Rome also existed in Japan. At the same time, he argued that ancient Japanese art, which had reached its climax in the achievements of Tenpyō sculpture (729–49), is a unique art form not found in Europe and China. The claim of such a unique cultural tradition led to the birth of the concept of 'national treasure' (*kokuhō*).

Modern Japan's creation or revival of ancient culture has two parts: first, the creation of a mythical ancient period and second, the creation of a historical ancient period. In the few years right after the Meiji

Restoration (1868), 'traditional culture' was under attack due to an extreme form of modernization/westernization. However, the Meiji Emperor's tour of the Yamato region in 1877 became a turning point in the revival of ancient Japanese culture, and the trend further developed in the 1880s when the Meiji constitution was drafted and promulgated.

The revival of the 'mythical ancient history' (*shinwa-teki kodai*) has a number of milestones. The visualization of the ideal represented by Emperor Jinmu's founding of Japan took the form of the construction of Jinmu's mausoleum in 1863 just before the Meiji Restoration. On the promulgation of the Meiji Constitution in 1890, the Kashihara Shrine was built and dedicated to Emperor Jinmu whereas all the imperial mausoleums were also officially identified. Then there was the construction of the 'shrine garden' (*shinen*) in the foothills of Mt Unebi (traditionally identified as the site of Jinmu's mausoleum) after Japan defeated China in the Sino-Japanese War of 1894–95. Finally, there was the 'state undertakings' (*kokkateki jigyō*) – a series of celebrations, public events and construction projects – initiated in the 2,600th year (1940) of Jinmu's founding of the nation. Thus, Emperor Jinmu, who had been known as 'Jinmu-san' – a god of good harvest – in the popular religion of the Edo period (1600–1867), was transformed into a bearded warrior figure under the influence of European historical paintings and image of the monarch (Figs 1, 2).

The revival of the 'historical ancient period' (*rekishi-teki kodai*) also has multiple components, namely, (1) the revival of old shrines and temples such as Hōryūji and Kōfukuji, both of which have been studied and promoted by Ernest Fenollosa (1853–1908) and Okakura Tenshin; (2) the formation of 'imperial property' comprising the Three Yamato Mountains (*Yamoto sanzan*) and the treasure of Shōsōin (on the ground of Tōdaiji); (3) the opening of the Imperial Nara Museum in 1889; and (4) the maintenance and preservation of famous sites such as Mt Yoshino and the Nara Park as well as the old capital Heijōkyō and ancient mausoleums. A nationwide provisional investigation of treasures conducted between 1888 and 1897 classified over 210,000 items of art from all over the country into genres such as sculpture, painting, and so on. The dates and authors of all these items were identified, and ranks (signifying their value) were assigned to them by the state. On this basis, the Preservation of Ancient Shrines and Temples Law (*koshaji hozonhō*) came into effect in 1897. It is the first cultural assets preservation law in Japan. Thus, ancient Buddhist statues were transformed from objects of worship into objects of appreciation as works of art.

This systematic investigation of cultural assets was the precondition for the establishment of Japanese art as an institution. Besides, the publication of Okakura Tenshin's *Nihon bijutsu shi* in 1890 established the periods of Suiko (or Asuka), Tenji, Tenpyō and Heian for the study of ancient cultural history while the publication of *Histoire de L'Art du Japon*

Figure 1: Image of Emperor Jinmu in the Edo era (from *Kashihara Jingū-shi*)

for the Paris World Expo of 1900 was an appeal to the international community.

THE FORMATION OF CONSTITUTIONAL GOVERNMENT AND THE PRESERVATION OF CULTURAL ASSETS IN NARA

In December 1867, with the imperial order for the restoration of imperial rule nullifying the rule of the samurai-class, began the Meiji Restoration aimed at realizing the ideal of Emperor Jinmu's founding of Japan. Here I would like to consider the progress in the preservation of cultural assets during the latter half of the nineteenth century by focusing on Nara prefecture, the putative site of Emperor Jinmu's nation founding or the 'sacred land' of Yamato according to prewar usage.

The Meiji government's March 1868 order to separate Shinto from Buddhism caused the shrines and temples of Nara to become dilapidated due to the suppression of Buddhism that it sparked off. Kōfukuji, which had had twenty thousand *koku* of dominion given by the Shogunate in the Edo period, was abandoned, and its five-story pagoda was put up for sale. The Eleven-Face Kannon in the temple (now called Wakamiya) belonging to Ōmiwa Shrine was transferred to Shōrinji some distance away. However, the order issued by the Office for the Preservation of Ancient Artifacts in 1871 and the investigation of ancient shrines and temples in the following year can be regarded as a reconsideration of the suppression of Buddhism movement. At the same time, Machida Hisanari and Ninagawa Noritane conducted examinations of the artifacts in Hōryūji, Kōfukuji, and Shōsōin. Their investigation had the duo purpose of examining the treasures belonging to the temples and identifying treasures associated with the imperial household, i.e. items that were 'sealed by imperial order' (*chokuhū*). Since there were hardly any imperially sealed treasures in the possession of the imperial family, it became necessary to transfer the custody of the treasures of Shōsōin from Tōdaiji to the Ministry of Interior, which managed the imperial household, in March 1875.

In the Nara Exhibition from April to June 1875, the treasures of Shōsōin were displayed along with cultural assets from other ancient shrines and temples. This was an opportunity for viewers to see the treasures of Shōsōin from close distance. Nonetheless, although the preservation of cultural assets in early Meiji aimed at unifying modernization (*bunmei kaika*) and the protection of ancient artifacts, it placed the greatest emphasis on the promotion of industries.

The Meiji Emperor's tour of the Yamato region in 1877 was the turning point in the move toward serious protection and promotion of 'cultural tradition', which included cultural assets (*bunkazai*). The significance of this imperial tour was primarily one of military operation, since the emperor stayed in the Yamato region for an extended period as the commander-in-chief of the government forces during the Seinan Rebellion (1877). On 11 February the same year, the emperor personally performed the ritual at Jinmu's mausoleum on the Kigensetsu, the national holiday commemorating Jinmu's enthronement. During the tour, the emperor paid his respects at Kasuga Shrine, inspected the treasures of Tōdaiji, Hōryūji, and Shōsōin, and viewed archaeological findings. Moreover, he made offerings at many imperial mausoleums and publicly commended individuals who had loyally served the imperial family in the past such as Fujiwara Fuhito.

After this, the commemoration and promotion of 'cultural tradition' as represented by imperial mausoleums, historical monuments, famous sights, and ancient shrines and temples came to be conducted in the name of the preservation of 'ancient customs' (*kyūkan*). In contrast to the suppression of Buddhism and the extreme form of modernization in early Meiji, 'cultural tradition' became important during the formative period of the Meiji constitution in the 1880s. To explain this change we must recall the international context.

'First class nations' in Europe at the time such as Britain, Austria, Russia and Prussia did not share a unitary 'European' culture. Just as England boasted its own 'tradition', every European nation turned to its unique 'cultural tradition' as the source of authority. The typically English ceremonies such as royal weddings and funerals as well as the daily rituals of the royal family were a 'tradition' created since the nineteenth century, the formation period of the nation-state. Similarly, coronation ceremonies such as the one in Austria where torchlight was lit and benefits were bestowed to the people, or the one in Russia that was staged in the 'sacred city' Moscow symbolized unique 'cultural traditions'. Thus, it was difficult for Japan to join the ranks of the 'first class nations' by just copying Western fashions as it had done in the case of Rokumeikan. It was necessary for Japan to create its own individuality and a native cultural tradition and to display these to the West. It had to create a culture that has been under the continual protection of the imperial family since Jinmu's time as well as an ancient Nara culture that rivals the classical culture of Greece and Rome.

In the field of art, the period in which Ernest Fenollosa and Okakura Tenshin preserved and promoted 'ancient art' and created 'Japanese painting' (*Nihonga*) overlapped precisely with the state policy of creating a national cultural tradition. In this sense, Fenollosa did not become the 'benefactor of Japanese art' by accident, for a figure like him was needed, socially and politically, by the Japan of the 1880s. Let us consider the development of the preservation of cultural assets in Nara by looking at some concrete cases.

The mausoleum of Jinmu, the fictional founding emperor of Japan, held the most important position since the restoration of imperial mausoleums began at the end of the Edo period. At the time of the Meiji

Restoration, 'Jinmu's founding of Japan' (*Jinmu sōgyō*) was promoted as representing the primordial political culture of Japan, preceded the culture brought in from the continent and the culture of the warrior class in medieval times. On the 17th of the second month 1863, it was decided that the mausoleum of Emperor Jinmu was located at Misanzai (Jibuta) on the site of a medieval temple that no longer existed. All of a sudden, a mound representing Jinmu's tomb was raised in the middle of a field. This site was chosen over Maruyama on the side of Mt Unebi, which had traditionally been regarded as the site of the imperial tomb. Maruyama was dropped because it was next to a cave belonging to a community of outcastes. So, Misanzai was chosen instead. From the following year, imperial messengers began to be sent to this Jinmu mausoleum. On 11 March 1872, the Festival of Emperor Jinmu became a ritual conducted by the emperor and thus part of the annual functions of the imperial palace at Tokyo.

The government's deliberation (*shingi*) over the question of impurity of imperial mausoleums that took place on the 7th of the fourth month of 1868 was decisive for effecting a change in the meaning of imperial tombs of which Jinmu mausoleum was the most important. The decision was that the traditional view of imperial mausoleums as places of death impurity was a fabrication by Buddhists, and that these tombs were sacred places as noble and dignified as the imperial ancestral shrine at Ise. This is because, as an *arahitogami*, the emperor would continue to exist as a deity even after the death of his physical body. This is the origin of the rationale given by the Imperial Household Agency in the present day for not opening the imperial mausoleums to the public.

In 1878, custody over imperial mausoleums was transferred from the Ministry of the Interior to the Ministry of the Imperial Household. Then on 3 June 1889, after the promulgation of the Meiji Constitution, the government officially identified the location of all the tombs of past emperors (Kunaichō 1997, vol.7). The opinion of Itō Hirobumi (1840–1909) is worth noting here. He claimed that it would be a hindrance to the government's diplomatic effort to revise the 'unequal treaties' between Japan and the western powers if Japan, despite its unbroken line of imperial succession, failed to identify the location of all of its imperial mausoleums. In his view, identification of all the imperial mausoleums was indispensable for the manifestation of the 'essence of the national polity' (*kokutai no seika*). Itō's ideas indeed represent the creation of a cultural tradition unique to Japan and its display to the west.

Since the imperial mausoleums thus identified drew upon the interpretation of the two ancient chronicles by national learning scholars (*kokugakusha*), from the point of view of present-day archaeology, hardly any of the imperial mausoleums are the actual burials of the emperors whose names are associated with them.

In addition to the mausoleum of Jinmu, in the year following the promulgation of the Meiji Constitution, Kashihara Jingū, in which the mythical Jinmu and his consort Himetataraisuzuhime-no-Mikoto were worshiped, was built in the southwest of Mt Unebi as a national shrine of the highest rank (*kanpei taisha*). Kashihara Jingu was a means by which the people could participate in the myth of Jinmu. Then, between the time of the promulgation of the Meiji Constitution (1889) and the 2,600th anniversary of Jinmu's foundating of Japan (1940), the area around Mt Unebi, which encompassed the mausoleum of Jinmu and the Kashihara Jingū, was turned into a sacred shrine garden modeled on the garden of the Ise Shrine.

The Three Mountains of Yamato, Mt Yoshino and Nara Park are representative of the famous sites (*meishō*) in Nara prefecture. In the Edo period, Mt Unebi, Mt Miminashi and Mt Amanokagu, which are central to the landscape described in the poems of the *Manyōshū*, were the common property of nearby villages. Peasants were free to enter them for firewood and other resources. In 1878, however, Sakai prefecture nominated these mountains as famous sites to the central government. After a proposal submitted by Matsukata Masayoshi, the Interior Minister, in 1880, the government incorporated these mountains into the imperial estate (*goryōchi*) in 1891.

It should be pointed out that, contrary to popular perception, the scenery of cherry blossoms on Mt Yoshino had not remained unchanged since the medieval period. Yamada Yoshio, who visited Yoshino in 1896, complained that all the cherry trees there had been cut down after the Meiji Restoration. What he saw, therefore, were all young trees (Yamada 1941). In other words, it was Nara prefecture and the Association for the Protection of Mt Yoshino who were responsible for reconstructing the world of medieval Japanese poetry in the modern era by planting cherry trees.

Nara Park was constructed around the area of Kōfukuji, which was abandoned at the time of the Meiji Restoration. The government gave permission to set up a park in 1880, which was later designated as a 'famous sight'. In 1888, the Nara Park was officially created with its present boundaries. During this period, it was stressed that the increase of visitors due to better maintenance would bring economic benefits and that the forest of Mt Kasuga was a public good as it was a suitable place for westerners to retreat to during the hot summer. Moreover, the Kasuga Association for the Protection of Sacred Deer revived the myth that the protected deer that grazed in the park were the messengers of the deity of Kasuga.

In 1889, it was decided that the Imperial Nara Museum was to be located in the Nara Park. The result was a neo-Baroque style building designed by the palace architect Katayama Tōkuma. Neo-Baroque was fashionable in Paris and Vienna in the same period as the architectural style that could best project the authority of the state. With this museum looming above all the thatched houses in the Nara Basin, it is not difficult to imagine how majestic the Meiji state must have appeared to the people of the time.

The restoration of Kōfukuji was of central importance to the effort to preserve ancient shrines and temples. In 1880, Sakurai Nokan, Director of the Department of Shrines and Temples, Home Ministry, proposed that the temple be restored. Then in 1888, Kōfukuji, together with Hōryūji, were made the headquarters of the Hossō sect.

Meanwhile, Hōryuji has also faced financial difficulties. For this reason, it presented 322 items of treasures to the imperial family in 1878 and received 10,000 yen in return. After the Second World War, the liquidation of the estate of the imperial family caused most of the items presented by Hōryūji to be transferred to the government, and are now kept in the Hōryūji Section of the Tokyo National Museum. However, among the Hōryūji treasures, items such as the Portrait of Prince Shōtoku and *Commentary on the Lotus Sutra*, which are the most precious of imperial treasures, remain to this day in the palace as the emperor's personal belongings. The presentation of the Hōryūji treasures in 1878 is a milestone in the creation of the imperial collection in modern Japan. It marks the beginning of the adding to the imperial collection of items unrelated to treasures that were 'sealed by imperial order' in pre-modern times.

On the other hand, Kōfukuji was the ancestral temple (*ujidera*) of the Fujiwara clan whose descendents included such important aristocratic families as Konoe, Takatsukasa and Saionji. Its restoration was thus planned with the imminent establishment of the House of Lords (under the Meiji Constitution) and the need to add authority to the newly created aristocratic class (*kazoku*) in mind. The same political motive was behind the granting of government aid to the Danzan Shrine dedicated to Fujiwara Kamatari, the founding ancestor of the Fujiwara clan.

Tōdaiji also received 500 yen as preservation expense from the Imperial Household Agency in 1883. However, the construction of the Great Buddha Hall, which had begun during the time of the fifth Tokugawa shogun Tsunayoshi, was completed only in 1915.

The objects of the effort to preserve cultural assets during the second decade of the Meiji period (1877–86) were restricted to Kōfukuji, Hōryūji, imperial mausoleums, the Three Mountains of Yamato and the Nara Park, all of which were closely related to the imperial family. In contrast, cultural assets preservation after the promulgation of the Meiji Constitution, namely, during the third decade of Meiji (1887–96), became a part of the systematic management of art, which is itself a component of the bureaucratic control of cultural affairs. Moreover, within this decade, the creation of the Provisional Bureau for the Investigation of Treasures Nationwide, the building of the Nara National Museum, the

Figure 2: Modern image of Emperor Jinmu (from *Kashihara Jingū-shi*)

implementation of the Preservation of Ancient Shrines and Temples Law, etc. were all inspired by the cultural policy of European countries. The cultural policy that lacks a proper sense of history and emphasizes the supremacy of 'art' that was created in this period became a characteristic of Japan until this day.

THE ESTABLISHMENT OF ANCIENT CULTURE

When was the contemporary textbook[2] image of a Tenpyō culture rich in international colors due to cultural influences from High Tang China created?

For instance, in the case of Kōfukuji in the Edo period, most visitors to the temple went to one of its many buildings called Nanendō, which is included in the thirty-three temples that make up of the Western Japan Pilgrimage Loop. Unlike today's visitors, these pilgrims did not associate Kōfukuji with its Tenpyō sculptures such as the statues of Ashura and the Ten Disciples of the Buddha. The same can be said for Hōryūji. In the Edo period, the temple's Saiendō, wherein the Healing Buddha (Yakushi Nyorai) and many swords were enshrined was the center of popular devotion. In contrast, after the 1890s, Hōryūji, with its golden hall, five-story pagoda, inner gate and passageway, became a symbol of Asuka culture with influences from Six Dynasties China. Today, with Hōryūji representing Asuka culture and Tōdaiji Tenpyō culture, both temples have transcended their cultic status in medieval and early modern times. They have been assimilated into the aesthetic values of ancient Japan created in modern times.

Reportedly, until recently archeologists working in Nara would simply remove the strata of early modern and medieval times to go straight to the ancient stratum from where serious excavation would begin. Clearly, the modern Yamato region has an image especially associated with ancient culture.

Now, before Nara could be placed in the temporal frame of the 'ancient', it was necessary for European historiography to be introduced to Japan. This new historical consciousness is different from the pre-modern idea of time that consisted of two temporal layers, namely, the origin – or 'the ancient' (*inishie*) – and the 'present' (*ima*). The modern concept of time is linear and has 'historical stages'. In other words, in the modern period, ancient culture is placed at the beginning of linear and continuous time. And it is at the forefront of this developing time that, according to Tenshin, 'future art is being contrived' (Okakura 1890).

Meanwhile, there emerged a national distribution of culture formed by the conjuncture of the temporal and spatial axis: ancient culture in Nara (western Japan), mid-to-late Heian aristocratic culture (*kokufū bunka*) in Kyōto (western Japan), and Kamakura and Edo culture in the

Kantō region (eastern Japan). This, however, is predicated on Okakura Tenshin's chronology as explicated in his lectures on Japanese art (1890). Let us look into this process. In 1882, Ernest Fenollosa, who was teaching political science and philosophy at Tokyo University, published *Bijutu Shinsetu* (*A True Theory of Art*). In it, he declared that art is 'contrivance' (*sakui*), namely, an effort or activity that has creativity as its aim, and that contemporary artists continue to create new works of art everyday. Historically speaking, his theory led to the understanding that since culture was created in different periods, it also changed over time.

Meanwhile, the year 1884 saw another round of investigation of treasures. This occasioned the discovery of 'Japanese aesthetics' (*Nihonbi*) by Fenollosa and Tenshin following their opening of the doors of the shrine-cabin containing the Kuze Kannon statue at Hōryūji. However, their discovery of 'Japanese aesthetics' must not be understood only in the context of nativism. It must be also seen as part of the strategy by nineteenth century 'first class nations' to promote their unique 'cultural tradition' to the international community of nations (Takagi 1997).

The first standardized nationwide investigation of treasures was conducted by the Provisional Bureau for the Investigation of National Treasures under the Imperial Household Ministry in 1888. The inspection report it produced between 1888 and 1897 listed over 215,091 items. It also specified the period, author, genre, etc. of each item as well as the rank given to it by the state. It was on the basis of this foundational work of classifying and evaluating each item of cultural asset that a historical consciousness of Japanese art – articulated in Tenshin's above-mentioned lectures at the Tokyo Art School in 1890 – as comprising the Suiko (Asuka culture), Tenji (Hakuhō culture), Tenpyō, early-Heian, mid-to-late-Heian (*kokufū*) and Kamakura periods became possible. In this way, the Suiko period is represented by the Buddha Triad in Hōryūji, which shows Six Dynasties Chinese cultural influence, and the Tenji period by the Indo-Greek style of the fresco in the same temple's Golden Hall (Kondō). Moreover, the ideal and 'mysteriously elegant' Tenpyō period, which was under the influence of the international culture of high Tang, engendered such masterpieces in Tōdaiji as the statues of the Four Devas of the Kaidanin and the statue of Shitsukongojin of the Sangatsudō. By the same token, in the Shōsōin collection, the glass items were considered to be similar to those found in Egypt, Greece and Six Dynasties China while artistic characteristics of West Asia were said to be discernible in the Persian-like patterns on the textiles. Finally, Tenshin argued that it was only through the discovery of the Shōsōin treasures that Nara culture, which reached its highest point in the Tenpyō era, could be explained.[3]

The establishment of the Imperial Nara Museum was decided in 1889 along with those in Tokyo and Kyōto. The characteristic of Imperial Nara Museum is that its collection consists of cultural assets donated by shrines and temples in the region. It is thus a museum whose exhibits are linked to the historical representation of the ancient period centered on Nara. Meanwhile, Kuki Ryūichi, Director of the Imperial Museums, pointed to the European example where the Christian priesthood did not have the right to sell off church assets. By comparison, he noted, it was nothing but tragic in the case of Japan when Buddhist statues were sold and taken overseas during the early Meiji suppression of Buddhism. He argued that since the cultural assets of shrines and temples were not private but public property, religious institutions have the obligation to allow them to be displayed in museums. In this way, he applied to Japan the European idea that cultural assets belong to the nation and the people. In the meantime, this effects a transformation in the value of Buddhist statues from objects of worship to objects of sculpture art.

In 1900, the Imperial Nara Museum changed its name to Nara Imperial Household Museum to make clear its ownership. In fact, the practice of having the monarch display cultural assets to the public to achieve national integration developed almost simultaneously in Japan and Europe. Exhibiting art and cultural assets to the public by setting up museums staffed by curators instead of treating them as the private collection of the imperial family was a trend that began in France with the Louvre after Napoleon's time and with the Hermitage Museum in Russia and the Kunsthistorisches Museum in Vienna, Austria in the late nineteenth century.

In Japan, the 1897 Law of Preservation of Ancient Shrines and Temples was the first law for the preservation of cultural assets. Under this law, the government granted subsidies to shrines and temples holding valuable cultural assets. The same law also explicitly articulated the concept of 'national treasure'. The practice of giving rankings to beauty began with the survey conducted by the Provisional Bureau for the Investigation of National Treasures. Thereafter the Imperial Household Museums carried on with the work of identifying national treasures. By the way, in the prewar period, the designation of national treasures favored artifacts belonging to the ancient period.

The compilation of a state-centered history of Japanese art began under Tenshin's leadership. It continued on, following his methodology, even after he has lost his position. This effort resulted in the 1901 *Kōhon Nihon teikoku bijutsu ryakushi* (*Manuscript of an Abbreviated History of Art of the Japanese Empire*). The 'history of Japanese art' first appeared in print as *Histoire de L'Art du Japon* (1900) aiming at the international readership at the Paris Expo. The next year, a Japanese translation appeared in a deluxe edition under the title *Kōhon Nihon teikoku bijutsu ryakushi*. The main contention of this history is that many of the treasures in Shōsōin are Japanese-made artifacts. Furthermore, in the Introduction, Kuki Ryūichi declared that, after the Sino-Japanese War (1894–95), only Japan, as the representative country of the east, could give an account of the history of the art of the east.

Japan's ancient culture came into contact with society in general and the common people only from the 1910s after the Russo-Japanese War (1904–05). After the war with Russia, the government implemented social reforms in the countryside to better mobilize regional society in the event of a total war. The aim was to model citizens who would die for the state. In 1919, the government passed the Law for the Preservation of Historical and Famous Sites and Natural Monuments and established steles on such sites to cultivate a sense of history in the citizenry. This law included for protection such famous landscape as Mt Yoshino and Tsukigase as well as historical sites such as Heijōkyō, all of which had fallen outside the scope of the Law for the Preservation of Ancient Shrines and Temples. After Tenshin's 'history of Japanese art', thanks to the influence of 'culturalism' (*kyōyōshugi*) in the Taishō period, represented by Watsuji Tetsurō's *Koji junrei* (a pilgrimage to ancient temples), as well as education and tourism, the image of Japan's ancient culture became a 'national common sense'.

CONCLUSION

Right after the Meiji Restoration, during the period of 'civilization and enlightenment' (*bunmei kaika*) from 1868 to the mid-1870s, the ancient temples and shrines of Nara suffered great losses in the suppression of Buddhism, and the country's cultural tradition was denied. This was to change in the formative period of the constitutional government. With the Meiji Emperor's tour of Kyōto and Nara in 1877 as the turning point, the effort to reappraise and preserve the cultural tradition represented by the ancient capitals of Nara and Kyōto began, and this was done with Japan's standing in the international community in mind. This effort included the maintenance of imperial mausoleums, public grants for ancient temples such as Kōfukuji, Hōryūji and Tōdaiji, the Imperial Household Ministry's takeover of the custody of Shōsōin, and the preservation of famous sights such as the Nara Park and the Three Mountains of Yamato. This effort was linked to the discovery of the cultural strategy that regarded that the appraisal of the national cultural tradition beginning in ancient times was essential for Japan to attain equality with the great powers, namely, Europe and the United States. Fenollosa and Tenshin undertook to construct a history of Japanese art against this background.

Tenshin first drew on the concrete image of Japan's ancient culture in his 1890 lectures on Japanese art, and his was a narrative of art history much influenced by western theories. Due to the work of Tenshin and the provisional investigation of national treasures, Japanese art history came to sub-divide the ancient period into Asuka, Tenji and Tenpyō periods, and to adopt such classificatory genres as sculpture, painting and craft. Cultural assets also came to be ranked according to a hierarchy with 'national treasures' as its apex. Institutions such as the Nara Imperial Household Museum were created and legislations such as the Law of Preservation of Ancient Shrines and Temples passed. Moreover, historical time came to be symbolized by geographical space. Nara, representing the beginning of Japanese culture, came to be distinguished from Kyōto, the embodiment of Heian culture, and the Kantō region, which embodies the culture of the Kamakura and Edo periods. In this way, the reappraisal of ancient culture in modern Japan glorifies the myth of the 'unbroken line of emperors' in which the modern emperor system is grounded. At the same time, it explicates the origin of Japanese culture to the international and domestic audiences, functioning as a cultural strategy in support of Japan's claim to be a 'first-class nation'.

REFERENCES

Commission Impériale du Japon. n.d. *Histoire de L'art du Japon*. Paris: Brunoff.

Fenollosa Ernest. 1975 (1882) *Bijutu Shinsetu*. In Tsuchikata Sadaichi ed., *Meiji bungaku zenshū* vol. 79. Tokyo: Chikuma shobō.

Kunaichō ed. 1997. *Meiji tennō ki*. 7 volumes. Tokyo: Yoshikawa kōbunkan.

Okakura Tenshin. 1922 (1890). *Nihon bijutsu shi*. In *Tenshin Zenshū*, edited by Nihon bijutsu in. Tokyo: Nihon bijutsu in.

Teikoku hakubutsukan ed. 1901. *Kōhon teikoku Nihon bijutsu ryakushi*. Tokyo: Nōshōmushō.

Takagi, Hiroshi. 1997. *Kindai tennōsei no bunkashiteki kenkyū*. Tokyo: Azekura shobō.

Inoue Mitsusada et al. eds. 1993. *Shin-shōsetsu Nihonshi*. Tokyo: Yamakawa shuppan sha.

Watsuji Tetsurō. 1979 (1919). *Koji Junrei*. Tokyo: Iwanami.

Yamada Yoshio. 1990 (1941). *Ōshi*. Tokyo: Kōdansha.

NOTES

[1] Translated by Tsuneda Yumiko
[2] The example used here is Inoue Mitsusada's *Shin-shōsetsu Nihon-shi* (1993).
[3] See *Okakura Tenshin zenshū* vol. 4.

9

Japan's Living National Treasures Program: The Paradox of Remembering

MICHELE BAMBLING

INTRODUCTION

It is generally thought that Japan's artistic heritage survives as an unchanging tradition, whose time-honored art forms are precisely remembered and unaltered in their transmission. Indeed it was not unusual for a single school or family to pass down the skills and secrets of their artistic tradition for many centuries. Until the end of the Edo period (1615–1868) artisans, musicians and theatrical performers held a fairly secure position in society, and the arts thrived. But with the intense modernization and Westernization that took place beginning in the Meiji period (1868–1912) the traditional arts were no longer regenerated in the same way that they had been in the past.[1]

Spurred by concern for the continuation of the traditional arts in a political climate of growing nationalism, the Meiji government enacted a series of measures aimed at the protection of the arts and the traditional Japanese culture that created and perpetuated them. In 1871 the Meiji government proclaimed that important old works of art should be protected and that the names of the possessors of such works should be reported to the nation. In 1929 the Preservation of National Treasures law recognized certain objects of art as National Treasures. In 1950, in response to heightened concerns that Occupied Japan was in danger of losing its cultural heritage, the government instituted an over-arching law for the Protection of Cultural Assets. This law expanded the earlier protective measures to include 'Intangible Assets'. The law defines 'Important Intangible Cultural Properties' as, 'art and skill employed in drama, music and the applied arts and other intangible cultural products, which possess a high historical and/or artistic value in and for this country'. The public applied the term 'National Treasure' (*kokuhō*) from the 1929 law that designated 'objects' as National Treasures, to 'living artists'. Hence those who are 'Holders of Important Intangible Cultural Properties' came to be popularly called 'Living National Treasures' (*ningen kokuhō*).

There is historical precedent for awarding outstanding artists honorary titles and certificates of achievement in Japan. However, the Living National Treasure program fundamentally differs from past honorariums. It has given rise to public controversy, as critics detect in it remnants of an ideology of emperor worship. The very notion of elevating the stature of a human being to that of a 'National Treasure', for critics, mirrors the concept that the emperor of Japan was an embodiment of the divine. Often the designated artists have elite ancestries – long histories of association with the imperial institution as well as deep genealogical roots, some even claiming to extend back to the Age of Gods.[2] Despite the unmistakable aura of divinity and mystery that accompanies the title, the Ministry of Education, contends that the title 'Holder of Important Intangible Cultural Property' is not intended to venerate artists, but simply to ensure that certain high-level skills are transmitted correctly to future generations.

The Committee for the Protection of Cultural Assets, which is appointed by the Ministry of Education's Agency for Cultural Affairs, is responsible for the selection of 'Holders of Important Intangible Cultural Properties'. According to a law implemented in 1954, the designation acknowledges 'an indefinite balance of artistry, technique, historical position and even personality'. To be considered for the title, an artist must 'display skill and artistry that is traditionally and technically correct'. Those designated should be 'highly trained, well versed in intangible cultural properties and capable of high artistic representation'. The criteria for the selection of 'Holders of Important Intangible Properties' is threefold: (1) those which are of particularly high artistic value; (2) those which hold an especially important position in the history of the applied arts; (3) those which have 'conspicuous local characteristics'. The government's determination of high artistic value, of which arts merit historical importance and which artists are capable of representing superior artistic or local achievement, thus significantly affects the future practice of traditional arts in Japan.

Through the Living National Treasure program the government makes a concerted effort to prevent Japan's traditional arts from vanishing. The government recognizes that sustaining memory is vital to the transmission of traditional arts. But, there is a paradox at the program's core: by trying to secure the art traditions, governmental measures often undermine the very institutions that they set out to preserve. This happens because memory of the past – its techniques, skills, aesthetics, expressions, meanings and models – is encoded in rituals, secrets and life-long practice that often lose their power when revealed in the explicit and overt manner that the program encourages. Bureaucratic efforts to record and store artistic methods through empirical means are necessarily limited in their potential to preserve and transmit the past to the present and future, for memory is fundamentally intangible, even traceless and embodied in human experience.

This analysis of the function of memory in the transmission of traditional Japanese arts and the impact the Living National Treasures program has on how past artistry is currently remembered and maintained is based upon my conversations[3] with nearly forty artisans, musicians and performing artists who have been designated as Living National Treasures.[4] Although the memories of these living artists offer insight into past pedagogical practices employed in the apprenticeship system as well as underlying cultural attitudes that have fostered the transmission of the arts through the generations, their recollections, like all narratives, are necessarily selective and randomly presented – for memories by their very nature are altered through revision and reinterpretation in light of subsequent experience and present need.[5]

Although an artist's experience of learning and passing along skills is necessarily personal, the Living National Treasures whom I interviewed have related certain commonalities of experience and attitude that can be used to construct a normative picture of the traditional pedagogical system of apprenticeship that leads to mastery of the arts.[6] While the approaches to an art education changed slightly over time and each discipline pursued its own particular methodology, apprenticeships tended to share similar teaching strategies, philosophies and challenges. Until the Meiji period, an artist's training, mastery and ultimate transmission of skills to a succeeding generation followed a common pattern. Typically, an artist's life began with exposure to the arts during early childhood, followed by an intensive and challenging apprenticeship. After gaining independence from the master, artists continued to refine their skills as their creative spirits matured. Leading artists eventually devoted themselves to nurturing successors in order to pass on their skills, secrets and perspective to future generations of artists. The general cycle of this process changed little over the generations and contributed to the uninterrupted continuation of many arts down the centuries.

In the first part of this essay I bring together numerous memories voiced by Japan's Living National Treasures as a means of gaining insight into how artists once experienced their apprenticeships and subsequent tenure as masters of their artistic practice. Their recollections reveal how traditional methodologies worked effectively within the socio-economic context of the past'.[7]

The long-standing apprenticeship system is largely failing in Japanese society today due to social, economic and political changes that have affected the very foundation of an art world held firmly in place over many centuries. The Living National Treasures program is a governmental attempt to compensate for obsolete cultural and socio-economic structures that once facilitated the transmission of the arts. The second part of this paper, through the joined voices of the Living National Treasures, argues that while government assistance is sometimes helpful in sustaining certain art traditions, bureaucratic involvement in the process of transmission has encouraged methods of artistic instruction that are not traditional. Governmental representations of the 'traditional artist' and the 'traditional way' of artistic practice coupled with a re-creation of the framework within which transmission occurs, all contribute to the construction of a national cultural identity that suits the political agenda of the State.

1. THE TRADITIONAL SYSTEM OF ARTISTIC TRANSMISSION

1.1 Childhood Introduction to the Arts

Training in the traditional arts ordinarily commenced before a child was aware of being taught, often at the toddler stage. *Shamisen* player Kikuhara Hatsuko remembered, 'I was born into a family of three generations of *shamisen* teachers. I grew up in an atmosphere of practice sessions (*keiko* or honorific: *okeiko*). I do not know precisely when I started, but by the age of five or six I could play the *shamisen* freely. I also played a musical instrument called *kokyū* that resembles a *shamisen*, but is smaller.' *Shamisen* player Tomiyama Sekin explained the importance of starting young, 'There is no alternative to practicing when young; once a child reaches two digits in age, the hands are already too stiff to play well and the voice will not project clearly.' Singer of *jōruri* ballad dramas Takemoto Tosahiro, recalled that, 'From a young age I developed a fondness for *jōruri* – I sang aloud in my sleep, I was told.' For these artists music and song were unconsciously absorbed early in life.

Artistic cultivation typically started at home. Often the residence and studio were adjacent, allowing a continuum between home life and artistic practice. Children were exposed to the arts during the course of daily routine and teachings were delivered incrementally. In this familiar context art skills became ingrained or second nature early in life. Takemoto Tsudaiyū, narrator (*tayū*) of *bunraku* puppet plays, said, 'I absorbed *bunraku* since an early age, just as a Buddhist monk who learns to recite scriptures which he was never taught, simply by growing up in a temple surroundings.' Fujima Fujiko, who was raised by her mother, an accomplished dancer, stated, 'In my youth daily life always revolved around dance. Our dinner conversations inevitably drifted to dance – even though I do not believe it is good to discuss dance while eating.'

A child's initial training involved menial tasks, such as errand running and chores. The first lessons taught preparation for work, such as setting out tools, sorting imperfections from clay or gathering wood for the kiln. Gradually a child was granted permission to experiment with scrap materials. These routine, simple efforts were intended to instill an early appreciation for materials, respect for the handling and care of tools and instruments and confidence in performing the most basic skills.

At this elementary phase of learning, child aspirants were not only initiated into their own discipline, but also broadly exposed to art and culture, as a means of cultivating their artistic sensibilities and developing an awareness of their social position within the art world at large. In *kabuki* circles, for example, actor Kataoka Nizaemon commented, 'A young actor was encouraged to "polish his spirit" (literally heart and mind) (*kokoro o migaku*) through various artistic pursuits, including dance, music, puppet performance (*bunraku*), flower arrangement (*ikebana*), tea ceremony (*chanoyu*), etc., all before advancing into formal training.' Onoe Baikō, a seventh generation *kabuki* actor of female roles (*onna-gata*), observed that in his family by the age of seven a child was versed in playing *shamisen* and *suzumi* drums, *gidaiū* (ballad narration) and dance.

From the start a respectful and devoted relationship was established between the master (*sensei*) and the apprentice (*deshi*), the foundation on which a career was built. If the master was a child's parent, early on the child came to recognize the parent as an artistic mentor as well. Often apprentices who were not related to the master by blood would leave their natal family to reside with the master as live-in apprentices (*uchi deshi*). Others lived near the master. *Bunraku* narrator Takemoto Tsudaiyū, for instance, recounted that, 'I lived near my sensei. I used to rise before him and go to his house to sweep his yard and do his laundry. Just as in the *sumō* world, *bunraku* is all male. I even had to repair his *tabi* (Japanese socks worn with *geta* sandals) and help cook *chawan mushi* (steamed custard).'

Historically the master–apprentice relationship (*shujū kankei*) was a clearly defined, superior–subordinate relationship marked by the apprentice's uncompromising allegiance to the master. Reciprocal obligations were implicit in the relationship between master and disciple (whether natural or adoptive). Such inescapable moral and economic indebtedness is called *on*. The master often assumed the role of a surrogate parent. The apprentice was in a permanent position of subordination to the master. Just as children traditionally repaid their parents for the gift of life and upbringing through filial piety, the apprentice was expected to compensate the master for providing training though maintaining the high standards of the master and his predecessors, keeping art secrets and continuing the art-line.

As a child Jōnokuchi Mie, an artisan who inserts silk threads into paper stencils used for dying kimono (a technique known as *ito-ire*), was taught the meaning of *on* by her mother-sensei through the following folktale:

> An aged, impoverished man came across a wounded crane as he was gathering firewood. He kindly mended the crane's broken wing and cared for the bird until it was strong enough to fly away. Some time later, a young women knocked at the door of the poor man's hut. It was snowing and she asked for shelter. The next morning the maiden gave him a roll of beautifully woven cloth and asked him to sell it at the market. When he returned that night, she asked if she could stay and weave more cloth for him. She requested that he not look at her while she worked. Each morning she offered the man cloth of ethereal beauty. The cloth became highly valued by the villagers. However, the man worried about the weaver, as she grew pale and gaunt. He pleaded for her to stop weaving so earnestly. Still, each night he heard the persistent shuttle fly back and forth through the loom and watched in dismay the shadow of her bent-over silhouette flitter across the sliding paper doors. One night his concern for her grew so acute that he peered in at her, only to discover a nearly bald crane plucking its last feathers from its body and inserting them, one by one, into the weaving. In the morning the now nearly expired women presented the old man a weaving of inconceivable beauty. She explained that because he had discovered her secret she must leave him. She told him that she was the crane that he had cared for in the mountain. Then she flew away.

The crane demonstrated *on* toward the old man who saved its life by returning as a maiden committed to helping him. This expression of mutual favor serves to connect individuals to each other, instilling the Japanese people with a deep sense of belonging in their culture. Thus, Japanese people, who are similarly bound together through experiences involving *on*, readily understand the mythic relationship between the crane and the man. Ultimately the *on* between master and apprentice provides a link between artist and society. Jōnokuchi's mother taught her to prepare the studio ritually before starting work. Ritual preparation, a time-consuming procedure that from some perspectives might easily be omitted, was for Jōnokuchi an expression of *on* for her late mother. Ritual preparation of the studio was meaningful to Jōnokuchi because it was an expression of gratitude that provided her a vital sense of connection to her mother, to her grandmother, to the artistic tradition itself and extensively to the whole of Japanese society.

1.2 Apprenticeship

The formal apprenticeship began in earnest by the time a child reached about the age of eight. Training was fully integrated into the apprentice's daily routine and often served as a child's primary form of schooling.

Often apprentices attended daily practice sessions (*okeiko*) at the master's studio. A context of immersion, *okeiko* sessions tended to last most of the day. At *okeiko*, apprentices had the opportunity to benefit from the example of the master as well as from competition with each other. The experience of practicing together engendered solidarity in the studio, providing a social context for learning. At the same time apprentices were expected to spend much time practicing on their own in order to become self-motivated and self-reliant. One day's exercises were reinforced and further developed the following day. At *okeiko* sessions the skills, processes, techniques, aesthetics, lyrics, gestures, patterns, sounds, attitudes, etc. of past art traditions were effectively ingrained into the aspirants' memories. Apprentices internalized the art-making, music, drama and dance created around them. There was no substitute for practicing in this formal environment.

Within this setting the master-apprentice relationship assumed a ritualized dimension. An attitude of respect for learning was instilled at the onset through ritual greetings. *Kyōmai* dancer Katayama Aiko, described, '*Okeiko* begins with a formal greeting. I place my fan and *hariōgi* wand down on a small box in front of me. Then the student bows, placing her hands before her in the correct way – otherwise she may appear to have only four fingers. From the beginning, every movement must be exactly correct. Success is reached through proper forms.'

The fundamental goal of the apprenticeship stage was mastery of established models through repetitive practice. Emphasis was on acquiring basic skills and techniques through imitation and repetition; expressions of individual creativity and novel approaches were discouraged. The so-called 'copy book method,' for example, initially placed greater attention on continuing precedents than developing new approaches or nurturing individual talent.[8]

Through his father's stern admonishment, basket weaver Iizuka Shōkansai learned to replicate conventional forms in a manner that was considered traditionally correct, 'When I was still learning I took one of my first baskets to my father and asked him to take a look at it. He did not say anything, but scrutinized it for a few minutes. Suddenly he stood up and crushed it with his foot. Then he told me to go make it again. He did not tell me what was wrong with it, as one might have expected. I could not understand what was wrong. I just had to do it all over again. However, while I was working the second time the weaving came out differently. Naturally, on my own, I came to know what had been wrong the first time. When I brought the new basket to my father he said, "this seems to be right". According to my father's method of training I had to think for myself.'

Memorization was a fundamental method of skill acquisition in the traditional arts. The meaning of the verb '*oboeru*' embraced 'to learn' and 'to remember,' two inextricable aspects of internalizing skills. In the process of memorizing no steps were skipped; compromises and short-cuts were not permitted. Correct and thorough memorization led to the automatic and fluid execution of skills. *Shamisen* player Kikuhara Hatsuko explained that, 'Traditionally everything had to be memorized in *okeiko* as there was no custom of reading sheet music. Blind people were largely responsible for continuing the *jiuta* tradition of singing ballads. Even pieces as long as thirty minutes had to be memorized. When I was a *deshi* learning to play the *shamisen*, each day I memorized sections of music correctly and thoroughly until I had memorized an entire piece. Because I learned gradually in this way I still remember everything now that I am eighty-four.'

Memorization was not strictly a cognitive or academic exercise; it demanded physical training. A central training methodology of the traditional arts was 'to learn and remember by body' (*karada de oboeru*). The aim was to 'embody' the teaching, to gradually internalize skills so that eventually artistry would become fully natural and fluently expressed. Repeated practice of prescribed actions and drills was thought to physically encode or ingrain the skills. Thus it became possible to execute skills automatically and involuntarily so that skilled performance became second nature. This pedagogical approach acknowledges the concept that the body, through habitual experience, can understand and remember well after the conscious mind forgets.[9]

Shamisen player Tomiyama Sekin remembered how skills were physically inculcated during his apprenticeship, 'My *sensei* was also blind. It was hard to learn from him. Actually we learned "body to body". He held my hand and instructed me. I touched my *sensei*'s hands. It was hard to be touched by him. The traditional arts were taught from body to body.' Tomiyama conceded that the physicality was sometimes harsh, 'In the past, if a *deshi* did not understand or follow what the *sensei* said, the *sensei* would slap the *deshi*. This method of instruction literally drives knowledge into the body of the *deshi*. This is why we say that we "learn by body". This is what we call the Spartan, severe or strict method of instruction.'

Repetitive physical training required disciplined, single-minded concentration. During his apprenticeship, sword polisher Honami Nisshū was guided by the maxim, 'In ten years I polish a single sword (*jūnen ikken o migaku*).' After years of determined polishing and sharpening it was not until he sliced his thumb that Honami was able to fully confront his fear of the blade, a painful physical experience that instilled deep respect for the uncompromising edge of the sword that enabled him to perfect his skills.

Although learning the traditional arts had concrete aspects – such as the correct execution of techniques, there was a corresponding element of abstraction whereby methods were not explicitly taught. Historically, learning occurred in the absence of words. If procedures or

theories were written down, this was usually in the form of secret
manuals that were protected by a recognized authority, such as the
head of an art family or school. Secret manuals were kept in the
exclusive possession of the artistic elite and unavailable to apprentices,
in the modern sense of a textbook. Instruction frequently took a non-
verbal form, and deciphering called for proactive discernment by the
apprentices.

Kakutani Ikkei, maker of tea ceremony kettles, insisted that apprentices should not rely on explanations, but learn by vigilant and discrete
observation of the *sensei*, 'Teaching and learning should occur without
words. For instance, if you were my apprentice, you should try to understand my feelings through looking at what I have made. You should
observe me while I am speaking, meeting with my friends, eating my
meals, and all times of my daily life. If you were to wait for the teacher
to explain, it would take too much time and besides, that is not the way
of a true *deshi*. You would have to ask questions for yourself. There is a
saying, "Read what is not written." You should feel the *sensei's kokoro* and
not his words.'

As apprenticeships progressed, aspirants sought to uncover the secrets
underlying mastery of the arts. Apprentices were encouraged through
unobtrusive observation to 'steal' (*nusumu*) secrets, and only the most
determined and perceptive of them succeeded in getting past the wall
masters were obliged by the craft to defend.[10] *Shamisen* player Tomiyama
Sekin reflected that, 'From the old days there was thought to be a magic
lesson in the *sensei's* words. But secrets were never simply told to *deshi*,
they needed to be gleaned by dint of observation and hard work. It is the
tone of the *shamisen* that tells the secrets.' Kettle maker Kakutani Ikkei
asserted that, 'A secret is already shown on the completed work. If one
were to attain a scroll bearing written secrets it would mean nothing
without physical knowledge.'

Secrets contributed to the distinctive character of each studio or
school. The tension between protecting and discovering secrets lay at the
heart of the transmission of art traditions. Kikuhara Hatsuko explained
that appropriating the knowledge of others was an important observa-
tional skill expected of the apprentice, 'I was not told how to play *shamisen*. Simply, I was expected to play on my own. All the Japanese arts are
like this. Apprentices must learn by themselves before being informed by
a master. It is not good to steal objects from people, but my father told
me in the case of the performing arts invisible things like style and ideas
should be stolen.'

Ritual provided the framework in which secrets could be regenerated,
unveiled and passed along. Through their connection to the past, they
helped to maintain memory. Implicit within ritual is an attitude of
respect for procedure, materials and instruments that contributes to the
attainment of excellence in the arts. Rituals helped refine technical skills

and elevate the spirit. The customary disassembly and reconstruction of the imperial family's tutelary shrine at Ise is an archetypal example of the significance ritual plays in the transmission of traditional art skills. Since the founding of Ise Shrine in the eighth century, nearly every twenty years priests and carpenters have ritually broken apart the inner sanctuary, then rebuilt in exactly the same manner. This *shikinen sengū* rite ensured that succeeding generations of artisans would not forget the secrets of its construction. This centuries-old ritual shows the importance Japanese artisans have placed on the repetition of forms through the hands-on experience of *deshi* working along side their *sensei*. Perhaps the period of twenty years seems a short time span to repeat such a monumental undertaking, but twenty years allowed a generation of artisans to complete apprenticeships, to establish themselves as independent experts and then, in turn, to train apprentices. Together, master and apprentice dismantled and rebuilt Ise Shrine, ensuring that nothing would be forgotten over the centuries.

A constant striving for perfection motivated apprenticeships, but this was rarely easy. The training was rigorous and masters were often very strict with their apprentices as a means of bolstering their resolve to learn. Challenges demanding perseverance and sacrifice tested the apprentice's commitment to learn and aspiration to pursue a professional career. Hardship was thought ultimately to strengthen the apprentices' spirit or '*kokoro*.' Narrator of *bunraku* puppet plays, Takemoto Tsudaiyū, described his relentless drive to learn during the impoverished conditions of wartime Japan, 'The *kokoro* is essential to every performing artist. The *taiyū* places beans under a sash that is tied beneath his groin. If the *taiyū* is singing properly from the abdomen, then the beans will not move up. After the war when there was a food shortage we boiled the beans because we were starving. The beans were terribly salty from perspiration. After each performance my collar is soaked in sweat. A life of performing art once meant that the performer went through a hard life and that effort enabled him to advance his art skill and *kokoro*.'

1.3. Independence
After gaining command of techniques, apprenticeships usually ended with independence from the master. In some cases apprentices gained independence only after the master retired or passed away. The majority of the Living National Treasures indicated that the most challenging stage of their careers began with independence, when the exploration of individual creativity and spiritual development became a priority. Fujima Fujiko reflected upon what it meant for her to attain independence as a dancer, 'When I was a child learning the fundamentals of dance there were so many patterns and gestures to be strictly memorized. Everything in traditional dance is decided, although there is a limit.

Once the techniques were learned, I had to create details for myself. Dancers must find their own way.'

While the competent execution of established skills is the hallmark of the apprenticeship years, innovation is the primary challenge of the period of independence. After apprenticeship ends, personal expression and new interpretations of traditional forms are permitted. Innovation has always been an inherent aspect of maintaining art traditions in Japan. It sounds paradoxical: that which stays the same must at the same time change. But otherwise, traditions would become stale and fade out. The ability to truly innovate while keeping the integrity of enduring forms is rare. Delicate balance is required. Living traditions need revitalization, but they cannot be lost to invention.

The Living National Treasures agree that Japan's traditional arts have remained vital through the centuries because innovation has continuously infused fresh life into established conventions. *Nō* flutist Fujita Daigorō stated that, '*Nō* is old, but a performance must have a newness to it.' Dyer of *yūzen* textiles Moriguchi Kakō declared, 'What I am today can be attributed to the artist Ogata Kōrin of the Momoyama era. Looking at earlier art helps me form modern ideas.' Wood worker Ōno Shōwasai, cautioned, 'reproduction is not tradition'. *Kabuki* actor Onoe Baikō advised that, 'Making changes within a tradition is difficult. Artists can destroy what has become perfect. Therefore, artists must consider every aspect very carefully; in order to make changes the highest level of skill is necessary.'

For many of the Living National Treasures, perfecting their art has become something of a spiritual quest. Artists through the ages have developed an extraordinary ability to concentrate and elevate their *kokoro* by attaining '*mu*'. *Mu* signifies a fully concentrated mind, one cleared of all distraction. By leaving behind a subjective preoccupation with the self and attaining a mental state of *mu*, artistic practice becomes close to the experience of enlightenment or *satori* achieved through Zen meditation. Ultimately, all the talents of the body must mesh to work freely and fluently, without direction by the conscious mind. This transformation of mind allows artists to forget themselves and their bodily limitations. Through self-subjugation *mu* enables the artist to channel inspiration, to innovate and achieve perfection in the arts.

Kirikane artist Nishide Daizō described working in a state of *mu* when cutting thin lines of gold leaf – up to eight hundred lines from a eleven by eleven centimeter foil. 'I have eye problems, but still can see with my mind. We come to be able to perceive what we cannot see. In Japanese archery it is very difficult for a beginner to hit the target. But skilled archers do not see the target in the way in which beginners view it, as invisible or impossible to hit. Instead, master archers see it as larger than it actually is – as if the center were the whole target. When I cut lines they appear thick, then thicker. I want to cut them as narrowly as possible, but

if I cut them too thin they will become weak and lose their expressive-
ness. It is terribly difficult work. When I get really involved in the process,
I do not plan what is next; something leads me. At the moment of completion my mind is extraordinarily acute, clear and sharp.'

Working in a state of *mu* is not only liberating for artists individually,
but also constitutes a means by which artists can break beyond personal
limitations to connect their artistic efforts with other artists in collaborative works. *Mu* unites *bunraku* puppeteers to each other and their movements to the narrator's voice and the *shamisen* player's music. *Mu* fuses
dancers' movements to the accompanying music. *Mu* integrates the skills
of cutting paper stencils with those of inserting silk threads to hold the
openwork patterns in place, with those of stencil dying. *Mu* connects the
sword forging process with that of subsequent sword sharpening and polishing. *Mu* is essential to achieving synchronicity between artisans and
performers in so many of the highest-level collaborative arts. Ultimately
this enduring intangible dimension of artistic practice contributes to the
perpetuation of the traditional arts, for *mu* spiritually provides the master
artists a profound sense of identity and unity with the achievements of
their predecessors.

Mastery of the traditional arts is generally regarded as a life-long
pursuit, a ceaseless striving for perfection.[11] *Bunraku* narrator Takemoto
Tsudaiyū explained that by pushing the limits of his talent throughout
his life he was able to reinvigorate the traditional songs that he perpetuated. 'Some parts of the *jōruri* narration require extreme amounts of
strength to perform. Such challenging passages sometimes cause the
throats of beginners to bleed. Blood falls onto their scripts because they
have to go through extreme high and low tones that are very strenuous
on the throat. As the *taiyū* (narrator) ages his physical strength declines.
Although he cannot exhale with the vigor of his youth, instead he has
attained the disciplined throat of fifty years narration experience.
Because a young man's breathing capacity is strong, it is said that a
women's role should be narrated by a *taiyū* who is over fifty years of age.
By the time the *taiyū* has reached fifty, he has mastered the best way to
adjust his strength in accordance with his breathing and voice control. I
am now elderly, and I can no longer utter high and low tones perfectly.
But, the perfection of performing art has no limit. If excellence could be
achieved so easily, it would not be very interesting. Because it is difficult,
it has always challenged me. Conquering something that is difficult
brings great joy. When inhaling and holding as much air as possible, I
feel as if my body will explode. It is coming to this limit that gives life to
my art.'

1.4. Mentorship

Historically the master's role was both that of artist and mentor. These
two vocations – making art and teaching art – were well integrated. In

the context of *okeiko*, masters pursued their artistic practice while apprentices sought to learn. Here teaching and learning occurred in tandem. Interpreting an old proverb uttered by *sensei*, 'I am not giving you a lesson', *bunraku* narrator Takemoto Tsudaiyū claimed that, 'Actually, giving a lesson is receiving a lesson for me.'

Mentoring was not viewed strictly as teaching. It was a stage in the career when master artists brought apprentices into their world, exemplified skills and techniques, helped cultivate their *kokoro*, permitted them to witness their perspective, offered them the opportunity to steal secrets and observe ritual. Mentors were responsible for disciplining apprentices to assure that they developed proper work habits, inculcating memorization skills gradually over time, and instilling time-honored values such as reverence for natural materials, regard for instruments and tools, respect for artistic processes and appreciation for the achievements of past generations of artists. Beyond this the mentor's obligations were to continue striving to learn through continued study and reaching for perfection.

Mentoring apprentices not only requires depth of knowledge and acute skill, but also demands a heavy commitment of energy, focus and financial resources that would sustain the duration of their *deshi's* apprenticeship years. The nurturing aspect of mentorship is reflected in the way the Living National Treasures described 'raising' rather than 'instructing' their apprentices and referred to the production of art works as their 'being born.' For *yūzen* dyer Moriguchi Kakō the desire to raise successors stemmed from a feeling of gratitude and indebtedness toward his own sensei. He declared, 'I have a sense of gratitude for the past generations who preserved their work and passed down their skills to us. We must, in turn, pass down this feeling of appreciation to the people of the future. Everything begins and ends with thanks.'

By offering apprentices exposure to select 'tangible' models particularly in the case of the applied arts, a mentor elevates their experience of art. For evaluating quality and developing the eye, wood worker Ōno Shōwasai argued, 'It is essential that the mentor expose apprentices to the highest quality examples and models. To nurture the *kokoro*, *deshi* must examine authentic works, not reproductions. Under the best conditions aspiring artists should be exposed to high quality art in their homes or studios. This will naturally refine aesthetic sensibilities and cultivate good taste. Artistic sense cannot be taught, but can develop naturally through exposure to art of the highest order.'

The mentor was essential for demonstrating the all-important 'intangible' aspects of the arts. *Kabuki* actor Kataoka Nizaemon emphasized that, 'It is very difficult to teach a young actor how to make something seem real. A *sensei* cannot explain how or why in words, but can point out to the *deshi* what seems correct and authentic.' Compared to the teaching of concrete skills, many of the Living Treasures contend that cultivating the apprentice's spirit or *kokoro* presents the mentor with the greatest challenge. *Shamisen* player Kikuhara Hatsuko insisted that, 'The way of teaching the *kokoro* is very important. The sensei should first discover the *deshi's* weak points. If the teacher corrects these areas, then and only then, will the good aspects remain. It is most difficult to teach the *kokoro*, for success depends on the *deshi's* self awareness.'

Dancer Katayama Aiko, remarked, 'I am always positioned opposite my students so that we face each other. If a student dances with her right hand, then I dance with my right hand in unison. If we are side by side, we dance together, moving the same hands in synchronization. If the student does not move correctly with me, I become *"hidarigi"* (a pejorative expression similar to "lefty"). Therefore, it is very important and of good manners for the student to move with me properly. This should not be exact imitation, one after the other, but simultaneous motion. It may seem that we are moving together, but actually the students are imitating me. There are many ways to study the arts; however, with the intangible arts the *sensei* is essential.'

Bunraku narrator Takemoto Tsudaiyū offered a metaphor for cultivating an apprentice's *kokoro* over the course of a lengthy training regime, '*Deshi* often ask me why skipping steps is not permitted. This is because learning *bunraku* is a step-by-step process. As with moss in a Japanese garden, one has to follow its growth over the years to discover how lush it becomes. A *deshi* has to work at it year after year, and when he looks back he hopes to see beautiful moss. But this cannot be guaranteed. Some moss just does not have the right color. During the course of training a *deshi* cannot fully recognize how he is progressing, nor can he know how he will turn out. *Bunraku* is subtle. When I decide if a *deshi* is ready to appear on stage, I must determine if he is both technically and spiritually ready. There are some people who are very good technically and others who are not; but, above all, a performer's personality, depth of character and *kokoro* are most essential.'

The traditional process for the transmission of the performing and studio arts down the generations in Japan engendered an integrated, life-long approach to artistic realization. The system fostered a meaningful experience over the entire course of an artist's life, beginning with intensive training during youth, independence in adulthood, and achievement as a master and mentor from mid-life onward. Furthermore, the mentorship stage provided a vital link between accomplished artists and aspiring artists of the succeeding generation. Although the traditional system was rigid in many ways, it was also highly dynamic and allowed the arts to evolve in ways that preserved their connection to society.

At the heart of this system was a series of rituals and integrated philosophies and attitudes that have made transmission an essential aspect of the actual production of art. The master's roles – artist and mentor – were inextricably entwined. Memory of the past – its rituals, techniques, skills, aesthetics, expressions, attitudes, philosophies, etc. – was kept alive through oral tradition and by 'body' transfer. Learning and teaching were seamlessly woven into the process of performing and producing art. The arts flourished under this system, which was highly conducive of maintaining a legacy of the past as well as cultivating fresh talent.

2. THE LIVING NATIONAL TREASURES PROGRAM AND ITS IMPACT ON THE TRANSMISSION OF TRADITIONAL JAPANESE ART

Today, Japanese society, culture, economics and politics have changed to such an extent that the system that supported the traditional arts in previous centuries is no longer viable. Compulsory education, industrialization, technological progress, and the increasingly strong and centralized national government have all dramatically altered the terrain through which an artist travels in the course of a career. Kettle maker Kakutani Ikkei lamented, 'As time advances artists have more time to improve, to experiment, to learn. It is sad, however, that many traditional arts are declining. Today there is no artist of wood block printing that comes close to the caliber of Edo period *ukiyo-e* printmakers.'

The enactment of laws during the late nineteenth century that led to the establishment of the Living National Treasure program reveals that the historically established way of transmitting the arts was already failing during the Meiji period. Today many of the artists designated as Living National Treasures are the last practitioners of their artistic lineages. Kikuhara Hatsuko, for example, realized that, 'I was awarded the title Living National Treasure because I am the only *shamisen* player who can still play *Honte no kumi uta*, which was composed more than three hundred years ago. My duty is to pass on all my knowledge of old music to the next generation.' Jōnokuchi Mie speculated that, 'There is no future for *ito-ire*, because so few people have the skill. My top successor and I have to carry the tradition on alone. Only the two of us remain. In the future there will be no way of knowing the *ito-ire* technique except for by looking at the old stencils.'

As a part of its effort to preserve the Important Intangible Cultural Properties, the government confers a modest annual grant to the Living National Treasures. The Ministry of Education encourages the titled artists to thoroughly document their accomplishments and openly share their knowledge. To this end, it sponsors video productions, publications and exhibitions that chronicle the lives and work of the artists. In addition the administration helps defray costs of public art exhibitions and performances. The government places no specific stipulations on the artists, but expects that they will train successors. Funds are allotted to help cover costs incurred by training followers to carry on the artistic traditions.

Most Living National Treasures felt an obligation to go along with some of the alternate methods of transmission endorsed by the government and necessitated by social and economic change. Governmental pressure on the Living National Treasures to make concerted attempts to perpetuate the art traditions has altered the focus of their efforts and the process by which the transmission of their skills takes place – sometimes in ways that undermine the effectiveness of that very transmission. By striving to record and store information about the production of Japan's dying art forms, the Living National Treasure program inadvertently helps to cleave the process of learning from the process of creating art, as well as its rituals, secrets, and other long-established accompanying practices.

The responsibilities that accompanied the title were burdensome for a number of the artistis awarded. 'Since being designated a Living National Treasure I notice my name in the newspaper and feel a tremendous sense of responsibility. Now I become tense and nervous when I perform. I often cannot fall asleep the night before a performance', singer Takemoto Tosahiro remarked with dismay. *Kirikane* artist Nishide Daizō declared, 'It is just a title. But, I feel uneasy being categorized by the title. I also have some sort of rebellious feeling toward the rules imposed on the title-holders. There are stereotypes and pressures associated with the designation which I resent.' Metalworker Kashima Ikkoku, concluded, 'Now that I am designated a Living National Treasure, I will probably die soon, just as my friend who passed away not long after receiving his title. It was a grave responsibility.'

As 'Holders' of the nation's 'Intangible Cultural Property', many of the artists admitted that they could no longer view their efforts strictly as their own enterprise. Accompanying the title is the expectation that those designated will create works or performances that will serve as exemplary or outstanding models of a tradition. This has had the effect of stifling an artist's ability to innovate, for improvisation becomes increasingly difficult when creativity is institutionalized. Acknowledging the importance of innovation, wood worker Nakadai Zuishin struggled with governmental pressure to create 'traditional' works, closely modeled on earlier examples, 'Now that I am a Living National Treasure, people look at my works as important examples of tradition; therefore, I can no longer make anything that might seem different. Until now I made things to sell. Now that I am a Living National Treasure people look at my work as exemplary of the wood working tradition, so I feel inhibited and cannot make anything unusual.'

In attempting to adapt the antiquated apprenticeship system to modern Japan, new approaches to art instruction are designed to make the rigorous training process more approachable to today's youth and the traditional arts seem easier to learn. New approaches to teaching traditional art include attempts to speed up or truncate the learning process so that successors might be trained in shorter-spans of time that require fewer financial resources. This often leads to a reduction of the *sensei*'s role from mentor to merely instructor. Reciprocal obligations between the master and disciple are thus weakened, strict discipline is relaxed and expectations placed on apprentices are generally lowered. The recent reliance on technological approaches to teaching and documenting traditional art contributes to the diminished role of the *sensei*. As a consequence of new pedagogical methods memorization requirements based on physical practice have decreased significantly. There has been a marked shift from bodily to cognitive approaches to skill acquisition, a move from proactive, self-motivated observation to passive absorption of knowledge. Moreover, by encouraging *sensei* to break their silence and interrupt their work in order to explain and demonstrate, rituals become demystified and secrets lose their meaning. All of this leads to a curbing of innovation, which lies at the heart of artistic transmission. Taken together, these modifications have led to significant changes in the life and work style of practitioners of traditional arts. As historic learning methods become increasingly irrelevant in Japanese society, fewer students are willing to devote themselves to the rigors of the traditional training regiment.

Although the Living National Treasures acknowledge that in order to remain vibrant the traditional arts must evolve with society, the artists were critical of the extent to which traditional pedagogical methods are changing today. Dancer Fujima Fujiko observed, 'Lately many students begin watching a new dance by taking notes. But I do not permit this, because I always memorized. Memorization is difficult for students who come to *okeiko* only one or two days a week. Nonetheless, my students still memorize everything the traditional way by remembering through body movement. It is critical that they watch me move. I could write explanations for them with a ball-point pen, but eventually all my notations would be crossed out because instruction of dance is physical. They would not be pleased if I taught them motion according to a text.'

Because students attend *okeiko* less often many teachers of the traditional arts today attempt to ease the task of memorization. Contemporary apprenticeships sometimes adopt cramming techniques used in preparatory schools (*juku*) as a substitute for the task of gradual and thorough memorization. Narrator Takemoto Tsudaiyū criticized this development, 'Traditional art should be understood through the *kokoro*. Education now depends on cramming. I think that cramming has ruined the novices' ability to learn through the *kokoro*. I believe too much is made of cramming and the short-term memorization of facts. Many children go to *juku* after school and study earnestly; they are always busy. This approach to education is detrimental for young musicians.'

The use of technology and texts for instruction has significantly diminished the importance of memorization in learning the traditional arts.

Sheet music, textbooks, diagrams, photographs, video and tape recordings are now widely utilized as teaching tools. Yet, use of these aids diminishes the student's reliance upon their own memories. It changes the memorization process and constitutes a shift in learning by 'body' to reliance on text or tape. This necessarily diminishes the importance of the mentor's role in embodying and transmitting skills. *Bunraku* puppeteer Yoshida Tamao argued that learning music from tapes undermines oral tradition and weakens memorization skills, 'Now memorization is easy because we have tape recorders. In former days we did not have such devices. Apprentices learning shamisen could only hear the music once. They could not rewind and replay the *sensei*'s music. Therefore, *deshi* relied on their memories. We faced each other during *okeiko*. There was only one chance. At present we can listen to a tape ten times, one hundred times, a thousand times over, simply by pushing a button.'

Technological advances may make remembering seem easier, offering the student endless opportunity to repeat their teacher's examples, However, *shamisen* player Kikuhara Hatsuko noted a marked decline in her students' ability to memorize, arguing that 'body-to-body' repetition during regular practice at *okeiko* is a far more effective way to remember. 'When I teach my *deshi* something as difficult as *Kurokami*, if they practice four times in a month, they will be able to play it. When I was a child learning that song, I had *okeiko* everyday; so it took me about four or five days to learn to play that piece. Instead of using sheet music, we separated a song into four or five parts. My teacher would play a part; then I would repeat. Mouth to mouth, ear to ear, we practiced together. After the third time if I made a mistake, my *sensei* would become very cross, even when the piece was difficult. If on the second day I forgot the previous day's music, I could not go on to a new part. My *sensei* had me memorize very strictly until I could get the last part down perfectly. I would absorb other people's *okeiko* while I was waiting for my lesson. By the time it came to be my turn I could easily remember those pieces. This is how I could learn to play two days worth of music in a single day.'

The use of sheet music and tape recording for Kikuhara posed a dilemma, for she recognized that, 'it is no good for me alone to know this music. None of my father's friends play *Honte no kumi uta* any longer, so I have to do my best on my own. Without sheet music many songs would not pass on to the next generation. We can no longer rely on oral tradition.' Despite resorting to recording her music, Kikuhara understands that the recordings will ultimately have the effect of distorting rather than preserving the tradition. '*Jiuta* originated in the Kansai area and has always been most popular in Kyōto and Ōsaka. *Jiuta* is a matter of regional taste. Since every performer interprets *jiuta* in a personal way and since learning is by way of ear and mouth, the native dialect of the *sensei* accounts for regional differences. Now that there are tape recorders the study and performance of *juita* will greatly change.'

Kikuhara was primarily concerned that today's emphasis on learning music by reading scores and listening to recordings will inhibit the students' intuitive understanding of music and lower their ability to play from the *kokoro*. 'Sheet music revolutionized the way of learning. Even if I ask *deshi* to play something they do not know, they can do so easily by reading sheet music. Perhaps that is why many more seeing people play *jiuta* now. It is a very convenient way to play; however, artistic feeling is not merely being able to read notes. Many musicians can read music, but the ear can decipher whether or not a song is played with artistic understanding. It is a matter of small nuances. Understanding this subtlety is very difficult. If I tell my *deshi* that she is playing according to score it is not praise. Many *deshi* do not understand why I am disapproving when they play by reading score. After the beginning stages of learning, it is not enough to follow sheet music strictly. One must play from the *kokoro*. This is how Japanese musicians have learned to play for centuries. They were not taught; intuitive understanding is fundamental to music.'

The collection of empirical information, procedural short cuts, reliance on technological rather than human memory, the loss of body-to-body training, the fading of oral tradition, the revelation of secrets, the disappearance of rituals, all these changes in the training of traditional art implicitly place importance on that which is tangible rather intangible. New teaching strategies do not have the cultivation of an artist's spirit or *kokoro* as a priority in the way that it had been in the traditional apprenticeship system. By adapting the traditional training system to contemporary society, knowledge of techniques will likely be preserved, but the Living National Treasures expressed a consensual concern for the disappearance of what they claim to be the most important aspect of creating traditional art: its spirit, heart and mind – the *kokoro*. This is evident in comments throughout the paper that resound *kabuki* actor Onoe's Baikō decree, 'High skill is essential, but one's *kokoro* is paramount. Skill without spirit goes nowhere.'

Perhaps in response to the pressures imposed by the government's attempt to secure a future for traditional Japanese art, the Living National Treasures have asserted an ideology that recognizes a spiritual essence or *kokoro* at the base of their artistic practice. According to their ideology the practice of traditional arts is akin to a spiritual quest, and the *kokoro* transcends technical skills. While it is tempting to accept the artists' rhetoric of remembering and their ideology, it is important to examine what prompted the construction of the ideology and why it is widely upheld. As with any narrative, the experiences and thoughts of the Living National Treasures voiced here are selective accounts that attempt to organize events in time, interpret reality, construct identities, establish coherency and enable social action.[12] Although their ideology may be born of nostalgia and reflect an idealization of Japan's artistic past, it implicitly raises critical questions: what initiated and continues to motivate the government's desire to recover, reclaim and protect Japan's forgotten past? Which past? What constitutes 'tradition' and why? How and why is 'tradition' utilized as cultural and political capital today? How can this lead to a reinvention of history? What bearing will this have on Japan's future? Why bestow titles on certain leading 'traditional' artists? Why make it their responsibility to create exemplary work and to perpetuate the dying art traditions? How do governmental representations of 'traditional' art and the 'traditional artist' contribute to its construction of a national identity? What then are the full implications of this desire for memory?

Because of its abstract, non-specific nature, the concept of *kokoro* resonates with artists not only on a personal level, but also holds meaning for a larger collective – the community of Living National Treasures. Bound together by their ideology, practitioners of various arts form a collective identity – one that ultimately emphasizes the importance of the artist's state of mind and heart (*kokoro*) over the refinement of technical skills for artistic mastery. By insisting that the *kokoro* is indefinable and elusive, the artists are able to claim the spiritual aspects of art production as their own and thus resist full compliance with the mandates of the program. Their ideology is fundamentally a stake for autonomy and at its extreme can be a subtle form of resistance, even a position of defiance. It is a political stance contending that over-emphasis of the empirical elements of art production will ultimately stifle the creative, individual and spiritual aspects of the artistic process that have always brought the enduring arts fresh life. Through this ideology the Living National Treasures express a shared opposition to some of the protective measures that, as this article has argued, distort rather than preserve Japan's artistic heritage.

The paradoxical and controversial aspects of the Living National Treasure program discussed here attest to the fact that reconstructing a memory of Japan's artistic past that can be shared by a nation is indeed a complex undertaking. The effort that the government exerts in sustaining and restoring traditional art practices through the Living National Treasure program demonstrates that the past continues to strongly impact the present in Japan. As 'agents of memory', the 'Holders of Important Intangible Cultural Property' hold significant cultural and political capital. Governmental control of their recollections of the past, by institutionalizing and documenting certain artistic efforts, facilitates its ability to mould and regulate images of Japan's past. The present agenda of the Japanese government – specifically, the appropriation of a certain image of Japan's artistic legacy in its construction of a national cultural identity – shapes the remembrance of Japan's artistic past. By bureaucratizing the traditional arts under the auspices of the Living

National Treasure program, the Japanese government substantially influences how the Japanese populace today, as well as tomorrow, will recall its artistic heritage.

REFERENCES

Ben-Ari, Eyal. 1998. 'Golf, Organization, and "Body Projects": Japanese Business Expatriates in Singapore'. In *The Culture of Japan as Seen Through its Leisure*. Linhart Sepp and Frühstück Sabine (eds). pp. 139–61. Albany: State University of New York Press.

Connerton, Paul. 1989. *How Societies Remember*. Cambridge: Cambridge Uiversity Press.

Irie, Hiroshi. 1988. Apprenticeship Training in Tokugawa Japan. *Acta Asiatica*, vol. 54, pp. 1–23.

Jordan, Brenda and Weston, Victoria (eds). 2003. *Copying the Master and Stealing His Secrets: Talent and Training in Japanese Painting*. Honolulu: University of Hawaii Press.

Lebra, Takie Sugiyama. 1993. *Above the Clouds: Status Culture of Modern Japanese Nobility*. Berkeley and Los Angeles: University of California Press.

Lowenthal, David. 1985. *The Past is a Foreign Country*. Cambridge: Cambridge University Press.

Plath, David. 1998. 'Calluses: When Culture Gets Under Your Skin.' In *Learning in Likely Places: Varieties of Apprenticeship in Japan*. Singleton John (ed.) pp. 341–51. Cambridge: Cambridge University Press.

Rimer, Thomas 1998. 'The Search for Mastery Never Ceases: Zeami's Classic Treatises on Transmitting the Traditions of the Nō Theatre.' In *Learning in Likely Places: Varieties of Apprenticeship in Japan*. Singleton John (ed.) pp. 35–44. Cambridge: Cambridge University Press.

Singleton John, ed. 1988. *Learning in Likely Places: Varieties of Apprenticeship in Japan*. Cambridge: Cambridge University Press.

NOTES

[1] Outside influences had frequently inspired Japanese artists, who after an initial period of absorption tended to integrate and transform borrowed models into a Japanese idiom. This phenomenon was most pronounced during the Heian period (794–1185), after the heavy reliance upon Tang dynasty (618–907) arts during the Nara period (710–794), and during the Momoyama period (1573–1615), following reception of Song dynasty art during the Kamakura (1333–1336) and Muromachi (1392–1573) eras. While Western influences in the arts opened way for new approaches to art production, particularly in the fine arts, many of the traditional aesthetic pursuits began to decline.

[2] See Lebra, Takie Sugiyama. 1993. *Above the Clouds: Status Culture of Modern Japanese Nobility*. Berkeley and Los Angeles: University of California Press.

3   Over the course of one year I held extensive interviews with nearly forty of Japan's Living National Treasures as a part of a Thomas J. Watson Jr. Foundation Fellowship in 1985–86.

4   In this paper I collectively refer to those who practice the theatrical, musical and applied arts as 'artists'. It should be noted that a general distinction between the use of the term 'artist' and 'artisan' has evolved out of the influence of the folk art (*mingei*) movement lead by Yanagi Sōetsu (1889–1961). In brief, an 'artist' is considered one who approaches art-making, usually painting or sculpture, as an individual pursuit and a form of personal aesthetic expression, while an 'artisan' is recognized as one who produces objects primarily for daily life, working within an established tradition of artistic production without explicitly aiming for unique or individual interpretations.

5   Lowenthal, David. 1985. *The Past is a Foreign Country*. Cambridge: Cambridge University Press.

6   For a full study of Japan's apprenticeship system, See *Learning in Likely Places: Varieties of Apprenticeship in Japan*. Singleton John, ed. pp. 341–351. Cambridge: Cambridge University Press.

7   The list of artists awarded the title 'Holders of Important Intangible Cultural Properties' is updated annually. The Living National Treasures are divided into two categories: performing artists and artisans. There are approximately thirty-five Living National Treasures in each group at any given time. The areas of performing art that have been recognized include: *bunraku, nō, kabuki*, dance and music. The recognized crafts include: ceramics, earthenware, textile weaving and dying, lacquer ware, metal work, wood and bamboo work, doll making, stained ivory engraving (*bachiru*) and paper making.

8   See: Jordan, Brenda and Weston, Victoria (eds.). 2003 *Copying the Master and Stealing His Secrets: Talent and Training in Japanese Painting*. Honolulu: University of Hawaii Press.

9   Plath, David. 1998 'Calluses; When Culture Gets Under Your Skin'. In *Learning in Likely Places: Varieties of Apprenticeship in Japan*. Singleton John, ed. pp. 341–351. Cambridge: Cambridge University Press; Ben-Ari, Eyal. 1998 'Golf, Organization, and "Body Projects": Japanese Business Expatriates in Singapore'. In *The Culture of Japan as Seen Through its Leisure*. Linhart Sepp and Frühstück Sabine (eds) pp. 139–61. Albany: State University of New York Press; Connerton, Paul. 1989 *How Societies Remember*. Cambridge: Cambridge University Press.

10   See Irie, Hiroshi. 1988. Apprenticeship Training in Tokugawa Japan. *Acta Asiatica*, vol. 54, pp. 1–23.

11   See Rimer, Thomas. 1998 'The Search for Mastery Never Ceases; Zeami's Classic Treatises on Transmitting the Traditions of the *Nō* Theatre'. In *Learning in Likely Places: Varieties of Apprenticeship in Japan*. Singleton John, ed. pp. 36–44. Cambridge: Cambridge University Press.

PART 3

Remembering Nature

10

Remembering the Wolf: The Wolf Reintroduction Campaign in Japan[*]

JOHN KNIGHT

INTRODUCTION

Wolves have been extinct in Japan since the beginning of the twentieth century. Two species of wolves existed on the Japanese archipelago: the Hondo wolf (*Canis lupus hodophylax*) on the main islands of Honshū, Shikoku and Kyūshū, and the Ezo wolf (*Canis lupus hattai*) on the northern island of Hokkaidō. The extinction of the Ezo wolf occurred in the late nineteenth century with the establishment of livestock ranches in Hokkaidō and the Hondo wolf disappeared at the beginning of the twentieth century against the background of a rabies epidemic. The last known wolf in Japan was killed on 23 January 1905 on the northern part of the Kii Peninsula, and the stuffed remains of this animal are today to be found in the Natural History Museum in London. Nearly a century after wolves became extinct, a Tokyo-based pressure group called the Japan Wolf Association (JWA) launched a campaign for wolves to be reintroduced to Japan. The JWA proposed that wolves from Chinese Inner Mongolia be used to establish gray wolf colonies in a number of areas across Japan.

In this chapter I shall reflect on the wolf reintroduction campaign with specific reference to the way wolves are remembered. In the most recent

---

[*] This paper draws on material contained in a recent book, *Waiting for Wolves in Japan: An Anthropological Study of People-Wildlife Relations* (Oxford University Press, 2003), which examines the issue of wolf reintroduction at greater length.

public opinion survey, carried out by the JWA in 1999, only 14 per cent of respondents agreed with the idea of reintroducing wolves to Japan. The JWA argues that this low level of support simply reflects the current lack of awareness of the issues, and that as its campaign develops this will change. A key problem faced by the JWA is that the dominant memory or image of the wolf in present-day Japan is that of a dangerous animal that threatens human safety. The JWA campaign of public education sets out to challenge what it sees as the misremembrance of the wolf, and to replace it with a more favourable representation of the animal. This chapter examines the rhetorical strategy employed by the JWA.

Much of the discussion refers to mountain villages on the southern part of the Kii Peninsula in western Japan, one of the areas for which wolf reintroduction has been suggested. It draws on long term ethnographic fieldwork in this area (which began in 1987), especially the municipality of Hongū-chō.

THE REPUTATION OF THE PREDATOR

Hostile attitudes towards wild predators such as lions, leopards and wolves have been widely recorded. Wild predators are feared and hated, first and foremost, because of the physical danger they seem to pose to livestock and to people. But such attitudes towards predators are not always reducible to the direct physical threat posed by the animal, but may also be infused by the negative associations of the animal in human society. Predators tend to be viewed as outlaws, criminals and killers, while human action to control or eradicate these dangerous animals is lauded as public-spirited heroism. This appears to be especially the case with the wolf, an animal that has long been associated with evil in western societies, and even portrayed as incarnations of the devil. There is a long history of wolf persecution in the form of recurrent eradication campaigns through trapping, poisoning and shooting. The assault against the wolf has been waged not simply in defence of life and livelihood, but also as a moral struggle of good against evil. Wolf elimination was not simply a utilitarian measure to remove a livestock pest, but also represented the removal of an immoral animal (Worster 1977; Steinhart 1995).

It is against this background of a widespread predator phobia in human societies that predator conservation policies tend to become controversial. Such initiatives often encounter suspicion, hostility and even outright opposition among local people who see these animals as threats to their interests or wellbeing. Wild predators may be viewed by hunters as competitors for game animals, by farmers as threats to livestock, and, more generally, by the people who live in or near predator ranges as potential threats to human safety. A high profile example of this is the long-running controversy surrounding the plan to reintroduce wolves to

Yellowstone National Park (Paystrup 1993; Fischer 1995). But there are also many examples of local-national antagonism over wild predators in Asia. In Armenia officially protected leopards threaten livestock, and this leads to clandestine leopard killings by shepherds and other livestock farmers (Khorozyan 1998: 9–10). In Gujarat, villagers next to the Asiatic lion sanctuary, on being told by government officials about the need to protect lions, respond by telling the officials 'to take all the lions with them to Delhi' (Sukumar 1994: 315). In the Indian tiger reserves established as part of the Project Tiger initiative, villagers react to tiger predations on their livestock by poisoning waterholes and salt-licks, causing forest fires, and manhandling reserve staff (Howard and Dutta 1995: 430; Rishi 1995: 417), while in Nepal there have been riots over man-eating tigers (Mishra et al. 1987: 456).

The negative image of predators presents a major challenge to conservationists seeking to protect or restore predators in the wild. First of all, a wary public must be persuaded that the predator is not the mankiller or even maneater that it is portrayed as in popular legend. In an effort to correct the what they see as exaggerated depictions of wild predators, conservationists have projected alternative representations of wolves, bears and wild cats, typically emphasizing the exceptional character of mankilling incidents and characterizing the predator mankilling incidents that do occur as reactive rather than aggressive in character. In addition to challenging this negative imagery, predator conservation campaigns may also project positive imagery of predators, such as the claim that their predations have benign ecological effects. In short, a condition of effective predator conservation and management is likely to be the corrective redefinition of the negative reputation of the animal in question. On top of this predator reintroductionists face another kind of obstacle. As reintroduction entails bringing in animals to the place where they have become extinct from other places where they still exist, it is also vulnerable to what we might call nativist objections – that the animal is an outsider out of place among indigenous flora and fauna and even a potential threat to it. Reintroduced predators can become symbols of national interference in local affairs and even arouse quasi-xenophobic local reactions to their presence (Capps 1994; Moore 1994; Wilson 1997). The wolf reintroduction campaign in Japan provides a recent example of how one conservationist organization has responded to this challenge.

THE REINTRODUCTION PROPOSAL

In 1993 the Japan Wolf Association (*Nihon ōkami kyōkai*, hereafter JWA) issued a public call for wolf reintroduction to be carried out in Japan. The JWA proposes that wolves from Chinese Inner Mongolia be used to establish gray wolf colonies (of up to thirty animals) in a number of areas across Japan. Ten (national park) areas have been identified as possible candidate sites for wolf reintroduction, including the Yoshino-Kumano National Park area on the interior of the Kii Peninsula. The reintroduction of wolves to Japan is a long-term goal rather than an immediate ambition. The first objective of the campaign is to stimulate a national debate by getting the issue of wolf reintroduction onto the public agenda in Japan. Largely through the efforts of the leader of the JWA, the zoologist Maruyama Naoki, an articulate and forceful spokesman, the issue has attracted extensive media coverage and become a topic of public debate in Japan. In the short and medium terms, the JWA aims to build up public support for wolf reintroduction, and to lobby the Japanese government to establish effective wildlife management institutions staffed by suitably trained personnel. Once these foundations of public support and state approval have been laid, the JWA will draw up detailed plans for the practical implementation of the reintroduction proposal, but the time-frame for reintroduction would appear to be in terms of decades rather than years.

The JWA has a membership of more than six hundred people, drawn largely from the professional classes, including university professors, schoolteachers, writers, journalists, doctors and artists. The association has a regular newsletter that carries specialized articles as well as contributions from ordinary members. There is a dedicated email message board on the JWA home page where members communicate with each other on wolf-related matters, and exchange information on a variety of topics – wolf literature, wolf memorabilia and other wolf websites; environmental and wildlife issues in general; opposition to wolf-culling overseas; wolf-watching opportunities around the world, and so on. Many of the JWA members express a strong identification with the wolf. At a JWA gathering in 1995 that I attended some members wore T-shirts and sweaters bearing images of the wolf (imported from America). Members refer to themselves and address each other as *ōkami fan* or 'wolf fans', *ōkami ningen* or 'wolf people', and even *ōkami furīku* or 'wolf freaks'. This sentiment is formally reflected by the association, which designates its three categories of members as 'alphas', 'pack wolves' and 'wolf friends', and divides its branches into the 'west pack' and the 'east pack'.

The JWA puts forward a number of reasons for wolf reintroduction. First of all, it argues that wolf reintroduction is a moral imperative. Wolf extinction is seen as a powerful testament to the excesses of industrialization and modernization. Wolf extinction is represented as a *machigai* or 'mistake' or *hi* or 'wrong' (Maruyama 2001). This sense that wolf extinction represented wrongful conduct on the part of the Japanese people is also indicated by the use of the the verb *okasu* (which normally denotes criminal-like behaviour) – as in *okashitekita hi* ('committed a wrong') (ibid.). The fact of wolf extinction demands a process of *seishintekina hansei* or 'spiritual reflection' on the part of the Japanese people and imposes on them a *rinritekina sekinin* or 'ethical responsibility' and *gimu* or 'duty' to do something about it (Maruyama 1999: 15). Maruyama Naoki sometimes argues that wolf reintroduction is a kind of 'apology' for past mistakes – using the verb *wabiru*, 'to apologize': 'We must honestly apologize for having committed a wrong' (Maruyama 2001). This language recalls that of the wolf reintroduction in North America which is justified as a kind of atonement for past mistakes (Primm and Clark 1996: 1038).

A second reason for wolf reintroduction is that it would restore Japan's forest. Wolf extinction has come to epitomise the decline of the forest in the course of national modernization. The term *mori*, which nostalgically evokes the traditional forest, is often used in this regard (as opposed to *shinrin* or *hayashi*, words that suggest a modern, productive forest). In the JWA literature the word *mori* appears almost as much as the word *ōkami*, and the wolf is seldom mentioned other than in connection with the forest. The title of the JWA newsletter is 'Forest Call' (English loanwords used), while the front cover of each issue bears the slogan 'Towards a good relationship between forest, wolves and people' (*mori-ōkami-hito no yoi kankei o kangaeru*). Furthermore, a circular JWA logo has been created that shows wolves chasing deer against a backdrop of forest trees. The wolf is sometimes referred to in the JWA newsletter as *mori o sukuu ōkami* or 'the wolf that will save the forest'. There is a strong sense that with the extinction of the wolf the *mori* too has ceased to exist in Japan. 'A forest without wolves is in a state of chaos' (*ōkami no inai mori wa daikonran*) (Maruyama 2001). The powerful rhetorical suggestion of the JWA is that the wolf, through its reintroduction, can serve as the means by which the Japanese people can recover, and reunite with, their *mori*.

In conjunction with this emphasis on the *mori* is an emphasis on the *shinrin seitaikei* or 'forest ecosystem'. The idea of nature as an *seitaikei* or 'ecosystem' is a central theme in JWA discourse, and the wolf is accorded a special place in the Japanese ecosystem. Based on a key notion of modern ecology, the JWA defines the 'forest ecosystem' in terms of the existence of top-line wild predators such as wolves that, through their carnivory, keep in check the numbers of wild herbivores. The extinction of the Japanese wolf at the beginning of the twentieth century left Japan with a *hakaishita shizen* or 'broken nature' (Maruyama 2000) and a *yugamerareta seitaikei* or 'distorted ecosystem' (Koganezawa 1999: 5) in which forest herbivores could no longer be kept in check. In order to re-stabilize the natural ecosystem, the extinction of the wolf must be reversed. The reintroduction of wolves to Japan would 'restore broken nature' (Maruyama 2000) and 'revive a healthy ecosystem' (Koganezawa 1999: 5). This argument tends to be specifically directed at the deer population. One of the main arguments advanced for wolf reintroduction is *shika taiji* or 'deer conquest', whereby wolves would serve to control the excessive numbers of deer. Many of the discussions of deer in Japan refer to the absence of the deer's *tenteki* or 'natural predator', the wolf.

A key tenet of the holistic science that is modern ecology is the idea that the natural world is a system consisting of interconnected parts and that this 'ecosystem' tends towards balance and stability. Predator–prey relations have often served as a favoured illustration of the principle of 'the balance of nature'. The basic idea is that predators moderate, regulate or control the numbers of prey animals. Such regulatory predation occurs where the rate of predation increases or decreases in response to the population density of prey animals. It is argued that the effect of this linkage between predator and prey populations is to generate related cycles of fluctuation that in the long-term make for equilibrium and stability. Predators at the top of the food chain are said to exercise a major controlling influence over the larger ecosystem, a special status indicated by a variety of terms, including 'top predator' and 'keystone predator'. The JWA argues that this regulatory mechanism operated in the past and that Japanese folklore gives expression to the principle of protective predation. The existence of the wolf helped to maintain a balance in the forest ecosystem.

A third reason advanced for wolf reintroduction, one that follows on from the ecological argument, is that wolves would relieve the problem of wildlife pestilence. The traditional role of the wolf as a protector of farmland from forest wildlife is invoked to justify the reintroduction proposal. The JWA argues that the ecological balance between carnivores and herbivores benefitted human society because it helped keep down the numbers of wild animals such as wild boar, deer and monkeys that caused damage to human farm crops. The opening paragraph on the JWA's main page on the website reads as follows: 'In Japan, a land of farming people, the wolf was a protective spirit that vanquished the beasts damaging the fields.' The JWA claims that restored colonies of wolves in remote areas of Japan would benefit farmers because the wolves would prey on wild crop-raiders such as the wild boar, the deer and monket. In this way, wolf reintroduction offers the prospect of a relatively uncontroversial (because 'natural') means of lethal pest control. Similarly, the JWA claims that foresters, in addition to farmers, would benefit from wolf reintroduction. The large numbers of forest herbivores are a cause of large-scale damage to timber plantations, as well as to remote farmland. The JWA argues that wolf reintroduction would be a solution to this problem because the new wolves would restore a balance to the forest by preying on deer and serow, the two main forestry pests. In this way, the restored 'forest ecosystem', with wolves once again at its apex, would be in the interests of Japan's timber-growers. As Maruyama puts it, the reintroduced wolves would be the *kyūseishu* or 'Saviour' of those people suffering from deer pestilence (*Chūnichi Shinbun* 7/3/2000).

THE MISREMEMBERED WOLF

The Bad Wolf
Wolves invite sinister associations. There are many Japanese word compounds containing the Chinese character for wolf that have highly negative meanings, including *rōsei* or 'wolf voice' (a frightening voice), *rōko* or 'wolfish look' (a menacing glance), *rōzeki* or 'wolf mess' (riot), *rōshitsu* or 'wolf sickness' (a terrible sickness), and *nakayama ōkami* or 'mountain wolf' (a savage). Dictionaries explain many of these Japanese wolf terms as metaphors of human greed: *rōko* ('wolves and tigers') is 'an expression applied to people who, because of their greed, harm others'; *rōshin* ('wolf heart') is 'a heart that is greedy like a wolf's'; and *rōtan* ('wolf greed') is applied to people who are 'insatiably covetous like a wolf' (Akatsuka et al. 1993: 682). An incorrigibly greedy man is an *ōkamimono* or 'wolf man', while the tyrannical mother-in-law who bullies and mistreats her son's young wife is an *ōkamibaba* or 'wolf granny' (Suzuki 1986: 244). This impressive Japanese lexicon of wolf terms has led one commentator to conclude that 'without a doubt . . . wolves are the most hated of animals' (Iwase Momoki, in Suzuki 1986: 244). In *Tōno monogatari*, Yanagita Kunio records the local view that 'there is nothing that is so terribly frightening as the growl of the wolf [*oinu*]' (Yanagita 1992: 34), while the scholar Ueno Masumi writes that the Japanese wolf has been 'deeply impressed on the memory of people as a dreadful carnivore' (Ueno 1987: 24). Another indication of the frightening image of the wolf was that, up until the end of the nineteenth century, parents on the Kii Peninsula would deal with the unruly behaviour of their children by warning them that 'if you do that, the wolf will carry you off!' (Nakamori 1940: 33–4). A great many other rural tales and legends likewise suggest that wolves were an object of fear.

The threat posed by wolves is not just a physical one. The wolf also poses a moral threat. These are the comments of Iwase Momoki (in the book *Hokuetsu seppu* [translated as *Snow Country Tales: Life in the Other Japan*]):

> All of this shows without a doubt that wolves are most hated of animals. Ah, but consider just for a moment: at least a wolf is a wolf and acts like a wolf. When men act like wolves they hide their wolfishness, and do not dare to show it openly . . . The wolfishness of men is far more terrible and hateful than that of real wolves. (Iwase, in Suzuki 1986: 244)

It is the wolf within the man that is the real fear. For when humans become wolf-like, they retain human form and are all the more dangerous as a result. The wolf offers a lesson in how *not* to be human – the wolf represents all that is bad in human beings, the (wolfish) corruption of humanity. When we worry about wolves from without, we are letting down our guard from within. The 'wise man' can spot people who have a 'wolf's heart' (*rōshin*). Iwase refers to Chinese literature about wolf shapeshifting. The wolf could stand for familiar negative moral qualities – and therefore serve edificatory purposes. The serves as a solemn warning of the potential for human degradation.

The werewolf motif, though absent in traditional Japanese folklore, is today pervasive in Japanese science fiction, horror and occult writings, as well as comics, video games and modern Japanese cinema. It has been suggested that interest in human-animal shapeshifting, especially involving the wolf, forms the basis of a 'Japanese subculture' (Ueba n.d.). The theme is also evident in the Japanese mass media, where the term wolf is sometimes used as a negative animal metaphor applied to danger-ous kinds of people such as criminals and delinquents. As one recent newspaper report on child abductions in Tochigi Prefecture put it, 'although the Japanese wolf became extinct in 1905 . . ., since the early spring [of this year] wolves in human skin driving cars have appeared in the prefecture', and the report ends by warning young children about the danger of these *nihon ashi no ōkami* or 'two-legged wolves' (*Shimotsuke Shinbun* 26/5/2000).

Red Riding Hood

The JWA argues that the legacy of the Meiji-era anti-wolf propaganda continues in present-day Japan. Despite the wolf's sacred associations in traditional Japanese culture, in modern Japan negative views of the wolf are widespread. 'Since the Meiji period a large part of the Japanese people has been thoroughly dyed in a Christian view of nature, in which nature, along with the wolf, is seen as subordinate to God and to Man, one which derives from the pastoralist view of the wolf as a harmful animal' (Maruyama 1999: 17). Maruyama Naoki refers to lingering popular views of the wolf as a mankiller and maneater as the *Akazukinchan shōkōgun* or 'Little Red Riding Hood syndrome' (*Kahoku Shinpō Yūkan* 13/3/2000). Most of the postwar generation of Japanese people have learnt the stories of Little Red Riding Hood and The Three Little Pigs at primary school (often the first year) by reading the picture books and even enacting the stories in a school drama.

The JWA associates wolf extinction with the post-Meiji westernization of Japan:

> It was a highly regrettable episode. Following the Meiji Restoration, Japanese society, in the name of modernization, introduced a great deal of Western culture. Included in this Western culture were 'anti-wolf sen-timents'. Without knowing much about the real ecology of the wolf, we Japanese were easily influenced by the Western anti-wolf campaign which was centred on folktales . . . . (Maruyama 1998: 1)

Japanese scholars have long debated the pros and cons of the Meiji Restoration in terms of social progress and cultural continuity. The impact of the Meiji Restoration has been one of the dominant intellectual issues of modern Japan, and one that has tended to be seen as a stark example of uncritical westernization that destroyed much traditional Japanese culture. There have been countless intellectual backlashes and reactions against Meiji Westernization in the name of reviving Japanese tradition. Here belatedly is yet another critical movement, only this time the argument is that in turning to the West, Meiji Japan inadvertently destroyed its own natural heritage. But the JWA criticism is directed not just to the exogenous Western influence, but also to the Japanese disposition at the time that allowed it to happen. If post-Meiji Japanese society uncritically absorbed Western wolf prejudices, this was because of its own state of ignorance about wolves. This is the background to the strong emphasis on knowledge in the JWA campaign. It is finally time for the Japanese people to take hold of their natural heritage – to correct the distorting effect of post-Meiji excess modernization. Here then we can see the wolf reintroduction movement as yet another manifestation of a recurring theme in the Japan of the late twentieth and early twenty-first century – the preoccupation with salvaging heritage. The difference is that this time the concern is with *natural* rather than *cultural* heritage – or, better, natural heritage that predicates cultural heritage. It can be seen as part of the trend of coming to terms with modernity, and reconciling the native and the foreign. Only when the legacy of Red Riding Hood (including werewolf lore, werewolf films, etc.) has been neutralized will the conditions be in place for the actual implementation of the wolf reintroduction proposal.

The theme also emerges in the exchanges among JWA members who reflect on how as children they absorbed negative images of the wolf that it has taken much time and effort to overcome. Contributors to the home page message board recall reading the Little Red Riding Hood tale as a child or even performing it in a puppet show at school, along with the difficulties they have had dispelling these negative images of the wolf from their minds (Kamata 2000; Matsuo 2000). This is the background to the strong emphasis on knowledge in the JWA campaign, with the task of public education heading its list of formal objectives. To this end, the JWA actively disseminates its message through public lectures, symposia and meetings; through the writings of its members for newspapers, magazines and the internet; and through its own media such as the *Forest Call* newsletter and the JWA website.

A COUNTER-MEMORY OF THE WOLF

The JWA is reviving the memory of wolf extinction, as well as the memory of the wolf itself. It argues that wolf extinction epitomises the loss of Japan's natural heritage in the course of national industrialization. The status of wolf extinction as a pivotal event in modern Japanese history has in fact come to be recognized in recent years – in the form of magazine articles, books and television documentaries devoted to the subject and in the issue of commemorative stamps (as in 1999 as one of the images of twentieth century Japan). The extinction of the 'Japanese wolf' is rhetorically central to the argument for wolf reintroduction: that it is a crime for which modern Japan must repent. In other words, the revival of the memory of the wolf's extinction provides a rhetorical lever for present-day action – for it sets up the conditions for repentence in the present-day population of Japan. This kind of *strategic remembrance* is of course familiar from the wider international environmentalist movement in which memories of species extinction or of environmental degradation serve to ground remedial environmental *action* – whether this takes the form of habitat protection or species restoration. Arguably, the JWA rhetoric is largely inspired by the American wolf reintroduction campaign in Yellowstone National Park in which the repentence or redemption motif was to the fore.

Wolf Lore
A favourable image of the wolf is evident in much Japanese folklore. Through folklore, the Japanese wolf is remembered as a 'good animal' which contributed positively to human well-being. The goodness of the wolf is in fact directly suggested by the written Chinese character for wolf. This character 狼 consists of two parts: the radical (for wild animal) 犭 and the character for good 良, together giving the meaning of 'good animal'. When I asked hunters and others on the Kii Peninsula about the wolf (its extinction, the prospects for its reintroduction, etc.), they would often respond by referring to or writing down 良 (on paper or just, with forefinger, on the palm of the hand) to show that in Japan the wolf was traditionally considered an *ii dōbutsu* or 'good animal'. Sometimes more specific qualities are read into the written wolf character, as in the following article from a municipal publication: 'as the character 狼 suggests, in reality the wolf is an extremely loving animal' (HYMKI 1987: 5). The folklorist Chiba Tokuji argues that up until the second half of the seventeenth century the wolf was considered an *ekijū* or 'benign animal' (Chiba 1995: 183). This is because the wolf catches deer and wild boar, just as the weasel catches mice. 'In particular, the wolf, by catching the wild boar, a harmful animal that destroys crops, becomes a benign animal for human beings. It is this on which the mountain dog [i.e. wolf] worship found in the different regions of Japan is based' (Nomoto 1990: 66).

Another theme that arises in Japanese wolf folklore is that of exchange and reciprocity. In Japanese folklore on the wolf, the wolf appears a *giri-gatai* or 'dutiful' animal that reciprocates any human kindness it receives

(Maruyama 1994: 139). One story from the Hongū village of Hiba tells of a wolf trapped in a pitfall that is set free by villagers and allowed to return to the forest. A few days later, villagers hear a wolf-howl from the vicinity of the pit, and discover a large deer in it – and realize that the wolf has made its return-gift (known variously as *ongaeshi* or *oreigaeshi*) (Hongū-chō 1969: 12–13). Similar examples of the wolf's sense of reciprocity, involving offerings of other animals or their parts (a wild boar, a pheasant, a bear's paw and so on), can be found elsewhere in the region and beyond. Some writers go on to suggest that the wolf is a symbol of the traditional Japanese relationship to nature that has been lost, like the wolf itself, in the course of national modernization. The folklorist Nomoto Kanichi concluded his survey of Japanese wolflore as follows:

> The relationship between Man and Wolf stands for the relationship between Man and Nature, for the Wolf can be viewed as the symbol of animal spirits, the symbol of Nature. Nature brings all manner of blessings. When, in return for those blessings and that protection, Man keeps his promises and obligations, the relationship will be one of harmony . . . It would be as well if the Japanese saw in the various tales of the Wolf, with their emphasis on exchange between Man and Beast, the way in which the relationship between themselves and Nature should be conducted. (Nomoto 1990: 68)

In the past, one widely recorded folk tale was that of the *okuriōkami* or 'escort wolf'. Sometimes when a person is walking alone along a forest road at night he or she is followed by a wolf all the way back home. On nearing the house the wolf disappears and the behaviour of the wolf is not overtly interpreted as threatening. However, the motif of predation is present to some extent in these tales. Some versions of the *okuriōkami* tale emphasize the danger of falling over while being followed by a wolf, something which may well invite the wolf to attack. This theme of danger is especially evident in the popular meaning of the term *okuriōkami* in contemporary Japan which refers to the seemingly well-intentioned young man who escorts his girlfriend back to her flat, but then on arrival pounces on her. Here man-eating predation on the part of a literal wolf in the forest becomes sexual predation on the part of a metaphorical 'wolf' in modern urbanized space, but in both cases the calculating predator waits to seize the opportunity when the victim (forest traveller or single woman) is most vulnerable. However, it is argued that in general the *okuriōkami* is a protector rather than a predator of human beings. The wolf follows the traveller through the forest until he arrives back home; once at home, the traveller should express appreciation to the escort wolf for its protection by offering it something in return, such as salt or water (perhaps the water with which he washed his feet on returning to the house, as this will tend to be salty) (WKMK

1987: 60). Indeed, this protective function of the wolf is evident in the scientific name of the Japanese wolf, *Canis lupus hodophylax* (conferred by C. J. Temminck), which is related to the *okuriōkami* legend (Hiraiwa 1992: 201). *Hodo* derives from the Greek for 'a way' or 'a path', and *phylax* from the Greek for 'a guard', together giving the meaning of 'guardian of the way'.

There are also wolf shrines in Japan. A wolf shrine is a Shinto shrine in which the wolf serves as the *otsukai* or messenger of the *kami* (a role that may be performed in other shrines by animals such the fox and the snake). Wolf shrines offered protection from a variety of dangers, including farm pests. There are estimated to have been more than twenty main wolf shrines on the main Japanese island of Honshu, including nationally famous shrines such as Mitsumine in Chichibu, attesting to the existence of an *ōkami shinkō* or 'wolf religion' among the Japanese people (Maruyama et al. 1996: 199; Hiraiwa 1992: 90). There were also many small, local wolf shrines, which tended to be related (through the *ofuda* charms enshrined within them) to the larger wolf shrines. One source of protection offered by the wolf shrines took the form of *ofuda* charms which farmers placed at the edge of the field to act as a *shishiyoke* or 'boar deterrent'. The *ofuda* of the most famous wolf shrine, Mitsumine Shrine in Saitama Prefecture, were used throughout Japan to establish the Mitsumine *kami* in local shrines as a ritual means of defending fields against the wild boar (Chiba 1995: 217–9). One such wolf shrine in Hongū (in the now abandoned village of Heichigawa) contains 'Mitsuminesama', the *ofuda* of the famous Mitsumine Shrine.

One of the tasks that the JWA sets itself is to diffuse a more positive image of the wolf among the Japanese public. The task of diffusing a more popular image of the wolf is discussed in the JWA email message board where suggestions are made for concerts, books (including new children's books), public lectures and other events. One JWA member points out that in recent years the image of the dolphin has been completely transformed so that it is now a *ninkimono* or 'favourite' in the public mind, at least among the young (Murayama 2000). In fact, wolves do feature widely in the print and electronic media of Japan: in *manga* comics, in computer games, on television, in the cinema, in magazine articles, and in literature. Wolf imagery appears on T-shirts, on posters, on calendars, in magazines and even on beer cans, while the sound of the howling wolf is available on compact discs in music stores. Indeed, this sudden ubiquity of wolf motifs, idioms and images in contemporary Japan leads some commentators to refer to an *ōkami būmu* or 'wolf boom' (*Sankei Shinbun* 27/5/1997). There is an important international dimension to this renewed Japanese interest in wolves. The wolf ranks alongside the tiger, the elephant and the whale as one of the foremost 'charismatic' animals of the modern world, as an instantly recognizable environmental symbol, and as an object of international conservationist concern.

But there is also a specifically American input into late twentieth century wolf iconography. The images of wolves that adorn the T-shirts and sweaters worn by Japanese youth, that are captured in calendars and posters in Japanese homes and offices, and that appear in the wildlife documentaries shown on Japanese television are typically those of North American wolves.

Mongolia as a Site of the Counter-memory
The JWA organizes trips to Inner Mongolia in which members of the association have the chance to observe wolves in the wild and acquaint themselves with the wolves of the wider region. The visit to Mongolia is an experience that can leave a strong impression on JWA members, not least because of its power to evoke the now extinct Japanese wolf. These are the comments of one such wolf-watcher, Takatori Kiyoshi, to his fellow wolf enthusiasts in an article posted on the JWA website:

> In Inner Mongolia I went out three times and I met the wolf three times. Each time it was for just an instant and I can say no more than that 'I saw it', as I was unable to calmly observe it or photograph it. But even now I can clearly remember it. Each of the three times there was only a single wolf. This wolf, which was small in stature with graceful, long legs, was far from the fierce image of a savage beast portrayed by Westerners. I had the impression that in the past the Japanese wolf must have had this kind of [unthreatening] appearance. (Takatori 2000)

The trip to Mongolia is not just a journey over to the continent, but also becomes, in effect, a journey back in time. This is possible because of the way the JWA, in response to nativist criticism of the reintroduction proposal (that focuses on the *foreign* character of the wolves to be brought in), emphasizes the similarity of the various wolf subspecies of East Asia and, in particular, asserts that there is a genetic continuity between Japanese and Chinese subspecies of the gray wolf – characterizing the Chinese wolves as 'close relatives of the Japanese wolves' (Takahashi and Maruyama n.d.: 6). The Inner Mongolian subspecies is said to be a cognate subspecies to the Japanese wolf.

REFLECTIONS ON THE JWA'S COUNTER-MEMORY

While the JWA condemns the popular memory of the wolf as Westernized and inauthentic, a similar criticism could be levelled at its own counter-memory. Of course, this is presented as the revival of traditional folk culture. The Japanese *mori* or forest would once more be protected by the presence of the wolf. But it actually draws on modern Western mechanistic ecology – both the idea of the balance of nature and, more specifically, the idea of predator regulation of prey populations.

The wolf reintroduction issue raises a number of different kinds of struggles over memory. The first memory battle is between opposed remote memories: *mukashi no ōkami* or 'the wolf of long ago' is remembered in contrasting ways, as we have seen: as a bad animal that threatened livestock and human safety and as a good animal that protected farms and people. As the wolf has been extinct for nearly a century (according to the official orthodoxy), both claims depend on testimonies and claims of people who are no longer around.

The second memory battle is between the recent memories associated with the JWRS and the remote memories of the JWA. Here the positive view of the wolf is a shared one. The problem that arises has to do with the time-depth of the memory – living memory versus remote memory. There are (claimed) living memories of the wolf in Japan. There have been many sightings of wolves in Japanese rural areas after the date at which they supposedly became extinct. Hiraiwa Yonekichi gives details of 26 separate claims made between 1908 and 1978 (Hiraiwa 1992: 250–283). These are either sightings or the finding of remains, and such figures do not include the countless claims to have heard wolf howls or to have found wolf tracks or wolf faeces. In his study of the folk history of Totsukawa Mura in southern Nara Prefecture, Tsuda Matsunae found many people who claimed to have encountered a wolf (Tsuda 1987). Wolf sightings continue up to recent times. A recent example of a claimed wolf sighting arose in November 2000 when a photograph of a wolf-like animal in the mountains of Kyūshū was obtained by the mass media, leading to a profusion of newspaper, magazine and television stories suggesting that a living Japanese wolf had been found. Neither this nor the many other claimed wolf-sightings in Japan have ever been formally confirmed or officially endorsed.

The JWA's memory of the wolf is a strictly non-biographical one. The above claims are not accepted by the JWA which generally subscribes to the Meiji wolf extinction orthodoxy. Indeed, these claimed living memories of the wolf are seen as a potential threat to the wolf reintroduction campaign: for they challenge the Meiji extinction orthodoxy and may even challenge the extinction view altogether – and suggest that wolves still exist in Japan! From this perspective, the task of wolf conservation in Japan would be to preserve existing indigenous wolf populations, rather than bring in exogenous wolves. The JWA remembers the Japanese wolf as an animal that disappeared at the beginning of the twentieth century, rather than as an animal that continued to exist duing the twentieth century. The JWA deals only with remote memories – pertaining to wolves that lived in times past beyond living memory.

CONCLUSION

On the face of it, the JWA campaign is an example of an instrumental remembering or counter-remembering: i.e. to achieve public support for the wolf reintroduction proposal. The memory of the wolf as an *ekijū* helps to legitimize the call for the restoration of the animal to the mountains. But would it not be possible for the JWA to simply justify wolf reintroduction in contemporaneous terms and without referring to the past? Could reintroduction not simply be justified in modern technocratic terms – as a measure supported by modern ecological science? America, with its wolf reintroduction programme, would remain a compelling precedent, after all. One reason why this would not be the case has to do with the obvious nativistic objections directed at the wolf reintroduction proposal, which after all entails bringing *foreign* wolves into Japan. By invoking the past, the JWA manages to circumvent these objections. It can claim that wolf reintroduction would not add something new to Japanese nature, but would instead fill a gap in nature, a gap created by modernization. To the extent it can fill this gap, wolf reintroduction would become continuous with tradition – traditional nature. Ironically, the part-to-whole discourse of modern ecology provides the basis for prospective wolf reintroduction to connect with the traditional past.

REFERENCES

Akatsuka, T. et al. 1993 *Kanwa jiten (Chinese Character-Japanese Dictionary)*. Tokyo: Ōbunsha.

Capps, K. 1994 'Wolf wars'. *Alaska* 60(6): 20–27.

Chiba, T. 1995 *Ōkami wa naze kieta ka (Why Did the Wolf Disappear?)*. Tokyo: Shinjinbutsu Ōraisha.

Chūnichi Shinbun 7/3/2000 'Shokugai no shika – ōkamitsukai taiji' (The deer pest: overcoming it with the wolf). Evening edition.

Fischer, H. 1995 *Wolf Wars: The Remarkable Inside Story of the Restoration of Wolves to Yellowstone*. Helena: Falcon.

HYMKI (Higashi Yoshino Mura Kyōiku Iinkai) (ed.). 1987 'Nihonōkami' (The Japanese wolf). Reproduced in Higashi Yoshino Mura (ed.) *Maboroshi no nihonōkami – nihonōkami ni kansuru shiryō (The Phantom Japanese Wolf: Materials on the Japanese Wolf)*. Higashi Yoshino: Kyōiku Iinkai, 5.

Hiraiwa, Y. 1992 *ōkami – sono seitai to rekishi (The Wolf – Its Ecology and History)*. Tokyo: Tsukiji Shokan.

Hongū-chō 1969 *Yamabiko (Echo)*. Hongū: Town Hall.

Howard, W. E. and J. J. Dutta 1995 'Animal damage control techniques'. In S. H. Berwick and V. B. Saharia (eds) *The Development of International Principles and Practices of Wildlife Research and Management: Asian and American Approaches*. Delhi: Oxford University Press, 421–433.

Kahoku Shinpō Yūkan 13/3/2000 'Shika shokugai taisaku ni ōkami yobō' (Let's call on the wolf as a countermeasure against deer damage).

Kamata, C. 2000 'Message 227'. Available at: http://www.egroups.co.jp/messages/wolf-japan/227 [Accessed on 1st June, 2001].

Khorozyan, I. 1998 'Leopard (*Panthera pardus ciscaucasica*) in Armenia: basic trends, dangers and hopes'. *International Journal of Sustainable Development and World Ecology* 5(1): 1–10.

Koganezawa, M. 1999 'Nikkō ni okeru shika no zōka to shinrin seitaikei no eikyō – soshite ōkami dōnyū no hitsuyōsei' (The increase of deer in Nikko and its effect on the forest ecosystem: the necessity of the wolf). *Forest Call* No. 6: 4–6.

Maruyama, A. 1994 'Ōkami' (The wolf). In Inada K. et al. (eds) *Nihon mukashibanashi jiten (Dictionary of Japanese Old Tales)*. Tokyo: Kōbundō, 139.

Maruyama, N. 1998 'Ōkami saidōnyū to wa nandeshō' ('What is wolf reintroduction?'). *Internet Forest Call*. Available at: http://www2s.biglobe.ne.jp/~wolfpage/topic.html [Accessed on 19th September, 2000].

Maruyama, N. 1999 'Ōkami no fukkatsu ni mukete' (Towards the restoration of the wolf). *Forest Call* No. 6: 15–23.

Maruyama, N. 2000 'Message 353'. Available at: http://www.egroups.co.jp/messages/wolf-japan/353 [Accessed on 1st June, 2001].

Maruyama, N. 2001 'Message 636'. Available at: http://www.egroups.co.jp/messages/wolf-japan/636 [Accessed on 1st June, 2001].

Maruyama, N, K. Kaji, and N. Kanzaki 1996 'Review of the extirpation of wolves in Japan'. *Journal of Wildlife Research* 1(2): 199–201.

Maruyama, N, Wada K and Kanzaki N. 1995 'Dai 38 kai shinpojiumu 'ōkami fuzai no ekorojii' ni tsuite no shusaisha sokatsu' (Review of the 38th symposium of the Mammalogical Society of Japan, 'Ecology Without Wolves'). *Honyūrui Kagaku* 35(1): 21–7.

Matsuo, T. 2000 'Message 165'. Available at: http://www.egroups.co.jp/messages/wolf-japan/165 [Accessed on 1st June, 2001].

Mishra, H. R., C. Wemmer, and J. L. D. Smith 1987 'Tigers in Nepal: management conflicts with human interests'. In R. L. Tilson and U. S. Seal (eds) *Tigers of the World: The Biology, Biopolitics, Management, and Conservation of an Endangered Species*. Park Ridge, New Jersey: Noyes Publications, 449–463.

Moore, Roland S. 1994 'Metaphors of encroachment: hunting for wolves on a central Greek mountain'. *Anthropological Quarterly* 67(2): 81–88.

Murayama, J. 2000 'Message 108'. Available at: http://www.egroups.co.jp/messages/wolf-japan/108 [Accessed on 1st June, 2001].

Nakamori, S. 1940 'Yoshino no ōkami no hanashi' (Tales of wolves in Yoshino). *Dōbutsu Bungaku* No.68: 26–36.

Nomoto, K. 1990 *Kumano sankai minzokukō (A Treatise on the Mountain and Coastal Folk Customs of Kumano)*. Kyoto: Jinbun Shoin.

Paystrup, P. 1993 *The Wolf at Yellowstone's Door: Extending and Applying the Cultural Approach to Risk Communication to an Endangered Species Recovery Plan Controversy*. Unpublished Ph.D. Thesis, Purdue University.

Primm, S. A. and T. W. Clark 1996 'Making sense of the policy process for carnivore conservation'. *Conservation Biology* 10(4): 1036–1045.

Rishi, V. 1995 'Human dimensions in wildlife management and development: two case studies in India'. In S. H. Berwick and V. B. Saharia (eds) *The Development of International Principles and Practices of Wildlife Research and Management: Asian and American Approaches*. Delhi: Oxford University Press, 415–420.

Sankei Shinbun 27/5/1997 'ōkami būmu ga kita' (The wolf boom is here).

Shimotsuke Shinbun 26/5/2000 'ōkami' (Wolves).

Steinhart, P. 1995 *The Company of Wolves*. New York: Vintage Books.

Sukumar, R. 1994 'Wildlife-human conflict in India: an ecological and social perspective'. In R. Guha (ed.) *Social Ecology*. Delhi: Oxford University Press, 303–317.

Suzuki, B. 1986 *Snow Country Tales: Life in the Other Japan*. (Translated by J. Hunter with R. Lester.) New York and Tokyo: Weatherhill.

Takahashi, N. and N. Maruyama n.d. *Is There Room Left for Reintroduced Wolves in Japan?* Paper (in author's possession) presented to the conference *Coexistence of Large Carnivores with Man*, Saitama.

Takatori, K. 2000 'ōkami to deatta toki' (When I met the wolf). Available at: http://www.egroups.co.jp/files/wolf-japan/takatori2.txt [Accessed 29th May, 2001].

Tsuda, M. 1987 'ōkami' (Wolf). In *Nara ken no dobutsu* (The animals of Nara Prefecture). Reproduced in Higashi Yoshino Mura (ed.) *Maboroshi no nihonōkami – nihonōkami ni kansuru shiryō (The Phantom of the Japanese Wolf: Materials on the Japanese Wolf)*. Higashi Yoshino: Kyōiku Iinkai, 107–8.

Ueba, T. n.d. 'Nihon sabukaruchā ni okeru jūnin' (Werecreatures in Japanese subculture). Available at: http://www.fang.or.jp/ueba/w_review.html [Accessed on 22nd September, 2000].

Ueno, M. 1987 'The last wolf of Japan'. [In English]. Reproduced in Higashi Yoshino Mura (ed.) *Maboroshi no nihonōkami –nihonōkami ni kansuru shiryō (The Phantom Japanese Wolf: Materials on the Japanese Wolf)*. Higashi Yoshino: Kyōiku Iinkai, 24.

WKMK (Wakayama-ken Minwa no Kai) (ed.) 1987 *Kishū-Ryūjin no minwa (Folktales of Kishū-Ryūjin)*. Gobō: Wakayama-ken Minwa no Kai.

Wilson, M. A. 1997 'The wolf in Yellowstone: science, symbol, or politics? Deconstructing the conflict between environmentalism and wise use'. *Society and Natural Resources* 10: 453–468.

Worster, D. 1977 *Nature's Economy: A History of Ecological Ideas*. Cambridge: Cambridge University Press.

Yanagita, K. 1992 [1910] *Tōno monogatari (Tales of Tōno)*. Tokyo: Shinchō Bunko.

ACKNOWLEDGEMENTS

I would like to thank Maruyama Naoki, Kanzaki Nobuo and Takahashi Masao of the Japan Wolf Association (*Nihon ōkami kyōkai*) for sharing with me their views and expertise on the subject of the wolf and for sending me various written materials on the issue of wolf reintroduction. I would also like to thank the organizers of the conference on *Monuments and Memory Making in Japan* in Singapore, 8–10 July, 2002.

11

Preserving the Memories of Terror: Kōbe Earthquake Survivors as 'Memory Volunteers'[1]

LENG LENG THANG

INTRODUCTION

At 5:46 a.m. on 17 January 1995, an earthquake struck the Hanshin-Awaji area of Japan with a magnitude of 7.2 on the Richter scale. It was an unprecedented catastrophe which caused 6,400 untimely deaths, and left 320,000 people homeless. The cost of physical damage was estimated at about 10,000 billion yen. Reconstruction and restoration work began soon after the earthquake. In July 1995, the 'Hyogo Phoenix Plan' – a ten-year Great Hanshin-Awaji Earthquake Reconstruction Plan was conceptualized not only to reconstruct the affected areas, but also to achieve the dream towards an idealized new society for the twenty-first century – a society dedicated to public welfare, open to the world, disaster-resistant, 'creatively citizen-oriented'; a society where industries flourished and communities well connected (Phoenix Hyogo 2001: 4).

Along with physical reconstruction, there are also private, civic and state efforts to remember the earthquake in various forms, such as through the erections of memorials, variously called 'monuments', *ireihi* (memorial stones) or *tsuitōhi* (mourning stones). These memorials were set up not only as a requiem, but also as *assets* in terms of the experiences and lessons the disaster convey to the future generations.

The disaster is also creatively remembered through various forms of expressions such as music, art, literature and drama. In this chapter, I attempt to study the preservation of disaster memory through a narrative group I called the 'memory volunteers'. I was introduced to the group during my study of senior volunteer groups established in the aftermath of the earthquake in late 2001. The group is unique among the volunteer groups formed by (and for) the earthquake survivors – which mainly revolve around welfare- or environment-oriented themes.[2] Here, I shall use the group as a case study to examine narrative as a form of memory preservation and discuss how social memory and personal memory intertwine with the past and present in shifting focus and changing context. As the volunteers – more precisely the narrators – are usually women, this chapter also addresses the issue of gender and social memory.

THE MEMORY VOLUNTEERS

The 'memory volunteers' was formed in September 1999, led by Mr Hasegawa,[3] a man in his early fifties who lost his house during the earthquake and had to spend four years in temporary housing before he succeeded in balloting for a unit at the public housing built for earthquake survivors. It is a small group comprising about ten members. As a survivor of the catastrophe, Mr. Hasegawa felt compelled to initiate a narrative group because 'It is important for people to hear the "raw" voice (*nama no koe o kiite*), the real experience, not just reports from the mass media.' Moreover, the group also perceived their action with a sense of urgency as social memories of the disaster are fast fading away in a rapidly reconstructed cityscape that leaves little physical signs to invoke reminiscence. When asked why the group was only formed four years after the earthquake, Mr. Hasegawa explained that it took time to recover from the trauma for one to feel he/she was ready to 'break the silence'.

One of the regular activities of the group is monthly meetings to share, interact and discuss the various issues relating to the group. In one of their meetings that I attended, they discussed issues as fundamental as 'What is the purpose of our group?'; they explored ways to improve their narrative with questions like 'What shall we speak about?' and 'How shall we speak more effectively?' Reflections at these meetings further refine and determine the objectives of narratives. The group also produces quarterly newsletters with reports of their past activities, announcements and appeal for sponsorship.

Since the group was formed, the volunteers have spoken to about 30 groups in the first two years. Most of these groups are made up of students who visited Kōbe as part of their graduation or year-end school excursions. Several of these events were covered by the media, which have played a significant role in popularizing the group's activities.

When the group receives a request to speak for a group of visitors, the volunteers would usually suggest that the visitors begin their study trip with a visit to the Phoenix Plaza situated at Sannomiya, the city centre of Kōbe. This is an Earthquake Reconstruction Promotion Center which among others, displays records of the earthquake and visuals of the damage. After which, the volunteers will lead the visitors (divided into small groups of 10 to 15 if it is a large group) to various areas where signs of the earthquake damage were still visible. Some of these have been preserved as memorial sites. The volunteers who are living or used to live in the area would give a narration on the extent of damage the area has suffered during the earthquake and how the landscape has changed with the restoration. They would also give a talk focusing on their own experiences at one of these sites. If there is time, the visitors could visit the reconstructed public apartments built for earthquake victims, or an orphanage housing children who had lost their parents during the disaster. The group has essentially developed a package of 'walking-down-the-memory-lane-of-the-disaster tour' consisting of sights and accompanying live narratives. Such a combination and live accounts through the victims *subjectify* what the visitors have read on news reports about the earthquake.

Over the three years as a narrative group, the memory volunteers have experienced a shift in their narrative focus.

Narrating the memory of terror
When the group began in 1999, its mission was simply to share with others their frightening memories of the few seconds of violent tremble, and their experiences in the aftermath of the quake, including their unsettling lives in emergency shelters and temporary housing. News reports of one of their earlier talks to Japanese elementary students from Gifu Prefecture reflected this focus:

> At first, at the Merican Park in Central District, Hasegawa described how the surrounding has been damaged by the earthquake. After showing the students a damaged building near the Nankin Street which has remained since the earthquake, Mr Hayashi (81 years old) took over to describe how his residence at the Higashi-Nada District was completely destroyed. He talked about the awful experience of becoming homeless in the cold winter with the lack of food. (*Yomiuri News*, 10 June 2000)

After the talk, students and visitors were usually asked to respond through writings. Reactions from the elementary school students reflected the objective of the talk:

> From the talk, I learnt how terrifying an earthquake is!

> I heard about the earthquake from volunteers who came to help in Kōbe. Today, I really got to understand how frightening it was!

Learning from the memory of terror
When the group first began their activities, the male members were usually the speakers. As new female members joined the group a few

months later, they started to take over as the main speakers, a change that was encouraged by the male members. Mr Hasegawa maintained that the female members are better speakers than the men; further claiming that since they usually speak to school groups, the female members – as mothers, could relate better to the children; and are able to bring themselves 'to the level of the children'. This change is accompanied by a shift in narrative.

Mr Hasegawa recalled that the shift of the narratives from mere narrations of the terror to using the experience as 'catalyst to learn about the importance of life' first came about as a female poet became affiliated with the group in mid-2000. Her poems on the earthquake basically dealt with the theme of the need to treasure life and how the victims struggled to rebuild their lives.

It was also the same period when Mrs Shimada (68 years old) learnt about the group from news report and called to participate as a member. Mrs Shimada lost her 29 year old son when her house collapsed during the earthquake. She was also seriously injured in the quake and was hospitalized for a few months. Since she joined the group, Mrs Shimada has become one of the most active speakers in the group. Her narration consistently takes the intergenerational approach focusing on transmitting to the young the values of life. In the following, I give a description of the group's activity at a middle school in Nara city to examine the extent to which the narrative interacts with the context.

A talk at a middle school
The group was invited to give a talk to 240 second year middle school students in Nara city in mid December 2001. I was allowed to tack along for my fieldwork with the four members 'on mission'. It tuned out to be quite a big group as the NHK film crew joined us for most part of the journey. The event (including the train ride to Nara) was filmed for a documentary special that was broadcasted on the seventh anniversary of the earthquake.

It was the first time for them to receive an invitation to speak outside Kōbe. Before this, their activities were mostly based 'on site' where they could speak alongside the social memories implicated from the memorials and traces of the disaster damages. To make up for the absence of the 'field trip', the students were shown a short television documentary on the earthquake before the talk began. After which they gathered in the sports hall. Mrs Shimada and Mrs Inoue were the speakers for the event while Mr Hasegawa was in charge of flashing visuals such as the photographs of Mrs Shimada's damaged house and the gravestone of Mrs Inoue's[4] demised daughter. Mr Yamaori[4] was the MC for the event. The whole event was filmed except for Mrs Inoue's talk; she was adamant about staying out of the limelight. This section focuses on Mrs Shimada's narration, which lasted about thirty minutes.

In the introduction, Mr Yamaori began commenting that it was cold in the sports hall (there was no central heater), but 'on 17 January when the earthquake occurred, it was a much colder day than today. On that day, the earthquake happened, I suppose everyone knows about this, it was really in cold places like this, in the sports hall of elementary and high schools, in the same coldness – or colder places, many people had taken temporary shelter there for one or even two months . . . . It was very cold and very difficult times . . . . It will be good if you can imagine (yourself to be in) such a hard situation when you listen to the talk.'

With the cold winter temperature setting the stage, Mrs Shimada – who was sitting behind a desk in front of the students – began her talk. She started by defining the objective of her talk, 'I really wish to ponder together with all of you on the importance of life through my talk about the earthquake.' Then she gave a brief comment about earthquakes saying that in the past, when she was a child, there was this saying of 'earthquake, thunder, fire, father' as four things to fear most. She only finally understood why 'earthquake' is placed as the first most fearful thing after the experience in 1995. She represents the people in Kōbe in their feelings towards earthquake.

> I am 60 years old. Until I turned 60, staying in Kōbe, I have sometimes felt the tremor at about three degree (three on the Richter scale). But for a scale of about three, things wouldn't drop from the shelves. It was just like when I started to feel that there was a tremor, it stopped. Because my life has been such (without fear of earthquake), I came to feel that there would be no earthquake in Kōbe.

With this explanation, she described how the earthquake which happened almost seven years ago was absolutely beyond her imagination.

> There was a little tremor at the beginning. Oh, earthquake, I thought to myself and thinking that I should wake up my son who was sleeping next door, I woke up and sat beside the *futon* (mattress).Then the tremor stopped. Oh, it stopped, just when I thought that, there was a feeling of a heavy blow, and the house collapsed on me. My first thought was I am dying, and I lost consciousness right after that. I was trapped under the house. But since I have fainted I didn't know what happened. When I re-gained consciousness, I thought, what happen, I could not move my body at all. It was pitched dark. Then from the house next door – not the neighboring room – I heard the old woman next door shouting ' help, help' in a very loud voice. What has happened to her, why was she shouting 'help, help'? I thought, not realizing that a huge earthquake has happened. Then I noticed that I was in total darkness without a slightest ray of light. What has happened? Did I meet with a car accident, was it what that has happened? That came right to my mind. And

since the old woman next door was shouting 'help, help', I thought I should also try shouting. I opened my month to shout 'help – ', but my whole body felt compressed, and it was so painful that I could not make any sound . . . .

Mrs Shimada described how she was trapped in the debris for hours until she faintly heard her daughter's voice from the outside calling her. She was frustrated, she could only hear them faintly, and they could not hear her at all. As the voices from the outside faded off; she thought the rescuers have given up and she was to be left to die. 'I began to think seriously how to die in an easier manner.' Finally, she was saved by her dog, whose barks had led her daughter and daughter-in-law to locate her. However, her son did not survive the tragedy; his body was only found the next day, and it was confirmed that he had died instantly during the quake when he was knocked on the head by falling objects. Mrs Shimada paused to weep a little when she recalled the moment her son's death was confirmed.

Then she turned the narration to her experience as a patient caught in a chaotic condition after the earthquake where medication and bed space were seriously lacking. There were delays in treatments and different medical opinions on her injury. She expressed with a sigh of relief that although doctors had suggested that her injured right leg be amputated, the main doctor who had also experienced the earthquake decided against it and helped her to recover through a long period of physiotherapy.

Next, her narration moved back to the day of the earthquake again, this time putting it in the context of learning. She emphasized that 'there's nothing we can do about natural disaster', but recalling why her son lost his life, she said:

> I was told by my daughter that beside her unconscious brother was the table, which still stood in the midst of the debris. If my son had noticed that it was an earthquake and hidden under the table, he would have been saved. So all of you, in any event, simply hide under the table . . . as long as you have your life, you can do anything.

In her talk, her narration frequently swung to and forth from the scene of the earthquake to her experiences during hospitalization, and to the death of her son. Sometimes, she brought in memories of her own childhood. In between these narratives, she intentionally sent out moral messages to the young. She explained to the students why she wanted to talk to them:

> We can't do anything with earthquakes and natural disasters, but just two years ago, I often read about news on youth violence such as youth

killing other youth, killing their grandparents, murdering their parents, bullying their friends, what is the world coming to? There was a time that it was happening so often. At that time, I thought to myself, 'It is so regretful that many people are dying, it is a regret that people are wasting away the only life that they are given, this should not be so.' With such thought, I joined the group, because I want to do it for those who have passed away, as a way of paying respect to the many people who have died.

Her messages to the students could be divided into the following emphasis:

1. Stop violence
Let's say among you there are two or three people who are bullying a friend. When you see this, you should have the courage to say, 'Hey, stop it, we should be good friends' even if you may get beaten up for it. It is inhuman not to stop your friends from bullying others . . . . When we get angry and wanted to turn violent, it could be detrimental if we do not immediately take two or three steps back. We will be like an animal if we just hit on instinct because of anger . . . .

2. Unconditional love of parents to their children
The unbearable sadness to a parent who lost her child – you will understand when you grow up and become adults. The girls, especially, from the time you give birth to a child and become a mother, you will at some point understand the unconditional love that your parents have showered on you all these years . . . . Mothers forget about the pains of childbirth when they look at their cute children – that's how much love parents feel for their children. Hence, don't tell your parents you want to leave them when you become a middle school student. It's because of your parents that you are what you are today . . . . I have many regrets even at this age. I wished I had listened more to what my mother had to say when she was alive. Therefore, when you are free, even when you are busy with your studies, listen to your parents and ask them for advice. Talk to your parents about things in the past, things happening now, anything . . . .

3. Connecting with the older generations and volunteering
Take advantage of the presence of your grandparents and learn various things from them. The knowledge will be useful to you as you grow up. . . . Nowadays grandparents are really lonely. Why is it so? Because few are still staying with their children. Most elderly are staying alone nowadays, therefore, when you walk on the street and meet an elderly in the neighborhood, greet them 'good day'. These elderly men and women will be happy to be greeted by young people; your greeting will be a source of happiness for them. This is a small way to volunteer – just by

greeting others. It may sound strange to say that this is volunteering . . .
but it is a form of volunteering as long as the kindness and desire to help
others begins from your heart. Volunteering does not only mean bene-
fiting others, you also benefit as you volunteer.

4. Be kind to others
You're in your second year now. I learnt from my son that in the second
year, you have *senpai* (senior) above you and *kōhai* (junior) below you.
You are sandwiched in between. If you think you want to bully your
junior just because your senior has bullied you, this is not good. You
should reflect upon your position and be nice to your junior. Don't you
want to become the senior that your juniors will always respect?

She ended her 30 minutes talk with the following:

You are given a life by your parents, it is precious, you should take good
care of yourself and do not become a burden to your parents. It will be
unfilial of you to hurt yourself or become disabled because you did not
take good care of yourself. I hope you treasure your life dearly.

Mrs Inoue's talk that followed continued on the same message of 'life
is precious'. Like Mrs Shimada, she gave a personal, emotional and
detailed recollection including the conversations she had with her 10-
year-old daughter when both were trapped in the debris of the fallen
house. Her daughter passed away one month after the earthquake while
she survived.

After the talks by Mrs Shimada and Mrs Inoue, a student representative came forward to give a short comment. At the end of the event, a
few students stayed back to ask questions and interacted with the
members. In written comments submitted by the students afterwards,
many said they were alarmed at the scale of the disaster; most had little,
if any recollections about the earthquake which happened when they
were about seven years old.

BETWEEN SUBJECTIFYING AND OBJECTIFYING MEMORIES

The shift from a narrative on memories about the earthquake to one that
focuses on lessons to be learnt from the disaster represents a shift from
the first instance of using the personal memory to *subjectify* the social
memory (of earthquake) to the second instance where the personal
memory is *objectified* in the context of the listeners. The shift also suggests a change in the narrators' perceptions of the self from a *victim* to a
survivor. Kōbe earthquake survivors commonly call themselves (and are
referred to as) *hisaisha* (victims/sufferers) rather than *seisonsha* (survivor).[5] Here, Jerome Bruner's (1994:41) idea of a victim Self and *victimicy*

may offer some explanation. The victim Self is controlled by an agency (i.e. the disaster) which directly or indirectly 'controls the circumstances in which we are compelled to live'. In contrast, 'survivors' has the connotation similar to the 'Self as agentive' where the victim Self reacted through resistance or other forms that are culturally-appropriate (Bruner, 1994). Hence, by moving away from the narrative of how terrible one has suffered as a victim to emphasize how we could learn from the terror, it entails a change in one's perception of the self.

On a pragmatic level, the shift is initiated by various developments on the local and national levels. The civic consciousness of the new group members such as Mrs Shimada plays a significant role in the shift of the group narrative. Mrs Shimada was willing to re-visit the painful memory because besides sharing the same concerns with the group in preserving the memories of the earthquake, she explained that as she ages, she began to feel the urge to contribute something to the society before she becomes too frail to do so. Her view relates to reminiscences in old age with the penchant for nostalgia. Moreover, the various incidents in Japan relating to youth violence have prompted her to give a narrative of lessons for the young, because 'If I don't talk about it now, I will surely regret in the future.' Such attitude resonates with the concept of *ikasu* – the Shinto concept of a continuation or new life with the loss of old ones. Here, the memory of a lost life is not only kept alive through narrative transmitted from the older to the younger generation, in the course of doing so, the experience/memory also *give others new life*. In this sense, telling becomes both an *ikigai* and a moral necessity for the narrator.

However, it is also arguable that by turning the story into a narrative with certain morals for behavior, the deeper problems relating to the earthquake are circumvented. Although the earthquake was a natural disaster, the tragedy has also been critically commented as a 'human error' reflecting the government's irresponsibility in earthquake prevention. This included criticisms of the government's ignorance to the faulty buildings in large parts of Kōbe,[6] and its failure to equip the city and its people with crisis prevention measures and consciousness.

The memory volunteers' choice of focus is a clear case of how remembering leads to (or is part of) a process of de-politicization. Today, the Kōbe earthquake is increasingly remembered as a lesson of hope: the disaster saw the springing out of unprecedented numbers of volunteers to disaster relief, which eventually led to the legislation of NPO (non-profit organizations) law in Japan in 1998. As a result of the heightened volunteer consciousness 1995 has even been recognized as the First Year of Volunteerism in Japan (although not entirely without contention). Hence, the memory volunteers' stress on learning from rather than about the earthquake fits well with the growing consensus of how the earthquake is to be remembered. For instance, the Hyogo Phoenix Plan promotes 'sharing and passing on experiences and lessons from the earthquake' as one way to create a 'disaster-resistant metropolis'. Since the end of 2001, the group has begun to strategize themselves more explicitly as a creative group using earthquake memories as 'texts' for moral education. This makes them directly relevant to the schools and increases the opportunities of speaking to the students under the new educational structure.[7] Their emphasis is reflected in a grant proposal titled 'education of the heart' (*kokoro no kyōiku*) submitted to a grant agency which funds volunteer groups. The development supports Paul Antz and Michael Lamberk's (1996:193) assertion that 'memories are most fully and vividly accessed and developed when they fit cultural templates and have a receptive audience'.

From a theoretical framework, the shift may be explained with Barry Schwartz's theory which states that 'collective historical memory has both cumulative and presentist aspects' (Coser, 1992:26). His proposal builds on Maurice Halbwachs' *presentist* approach which stresses that our conceptions of the past are affected by the mental images we employ to solve present problems, so that collective memory is essentially a reconstruction of the past in the light of the present' (Coser, 1992:34). In addition, I propose that the shifted narrative and its focus on intergenerational transmission suggest the need to link not only the past with the present, but also with the future. Following the discipline of '*kogengaku*' (study of things and life in the present) created by Kon Wajirō, the memory volunteers – in their detailed descriptions of their earthquake experiences and the extension of these experiences into 'lessons to learn', are packing the past with the present for the future (see Jan van Bremen's chapter in this volume for a discussion on Kon Wajirō). Here, intergenerational transmission is more than just the functionalist definition of 'inculcating norms', but also entails active and cumulative processes of learning[8] and intergenerational interaction for both the narrators and the listeners. Mr Yamaori (a psychologist and member of the group) observes the event to be an interactive one. While the students are deeply moved by the narrative, the narrator's socio-psychological world as a victim is also altered in the course of the narration. To students who attended the talks, their empathy towards one of the narrators has prompted some to start regular correspondence with her.

This links to the issue of gender in the study of social memory. G-117 has stated the preference for women as narrators in the group noting that women are considered better at communicating with children. Linking narration/storytelling with women replicates images of gender roles and situates women more aptly as intergenerational transmitter of social norms and values. This fits the image of grandmothers and mothers as storytellers to younger generation.[9] Such gendered perception parallels the thesis of gender differences in one's identification of the self: where women tend to talk of 'a network of relationships in which "I" was one pole of a relation'; men structured the "I" as a subject of action' (Tonkin, 1992:135).

CONCLUSION

As a form, narrative is an intangible artifact in the preservation of memories. Compared to concrete forms such as monuments, 'narrative' engages in more constant conversations (as well as tensions) among the narrator, the present context, the social and personal memories.

As a result of the publicity gained from the NHK program in January 2002, G-117 has seen a marked increase in requests for their talks not only in Kōbe area, but also beyond the Kansai region. However, at the same time, the group leader expressed concerns that some members are beginning to feel reluctant about over-exposing themselves in narrating their experiences. The tension between keeping their memories in the private realm versus releasing it to become part of the social memory has been an on-going struggle for members like Mrs Inoue (who refrained from the media), who on the one hand thinks that the volunteer activity represents a tribute to her demised daughter – a form of empowerment of experience, but on the other hand, still feels withdrawn with survivor's guilt. To the memory volunteers who must constantly evoke their memory of trauma, to belong to the group is in a way similar to membership in a 'healing circle', where each telling is a therapeutic process towards healing.

The attempt to study narrative as a form of memory preservation is a challenging one. It is all the more exciting when the event in question is such a recent one. The preservation of the earthquake memory is still very much an on-going process. Everyday, more forms of preserving the memories of the disaster are being conceived, performed, erected and collected. The 18,000 sq m Memorial Center situated in Eastern Kōbe has just completed in 2002; in 2003, Shijimi-chō in Miki city will open the Miki Earthquake Disaster Memorial Park covering over 300 hectares in area.[10] Together, these various manifestations of memories will continue to transform the present social memory of the earthquake in Japan that happened at 5:46 a.m. on 17 January 1995.

REFERENCES

Antz, Paul and Michael Lambek 1996. *Tense Past*. London: Routledge.

Babcock, Barbara A. 1993. 'At home, no women are storytellers: ceramic creativity and the politics of discourse in Cochiti Pueblo'. In *Creativity/Anthropology*. Smadar Lavie, Kirin Narayan and Renato Rosaldo, eds pp. 70–99. Ithaca: Cornell University Press.

Bruner, Jerome. 1994. 'The "remembered" self'. In *The Remembering Self: Construction and Accuracy in the Self-Narrative*. Ulric Neisser and Robyn Fivush (eds). Cambridge: Cambridge University Press.

Coser, Lewis (ed. And translated). 1992. Maurice Halbwach's *On Collective Memory*. Chicago: University of Chicago Press.

Fentress, James and Chris Wickham 1992. *Social Memory.* Oxford: Blackwell.

Iwasaki, Nobuhiko 2002. 'Hanshin dai shinsai wa tensai datta no ka, jinsai datta no ka'. In *Dai shinsai wo katari tsuzuku* (Volume #5). Kōbe daigaku shinsai kenkyukai, ed. pp. 236–267. Kōbe: Kōbe shinbun Sōgō shuppan sha centa.

Kenny, Michael 1999. *A Place for Memory: The Interface between Individual and Collective History. Comparative Studies in Society and History* 41(3): 420–37.

Phoenix Hyogo 2001. *Creative Reconstruction from the Great Hanshin-Awaji Earthquake.* Kōbe. 2001.

Ross, Bruce 1991. *Remembering the Personal Past: Descriptions of Autobiographical Memory.* New York: Oxford University Press.

Shinfuku, Naotaka 1999. 'To be a victim and a survivor of the great Hanshin-Awaji earthquake.' *Journal of Psychosomatic Research* 46 (6): 541–548.

Tonkin, Elizabeth 1992. *Narrating our Pasts: The social construction of oral history.* Cambridge: Cambridge University Press.

NOTES

[1] I am grateful to fellow participants of the 'International Conference on Monuments and Memory Making in Japan', National University of Singapore, 8–10 July 2002, in particular, Vered Vinitzky-Serroussi, for their valuable comments and help in revising the paper. Thanks also to Lim Boon Hock for his help with transcription, and friends of G-117 who has been most helpful in the research. I am also thankful to Toshiba International Foundation for funding the research in FY 2001–2002.

[2] In end 2001, G-117 is said to be the only group of such nature in Kōbe although I noted another group doing similar activities of recalling about the earthquake to visitors to Kōbe. The group is formed mainly of retired principals and many focused their recollections on how their schools have turned into temporary rescue centers right after the earthquake. The G-117 members criticized this group as consisting mainly of people whose own dwellings have not been affected by the earthquake, so they should not perceive themselves as 'earthquake victims' in the strict sense. As one G-117 member commented, 'they could not understand the experience of those who have lost their homes and family members to the disaster'.

[3] Pseudonyms are used for some informants at their requests.

[4] Mr Yamaori is the co-leader of the group. He is the only member who is not an earthquake victim. As a psychologist and currently an associate professor with Nara University, he joined the group partly as participant-observer to study the impact of earthquake on the survivors.

[5] This is related to the dominant modes of remembering in postwar Japan as 'national victimology'.

[6] In the earthquake, 5,520 people had lost their lives because of collapsed homes and buildings. Of the buildings that have collapsed, 95% were built before the 1981 new law of ensuring earthquake-safe buildings (Iwasaki, 2002:242).

7   One of the new educational initiatives is the weekly 'integrated learning' time implemented as part of the 'Rainbow Plan' in the educational restructure plan in 2001. Along with other measures such as five-day school week (from April 2002) and the expansion of the community's role in school education, the state hopes that a wider education beyond textbooks and classroom teachings could elevate crisis such as youth crimes, school violence, bullying, school refusal, the decline of moral standards among children long faced by the educational system.

8   Tonkin (1992) has criticized Halbwauch for missing out 'socialization' as a structuring and creative process in his analysis of memory (p. 105).

9   Although we should note the exception of the famous storytellers dolls created by Helen Cordero, a Cochiti Pueblo potter, who is imaged after her grandfather. After she became famous in the 1960s and 1970s, there were many imitations of her storyteller dolls, many of these imitations are female figures, which shows the stereotype of relating women as storytellers in many cultures (Babcock, 1993).

10 The Memorial Center, besides artifact exhibition, also serves as a center to train disaster management experts and carry out related research. The Memorial Park will be a station for disaster management; it will also house the world's largest earthquake simulation facility.

12

The Violent and the Benign: How Kōbe Remembers its Rivers[1]

TSU YUN HUI

INTRODUCTION

For over two decades, as spring gives way to summer each year, rivers in Kōbe undergo a symbolic transformation. In June, the 'earth-disaster prevention month' (*dosha saigai bōshi gekkan*), authorities launch a campaign to educate citizens about the danger of floods and landslides caused by heavy rain and overflowing rivers. Come July voluntary groups encourage residents to come out to the riverfront. With fanfare and ceremony, suitable rivers are declared open for people 'to befriend the water' (*mizu ni shitashimu*). Almost literally, at the turning over of a calendar page, capricious rapids become benign and pleasurable neighborhood streams. While this change may seem artificial and abrupt, both sets of meaning are grounded in memories that are carefully fashioned and skillfully presented. The purpose of this chapter is to analyze (1) why Kōbe maintains two opposite understandings of rivers, (2) how it constructs them with the help of crafted memories, and (3) how it deals with the contradiction between riverine violence and benignity in the context of the rhetoric of 'community making' (*machi-zukuri*).

By conventional standards, Kōbe is not an obvious choice for studying rivers. It is not the only city to hold two apparently incompatible views on rivers. Nor can it lay claim to any watercourse of distinction. None of its rivers are big and long winding, historically famous, exceptionally beautiful, or particularly controversial. The rivers – indeed, ravines in many cases – are not navigable, and a few regularly dry up in winter. That the city should spend not only lavishly on beautifying them but also promote a 'river culture' (*kawa no bunka*) – sometimes also called 'water culture' (*mizu no bunka*)[2] – suggests that social and cultural forces with significance going beyond technical river management are at work here.

Until the 1970s, Kōbe's justification for making huge investments in riparian works was simply utilitarian: reclamation and flood prevention. The urbanized part of this city of 1.5 millions, the sixth largest in the country, occupies a sliver of land no more than 30 km long and 2–5 km wide, including substantial areas reclaimed from rivers and the sea (Hyōgo-ken n.d.; Kōbe-shi 1991; Rokkō sabō, n.d.).[3] Squeezed between the Rokkō Range in the north and the Ōsaka Bay in the south, the seven seaboard wards (*ku*) are packed with residential and commercial buildings, railroads, highways, tunnels, a monorail, an international container port, and factories of all sizes. Moreover, extending as it does along a string of river deltas, this crowded urban corridor is sliced up by as many as 36 rivers.[4] Geological, topographical, and climatic factors contribute to the hazard of these rivers. Craggy and full of internal cracks, the Rokkō Range is highly susceptible to erosion by water. And water there is aplenty: precipitation in the hills approaches 2,000 mm per year. Heavy rains accompanying a slow-moving front or typhoon would cause the rivers to swell up quickly. These torrents could become highly destructive debris flows (*dosekiryū*) after causing extensive erosion upstream. Feared as 'cannon currents' (*teppō-mizu*), they could crash through dikes to inflict huge damage to settled areas downstream. In July 1938, flash floods of this kind paralyzed the city, damaging some 15,000 buildings and claiming over 600 lives. This Hanshin Deluge (*Hanshin daisuigai*) left a deep impression on the city's collective memory, and has since been invoked regularly to illustrate the hazards of nature.

In view of the economic and strategic importance of the city and the history of repeated flooding, for a long time it was taken for granted that ever more dams were needed to capture the endless flow of silt, and that ever higher dikes were necessary to safeguard life and property. However, just when it appeared in the early 1980s that the last trickle had been hemmed in by massive structures, the city began to undo its handiwork. Here and there concrete dikes were remodeled into landscaped greenbelts, gentle slopes replaced vertical retaining walls, protective rails made way for stairs and ramps leading to the riverbed, stepping-stones are placed in mid-stream, and billboards giving information on river ecology overshadow warnings about drowning hazard. Meanwhile, from government to businesses to voluntary groups comes a steady flow of images and information extolling the virtue of 'hydrophilia' (*shinsuisei*). On their part, citizens respond positively to this overture. A number of 'river protection associations' (*kawa o mamorō kai*) were formed over the years, students and retirees come to the riverfront to observe nature, joggers and strollers make use of the remodeled banks, and children play in the water.

For a crowded city like Kōbe, any open space is welcome. Nevertheless, the landscaped rivers are no mere parks: they are privileged sites where urban residents are to recover through hydrophilic activities not only a proper human–nature relationship but also the heart-warming 'home-town' (*furusato*). With the memory of wholesome but endangered nature *and* community inscribed on the banks, floodplains, and river-beds, these rivers are to provide an arena where a vanishing past could be revisited and, hopefully, revived. This chapter advances the interpre-tation that Kōbe's enchantment with landscaped rivers is, at bottom, an environmentalist expression of Japan's continual and multidimen-sional critique of modernity in terms of nostalgia for an idealized, nati-vist nature and culture.[5] Moreover, like past attempts to 'transcend modernity', this particular effort too is fraught with contradictions. On one hand, it questions the current mode of urban living while making demonstrable improvements. On the other hand, the recreation of human-friendly rivers aggravates the burden modern human beings impose on nature.

FLOOD COUNTRY, RIVER CULTURE

Kōbe's ambivalent relationship with rivers reflects the national experi-ence. The country, like the city, is beset by the problem of unruly rivers. It gets around 1,700 mm of precipitation per year, more than double the world average and mostly in spring and summer.[6] Craggy mountains running the length of the main islands frequently come right up to the edge of the sea, creating numerous short and high-gradient rivers (Iketani 1994:17–18). In many places, the topsoil is soft and porous, being volcanic deposit, whereas the bedrock is full of cracks created by frequent tremors underground. Consequently, runoff carries away large volumes of sand and pebbles while swelling torrents remove boulders and tree stumps. Downstream, deposition raises the riverbed and desta-bilizes the course of the flow. Between 1985 and 1994, floods affected 80% of cities and villages (Seki 1994: 12), although the problem was most acute in the two decades after the Second World War. From 1946 to 1969, floods claimed on average 1,340 lives per year (Takahashi 1971:3). The situation began to improve in the 1960s thanks to substantial invest-ments in river conservation. Between 1970 and 1993, natural disasters of *all* kinds claimed over 500 victims in only three years (Iketani 1999:64). Nonetheless, rivers are unpredictable and occasionally deadly even now.[7] The government estimates that no more than 47% of the country's rivers have been properly fortified against floods (Seki 1994:83).

Technically, floods are natural phenomena: they become 'disastrous' only when humans get in their way. It is the fate, however, of the Japanese to live close to, nay, on the very sites of, these phenomena. Only 10% of the country is flat, and most of this consists of delta plains that are inherently susceptible to flooding. Yet, 60 million people – half of the country's population – and three-fourths of the country's wealth are concentrated on alluvial plains (Seki 1994:72). Moreover, many rivers in the big cities, including Tokyo and Ōsaka, have risen well above the surrounding land due to silting (Seki 1994:75). This creates a particularly dangerous situation since, should a dike be breached, swathes of densely populated areas would be inundated in no time. Meanwhile, deforestation and mining in the hills have destabilized slopes and facilitated erosion whereas rampant development on floodplains has all but eliminated any buffer zone that had existed between rivers and humans (Iketani 1994:38).

The quarter century after the Second World War has been called a period of 'persecution' for rivers (Seki 1994:124–128). As the country rebuilt, the breakneck speed of economic growth taxed the environment beyond sustainable limits. Together with the economic miracle, Japan experienced such serious public health problems as heavy metal poisoning and photochemical smog (Kamioka 1987). Rivers were among the first casualties of this onslaught on the environment. Water was pumped out to satisfy the unquenchable thirst of factories and homes, and what remained became convenient dumping ground for industrial and domestic waste (Mitsuoka 1985:5–7, 25–28, Sakai 1973:27–29, Tanimura 1977:1–6, Yasuoka 1973).[8] Development pressure caused many urban waterways to be declared 'useless' and filled in. The rest were either straightened or covered up to yield yet more building space. Shoals and boulders in mid-stream were dredged and embankments were stripped of trees and bushes (Seki 1984:128, Kerr 2001:13–50). The result was kilometers after kilometers of unsightly concrete chutes whose sole purpose was to dump water into the sea with minimal contact with humans. It is not surprising that the authorities should have marked them off-limit to citizens. There was the risk of falling over steep dikes, and any contact with the polluted water would be extremely unpleasant if not detrimental to health.

Degradation of riverine environment came to a head in the early 1970s. While the central government belatedly drew up regulations, citizens' groups and local authorities took matters into their own hands. Slowly but surely, the situation was turned around. An early example is the Edogawa Protection Association (*Edogawa o mamoru kai*). Formed in 1964 by residents from six municipalities and wards in Tokyo and Chiba prefecture, it aimed to urge the authorities to enhance wastewater treatment capability, to persuade factories to reduce the discharge of untreated fluids, and to educate residents to refrain from polluting the river (Tanimura 1977:28–30). Declaring Edogawa the 'spiritual ancestral home' (*kokoro no furusato*) and a place of 'spiritual relaxation' (*kokoro no ikoi*) for the inhabitants on its banks, it resolved to conserve 'the nature of the river' (*kawa no shizen*). Nonetheless, it was interested mainly in improving water quality, paying little attention to other aspects of the river ecology.

Japan's first 'hydrophilic park' (*shinsui kōen*) appeared in 1973 just a stone's throw away from Edogawa. With half a million residents, the old and crowded Edogawa wards rivers were moribund if not downright toxic by the early 1970s (Mitsuoka 1985:48–49). Striving to 'recover a human lifestyle' (*ningen seikatsu no kaifuku*), the ward office decided to revive Furukawa, which was no longer needed for flood control. Clean water was piped in, allowed to flow for 1.2 km, and pumped out and disposed of (Mitsuoka 1985:54–56). With a concrete bed and landscaped banks, and measuring 2–3 m wide and 20 cm deep, the regenerated 'river' caused a sensation. It won the Japan Construction Engineers' Prize (*Zenkenshō*) in 1974 and was introduced to the world in the 1982 United Nations Conference on Human Environment in Nairobi. In retrospect, it is clear that this river is completely artificial and crudely designed, little resembling a natural river (Mitsuoka 1985:55). Nonetheless, the project indicates that, in the early 1970s, some local governments were already thinking beyond water quality. They were ready to experiment with reengineering and managing rivers as recreational sites where urban inhabitants could restore their humanity.

It was from the relatively new residential areas in western Tokyo that emerged a movement whose vision of river conservation anticipated the trend in the 1990s and beyond. In 1970, the Association for the Protection of the Nature of Tamagawa (*Tamagawa no shizen o mamoru kai*) joined force with a group of housewives from Komae city to protest government plans to build on the banks of Tamagawa.[9] The Ministry of Construction, whose River Bureau (*Kasenkyoku*) oversaw such projects nationwide, was heeding a 1965 resolution by the Lower House's Special Committee for the Promotion of Sports (*shūgiin taiiku shinkō tokubetsu iinkai*), which called for converting 'unused' banks and floodplains into sport facilities and parks (Tanimura 1977:20). The activists countered with 'A Plan for the Tamagawa Nature Park' (*Tamagawa shizen kōen keikaku*), which gave first priority to preserving the ecosystem. It envisioned the creation of zones for bird and insect watching and nature study. In addition, there was also to be ample space for such casual and low-impact activities as 'lying around' (*nekorobi*), 'water play' (*mizu asobi*), and 'mud play' (*doronko*) (Tanimura 1977:23).

For more than a decade, the government dismissed the views of this and other environmentalist groups as amateurish and idealistic (Tanimura 1977:23–27). In a meeting in 1976, the director of the Keihin Work Office (*Keihin kōji jimusho*), which is directly in charge of Tamagawa, basically told concerned citizens that river management was none of their business (Tanimura 1977:26). Pro-development government advisors like Tanimura Kiyoshi proclaimed that resource-poor Japan cannot afford 'real' nature.[10] As it turned out, the government was to gradually shift its position not just on Tamagawa but the whole issue of river conservation. Citizen's movements, experimental projects by local authorities, and the search by individual government specialists for new models of river management converged in the early 1990s. Change in national policy first came in the form of a 1990 directive on 'The Principles of Multi-natural River Engineering' (*Tashizengata kansen-zukuri no jisshi yōryō*) issued by the River Bureau's flood control department (Seki 1994:20).[11] According to its most vocal bureaucrat-advocate Seki Masakzu, the new approach seeks to restore nature to what has become little more than concrete gutters (Seki 1994:202–225). Natural features such as curves, marshes, pools, and shoals are to be reintroduced. Artificial building materials, if unavoidable, are to be disguised under vegetation or some natural-looking finishing. This influential but low-level administrative guideline received full legal backing in 1997 when the Revised River Law (*Shīn Kasenhō*) came into effect. The law enshrines, for the first time in the history of modern Japan, 'the preservation and improvement of river environment' as one of the three principal aims of river management, along with flood control and water resource exploitation.[12]

The new mood in the country is best captured by Sasayama Kyūzō's 1987 fiction *Shimantogawa: Atsuyoshi no natsu* (*The Shimanto River: Atsuyoshi's summer*). It is a simple story about the summer vacation of a 10–year-old boy in rural Shikoku. Life in this 'republic of affection' (*jōai no kyōwakoku*, Kiriyama 1991:200) revolves around Shimantogawa, which displays the hallmarks of the idealized river. First, it is abundant and benign. It has not only crabs and crayfish for children to play with but also carp and eels that can supplement dinner. Second, the people in the community are simple and innocent like the river. Tellingly, the author invites the reader to see the river and the everyday drama that unfolds along it through the eye of a child. With its natural setting, simple plot, plain language, and unabashed nostalgia, the fiction struck a chord in the national psyche, awakening the child in the urban adult, and triggered a 'Shimantogawa boom'. The river comes to symbolize Japan before the ecological Fall while holding out hope for human–nature reconciliation. Every year thousands of tourists flock to see it. Others are inspired to replicate it in their own neighborhood. Seki Masakazu depicts in his visionary book *Daichi no kawa* (*Rivers of the great earth*), which went through 13 editions in five years, a future where children all over Japan can swim in a river as clean and beautiful as Shimatogawa (1994:171–175).

VIOLENT RIVERS

In Kōbe, various social agents work to keep the memory of runaway rivers alive. Although there have been many floods in the past (Wakabayashi 1987:117–122), it is the Hanshin Deluge that is widely taken to epitomize the city's tumultuous relationship with rivers. Government agencies, schools, organizations, and private citizens invoke it to emphasize how precarious modern city life is and, consequently, the need to prepare for any eventuality. Individuals and collectives also use it as a milestone in their historical self-narratives, often to highlight their ability to overcome adversity.[13]

The most visible and extended display of the memory of furious rivers is the annual Exhibition on the Disasters of the Rokkō Range (*Rokkōsan no saigai ten*). Produced by the Rokkō Sabō Work Office (*Rokkō sabō kōji Jimusho*, under the Ministry of Land, Infrastructure, and Transport) and co-sponsored by the municipal government, it coincides with the Earth-Disaster Prevention Month.[14] The 2001 exhibition, for example, has three parts. The first part employs maps, diagrams, aerial photos, and landscape models to explain the causes and history of floods and land-slides in the city.[15] This background information frames a particularly painful memory, namely, the Hanshin Deluge. The second part comprises a series of black-and-white photos documenting the extent of this calamity: landslides, collapsed homes, overturned streetcars, half-buried bridges, mounds of rubble, etc. The images are especially shocking for any one who knows the city as they show familiar spots and landmarks in a state of such devastation that they would not have been recognizable but for the captions. The third part focuses on the flood of 1967. Another selection of photos juxtaposes scenes of moderate damage with earth-filled but intact dams and frothy but contained rivers. The point is that this flood caused much less destruction even though there was more rain than in 1938. Preventive engineering undertaken in the interval years, it is explained, has reduced the threat of rivers. In addition to information on the latest disaster prevention technology and personal safety advice, this part gives a brief history of the city's fight against soil erosion. Toward this end, it features a life demonstration of the effects of debris flows. Using a landscape model, water, and sand, an employee from the Sabō Office shows (mainly) children what has happened in their grand-parents' time (1938) and what has been done since to prevent its recurrence. Finally, underlying the whole exhibition is the warning that the catastrophic Hanshin Awaji Earthquake in 1995 has increased the danger of rivers by shaking up everything from slopes and embankments to retaining walls and the foundations of buildings.

The exhibition thus takes the viewer through three stages. In the first stage, it imparts the viewer with basic knowledge about the city's natural environment. The narrative adopts an impersonal tone and the objective authority of science. As a flashback to the recent past, the second part has a completely different feel. The monochromic snapshots meticulously document a city in ruin, and to good effect. The spectacle of utter devastation is disturbing if not shocking. The third part counterpoises the 1967 flood with that of 1938 to drive home the message that foresight and engineering ingenuity have succeeded in containing nature. The same strategy of contrasting a deficient past with an improved present underlies the presentation on erosion control and the life demonstration of debris flow.

In addition to the annual exhibition, the Sabō Office reaches out to the public by its homepage, newsletter, and public relations brochures. The goal is to make sure that an awareness of the deadly potential of rivers forms an integral part of the public's perception of nature. In a series of essays that appeared in *Rokko I-Net News* in 1996–1997 under the general title *Rokkōsan e no omoi* (*Reminiscences of the Rokkō Range*), long-time residents reminisce about life in proximity to the hills, stressing the bond between them and the local landscape.[16] Three of the essays recall not the benign but the ferocious aspect of the hills or, to be precise, the rivers that issue from them. In one of the essays, an 83–year old man describes his narrow escape from a roaring 'black wall' of water and mud. Another piece by a 77–year old woman gives a chilling account of frothy swirls engulfing houses in her neighborhood. The third piece is by a 64–year old man who had no experience of the 1938 flood but lived through the one in 1967. In addition to his own scary experience, he also writes about how the railway company he worked for weathered these disasters. A similar appeal to personal memory is employed by a four-part series titled *Rokkōsan o kataru* (*Talking about the Rokkō Range*) in the same e-publication (1997). Although a report on the views of four experts of 'disaster prevention' (*bōsai*) articulated during a colloquium organized by the Sabo Office, the series dedicates the first part to one expert's recollection of the Hanshin Deluge. It is only after presenting his personal account that the series reports on the discussants' opinions on slope stabilization, the function of greenbelts, and the pleasure of walking in the woods.

In its effort to heighten public awareness about disaster prevention, the municipal government also invokes the Hanshin Deluge. The PR materials of its construction department, river section, *sabō* section, park section, fire department, etc. make frequent reference to it to impress upon residents the need to remain vigilant at all time. As much of the information duplicates what the Sabō Office disseminates, one example should suffice here. The June 1996 installment of *Kōbe Repōto*, a 30–minute TV program produced by the public relations office and aired on local channels, was given to 'disaster prevention measures'.[17] Its main topic was natural disasters in the rainy season. After observing that the already fragile Rokkō Range was further shaken up by the 1995 earthquake, the program flashes back to the Hanshin Deluge. Characterizing it as an event that will be 'told and retold' (*kataritsugareru*), the narration affirms that the disaster not only marks the beginning of systematic erosion control in the city but also serves as the model disaster with reference to which all later contingency plans are designed. The narration cites the 1967 flood as proof that erosion control measures since have been successful. Toward the end of the program, the female narrator observes that although Kōbe is blessed with beautiful nature, the latter is also a source of grave danger, which is why residents must learn from past tragedies.

Given the emphasis on learning from history, schools play an important role in articulating and perpetuating the memory of floods. This is particularly so after the Hanshin Awaji Earthquake, when 'disaster prevention education' (*bōsai kyōiku*) comes to be stressed. The subject is sometimes taught independently, sometimes as a component of social studies or science. In 2002, Hyogo Prefectural Maiko High School became the first in the country to establish 'environment and disaster prevention studies' (*kankyō bōsai ka*) as a major. Its lectures and projects tend to pay most attention to the recent earthquake, although the Hanshin Deluge is never absent from the background. In his memorial speech at the school on 'Learning from the Hanshin Awaji Earthquake' (*Hanshin Awaji daishinsai ni manabu*), former prefectural governor Kaihara Toshitami spoke at length about the earthquake to illustrate his idea that history is about humans protecting themselves against natural calamities.[18] He cited the Hanshin Deluge to show that people are compelled to come ever closer to unruly natural forces. He noted that whereas in 1938 housing development in the Rokkō Range stopped at an altitude of 100 m, it has now reached the 300 m mark. The great flood notwithstanding, people have advanced deeper into dangerous terrains. The prudent thing to do, so advised the former governor, is to understand natural threats and keep a constant guard against them. Like the former governor, two speakers for the school's public lecture series in that year also made references to the 1938 flood as a memorable event in the city's uneasy relationship with nature.

The Municipal Minatogawa Middle School differs from Maiko High School in an important way when it comes to disaster prevention education: the former was inundated in as recent as 1989 and 1999. Consequently, its disaster prevention curriculum gives almost equal weight to earthquake and flood.[19] The flood component consists of reviews of the Hanshin Deluge, the history of flooding of the Old Minatogawa, and the recent floods caused by the New Minatogawa. The same parity between earthquake and flood is maintained in an elective science project titled 'My Neighborhood: Mintogawa'.[20] The first four parts of it comprise social, historical, religious, and ecological surveys of the Minatogawa ward. The last two are given to floods and the 1995 earthquake. The segment on floods begins with recent pictures of a schoolyard turned into a swamp, flashes back to a black-and-white picture of the Hanshin Deluge, and moves forward again to a series of color pictures showing Minatogawa rising and eventually spilled over. In the end is the observation that the neighborhood has suffered recurrent flooding. There is, however, no attempt to pin down the cause of it.

Non-governmental organizations and private citizens tend to treat the

Hanshin Deluge as a milestone in their self-constructed histories. Coop, which operates an extensive grocery distribution chain in Kōbe and elsewhere, presents on its homepage a synopsis of its history in 26 essays, one of which is given to the flood (four on the 1995 earthquake).[21] This essay first gives a general outline of the event: the amount of rainfall, the nature of the disaster, and the types of damage resulted. It goes on to relate the experience of Coop's branches, recording on one hand the damage they sustained, on the other hand, their employees' valiant salvage and relief activity. It stresses how quickly they resumed operation, arranging deliveries of essential goods to members and non-members. The essay concludes with the claim that Coop initiated 'psychological rehabilitation' (*kokoro no kea* or literally 'care for the heart') for flood victims, which is a reference to the Hanshin Awaji Earthquake, in the aftermath of which much attention was focused on the psychological effects of the disaster. Similarly, businesses in Motomachi, Kōbe's oldest and, until 20 years ago, most popular shopping district, have identified the Hanshin Deluge as a critical event in their history. The history given on the homepages of the Motomachi Shopping Arcade and Motomachi Avenue 1 both refer to the 1938 flood. In the first case, under the general title of 'Past and Present' is a section on 'Earthquake and Motomachi,' wherein the flood is identified as one of three major disasters (together with the air raids at the end of the Second World War and the 1995 earthquake) that have struck the area.[22] Under another heading called 'Snippets of Motomachi' are a brief description of the Hanshin Deluge and a picture of people picking their way through a street strewn with rubble. In the second case, a 'mini-history of Motomachi' refers to the Hanshin Deluge as one of three 'natural [*sic*] disasters' (including the air raids!) from which the neighborhood has emerged stronger.[23] Even small businesses are no exception. The restaurant Jūjiya, which is famous for its beef, affirms its commitment to high quality boasting that the taste of its food has not changed a bit even though the premises were inundated (1938), bombed out (1945), and shaken up (1995).[24] Like the businesses in Motomachi, this restaurant too derives strength from the trail of the 1938 flood.

The Hanshin Deluge figures as prominently in biographical narratives, although in this case too it pales against the recent catastrophic earthquake. In his testimony to the Association for Recording the Hanshin Earthquake (*Hanshin daishinsai o kiroku shitsuzukeru kai*), a Kōbe university professor singles out the 1938 flood, the air raids, and the 1995 earthquake as the three major disasters in his lifetime.[25] He relates how, as a primary two student, he waded through rising water to reach home with the help of older students and a neighbor. The conversation among adults about children being washed away, homes swallowed up by torrents, and streetcars buried in mud left indelible impressions on his tender mind. Another victim of the 1995 earthquake refers to the flood

60 years ago in his diary.[26] Staying in temporary shelter after being rendered homeless by the tremor, he began to worry one day in early May
when it rained in one night more than the month's average. Recalling
that heavy downpour was the direct cause of the Hanshin Deluge, he
watched anxiously as water leaked from the roof of his children's room.
He was concerned that the rain would seep into gapping cracks on the
ground and the surface of buildings to cause secondary damage. That
these people are no exceptions in their anxious recollection of the 1938
flood is evident from the 'slanted view' (*shasetsu*, a pun on the Japanese
word for 'editorial') in the e-magazine *Kazamidori*.[27] According to it,
there is a popular 'theory' (*setsu*) that calamitous floods hit the city at
30–year intervals. After 1938 was 1967, and now is about time for the
third to come. Although this piece claims to only report about the
theory, the fact that there is such a rumor circulating shows that the 1938
flood does cast a long shadow on Kōbe's collective consciousness.

BENIGN RIVERS

Despite the history of flooding, Kōbe's rivers elicit strong nostalgic sentiments from residents, who fondly recall them as the site of childhood
merrymaking, discovery, and freedom. It is the affirmation of this
memory and the commitment to its recreation that justify many of the
programs for the protection of riverine ecology and re-landscaping of
rivers. Take for example the Togagawa Protection Association (*Togagawa
o mamorō kai*), the oldest such organization in the city and the one whose
activity was featured in the national government's *White Paper on the
Environment* (*Kankyō hakusho*) in 2000. In its 20th anniversary publication, the president affirms that the association's founding idea was to
make available to children what the older generations remember from
their childhood (*Togagawa o mamorō kai* 1996:18).[28] The secretary echoes
this dedication to recreate and perpetuate a memorable past. He stresses
that the association believes children should be encouraged to play
in the river as in the old days, even though there is some risk involved
(*Togagawa o mamorō kai* 1996:19). He further explains in an interview in
2002 that his commitment to Togagawa is rooted in his own pleasurable
experience at the riverfront as a child.[29] This relationship between
memory, play, and memory-recreation underlies the association's 1976
founding declaration (*setsuritsu shuisho*). Its call for civic action takes the
form of a narrative that articulates the memory of an unspoiled
Togagawa in an indefinite past (*mukashi*), laments its degradation in the
era of high growth (1950s and 1960s), and urges the creation of a similar
memory for younger generations (*Togagawa o mamorō kai* 1996:44). Thus,
the memory of benign rivers, unlike that of violent rivers, functions as a
justification for reproducing the original memory as a living reality. In
the case of the Togagawa Protection Association, the event to which it

devotes most effort organizing is the month-long open river season in summer when children are not just told but taught to play at the river-front.

As schools close for vacation in late July the ward office puts up posters on neighborhood notice boards announcing the date on which Togagawa is to be officially opened (*kawabiraki*) (Togagawa o mamorō kai 1996:24–27, Suishinka 1999). As the main organizer, the association plans the whole event in coordination with the relevant municipal offices, schools and kindergartens, youth and women's associations, the Lion's Club, and other volunteer groups. It plants banners along the banks, mobilizes children to clean up a section of the river for the ceremony, procures fish for the release-and-catch event, and recruits volunteers to fill lookout positions during the season. On the day of the opening ceremony, after the dignitaries from the municipal government have given their speeches and cut the ribbon, and after bands from the fire department and neighborhood daycare centers have played, comes the most eagerly-anticipated activity, namely, catching fish with bare hands (*tsukamidori*). Cheered on by parents and onlookers, hundreds of children in swimsuits, some equipped with goggles and snorkels, rush into calf-deep water to grab or scoop up goldfish, baby carp, and eels, which have just been released. In most years, this event attracts some one thousand participants.

That is only the beginning; two more events are planned for the season. First, because of the popularity of the fish-grabbing game, three more days in early August are dedicated to it with additional release of fish each day. Altogether, it draws upward of two thousand children and their guardians, all of them becoming thoroughly soaked in their single-minded pursuit of fish. Second, toward the end of the season is a one-day 'water and water gun classroom' (*mizu to mizuteppō kyōshitsu*). Taking place on the ground of the Ōtsuchi Shrine upstream and the open space between the shrine and the river, this day's program comprises observation of small water creatures, the making of bamboo water guns and target practice, a picnic, and the standard summer game of 'watermelon smashing'. In 1992, the mayor put in an appearance. In addition to holding a dialog with citizens, he also helped children in making bamboo water guns. On both occasions, the association solicits essays from participating children and publishes the best-written ones in its newsletter.

Although summer is the time of the greatest fun, the association maintains a year-round schedule of activities to keep the river clean and remind people about the continual relevance of environmental protection. There are five full-scale cleanups in spring, summer, fall, winter, and year-end involving about a hundred volunteers each time. Sometimes wading in knee-deep water, they remove solid waste from the entire length of the river. On the 20th of every month, the association observes the 'river protection day' (*kawa o mamoru hi*) displaying banners on the banks and broadcasting slogans from a cruising car. To revive the river, it sponsors the release of baby trout (*ayu*) by children from kindergartens and daycare centers every May. In late October, there is a 'Fall Getting Together Festival' by the river (*fureai aki matsuri*) with performance and food stalls. And to emphasize that the river is a part of the community, it raises colorful cloth carp (*koi nobori*) in May to celebrate the health of all children in the ward, and co-sponsors the Cherry Blossom Festival (April), Rokkō Family Festival (June), and blood donation drive (October), which are organized by the ward.

Other river protection associations have similar though sometimes less elaborate year-round schedules. Typically, they have a summer riverfront celebration, which may go under such names as 'waterfront festival' (*mizube matsuri*), 'parent-child waterfront fiesta' (*oyako mizube fesuta*), 'waterfront classroom' (*mizube kyōshitsu*), or 'river fiesta' (*kawa fesuta*) (Kōbe-shi 1991:51, Sumiyoshigawa seiryū no kai 1999:58). In the case of Sumiyoshigawa, which is under the care of the city's second oldest river protection association, the Sumiyoshi Clear River Association (*Sumiyoshi seiryū no kai*), the summer climax is a 'parent-child waterfront fiesta' comprising speeches, performances, games, and, of course, a fish-grabbing (Shumiyoshigawa seiryū no kai 1999:5). The association cleans up the river twice a year with volunteers from primary schools and youth and women's clubs, conducts a biological survey with the help of middle and high school students, organizes an exhibition of paintings of the river by residents, deploys patrols to monitor and advice people walking dogs, and co-sponsors the release of fish and firefly larvae. It also puts in place and maintains garbage bins, banners, commemorative plaques, bulletin boards, and so forth along the banks.

All this started in Kōbe in the mid-1970s when concerned residents began to formally organize themselves into river protection groups. The two earliest ones were for Togagawa and Sumiyoshigawa, established in 1976 and 1979 respectively. In 1981, the municipal government set up the Kōbe Citizens' Waterfront Network (*Kōbe-shi shimin no mizube renraku kai*) to facilitate communication among these groups as well as between them and the authorities. In 1997, the network has nine members, five of which are concerned with urban rivers. Over the years, members have received many awards and commendations from municipal and prefectural governments as well as ministries in the central government. In particular, Togagawa Protection Association received the *Furusato*-Making Award (*Furusato-zukuri shō*) from the Hyōgo prefecture in 1988. The Sumiyoshi Clear River Association received the Hand-made Hometown Award (*Tetsukuri kyōdō shō*) from the Ministry of Construction in 1988, and was designated a 'hometown of *furusato* living creatures' (*furusato ikimono no sato*) by the Environmental Agency in 1989. Ikutagawa too was designated as a 'model *furusato* river' (*furusato no kawa-moderu kasen*) in 1988 (Kōbe-shi 1991:43). As if confirming Seki's contention that rivers are integral to the 'original landscape' (*genfūkei*) of the country (Seki 1994:40–51), the government, through these citations, acknowledges what these organizations do as contributions toward realizing the sublime but elusive ideal of *furusato*.

What is to be accomplished by urging citizens, especially children, to come out to the waterfront? After all, rivers are by no means safe in summer, which has its share of downpours and typhoons. Nevertheless, meteorological patterns cannot dissuade functionaries and neighborhood river enthusiasts from trying to inspire among residents a collective nostalgia for a recent past when, it is believed, people routinely engaged rivers in leisure. To their credit, the general population eagerly responds to the invitation to play in the river. A composite picture of this officially sanctioned and popularly received memory looks something like this.[30] The protagonists are active, healthy-looking boys and girls who revel in the freedom of summer vacation. The stream they play in abounds with small creatures, waiting to be observed or caught. The water guns and fishing tools they carry are typically homemade and crude. Their games too are simple and spontaneous: they try to grab fish with bare hands and splash water at each other. But their faces and comportment exude happiness and energy: they are shown laughing, running, exploring, calling out to each other, or in hot pursuit of some desperate fry. Adults, when depicted at all, are shown playing the parental role providing guidance and companionship. These images depict a *furusato* that is socially and environmentally wholesome, where children are adept at play, families are whole, neighbors interact (*fureau*) (Kōbe-shi 1991:40), and nature and humans are in harmony.

It should be pointed out that it takes much planning and investment for this dreamy past to be relived even in a fragmentary way. Most of Kōbe's rivers are moribund and boxed in by concrete. Although water quality has improved appreciably, it is necessary to release thousands of small fish into the river just so that people have something to watch or catch. It costs even more for the morphology of a river to be re-engineered to accommodate large numbers of people and the types of activity they are encouraged to engage in. Banks must be widened to allow people to gather, gentle slopes and stairs must be built to provide easy access to the bed, and artificial features such as shallows, curves, and stepping-stones must be added to entice people into the water. For some twenty years, Kōbe has been busily tearing down old riparian work to recreate the 'natural' contour of rivers. Daunting obstacles, however, remain. Human-friendly rivers like Togagawa and Sumiyoshigawa are a small minority. Most are so hemmed in by developments that there is no room left between buildings or roads and the riverbed.[31] Although the city tries to buy up land along rivers whenever possible, at least in the near future there is no realistic hope of turning many other rivers into another

Togagawa or Sumiyoshigawa. This reality, however, does not stop the city from falling deeper in love with rivers after the Hanshin Awaji Earthquake.

A catastrophic tremor struck Kōbe on 17 January 1995 causing over 5,000 deaths, thousands of buildings to collapse, and fires across the city. This tragedy adds a new and unexpected dimension to the city's favorable memory of rivers. Severe water shortage in the aftermath of the tremor allows citizens to cast the river in the light of a lifesaver in an emergency. Just as it was the case in the 1923 Kantō Earthquake, in Kōbe too fire caused extensive secondary damage. As deadly blazes raged, citizens and firefighters found out to their horror that, first, fire engines could not reach the fires because of blocked roads, and, second, fire hydrants were dry due to damage to the water transport system. In desperation, people turned to rivers for water. After the fires were put out (or died down by themselves), water shortage continued for two months. In desperation, people procured drinking water from wells and water for other domestic purposes from rivers. In retrospect, both citizens and government reached the conclusion that modern infrastructure could be rendered dysfunctional in another catastrophe, and that, when that happened, the city's population would have to fall back again on the river as 'lifeline' (*raifu rain*). The city thus comes to regard the landscaped rivers in a new light: greenbelts on the banks will stop the spread of fire, puddles and cascades will retain water for emergency use, ramps and stairs will make it easy to fetch water, and fountains and placards in riverfront parks will direct people to underground stores of drinking water.

After 1995, therefore, Kōbe remembers its rivers not only as life-enriching eco-playground but also as a life-saving eco-refuge. While there is no guarantee that there will be water in the rivers when needed, there is nonetheless a widespread willingness to believe that rivers might just make the difference between life and death when the next catastrophe strikes.

RIVER CULTURE

Kōbe's effort to recover the benign river is reinforced by a concomitant attempt to recall and reaffirm a river culture. As a national phenomenon, the interest in river culture is driven by the belief that traditional Japanese life is premised on heavy but responsible use of freshwater as evident in paddy cultivation, food processing and cooking, handicrafts, and, of course, the bathing habit. This affinity to water is taken to be the natural outcome of climate and geography, which endow the land with numerous rivers and springs. However, an acute sense of crisis often underlies this view of native culture. Although once an everyday reality, it is believed, this water-intensive lifestyle has been pushed to the brink of extinction by such forces of modernity as urbanization, industrialization, and infrastructure construction. Thus, the promotion of river culture generally entails some inculcation of nature-friendly values and behavior.

Kōbe constructs its river culture around the theme of 'the water of Rokkō' (*Rokkō no mizu*), whose reputed abundance and quality not only benefit the local economy but also enrich citizens' daily life. Until the recent past, rivers and springs in the Rokkō Range were central to people's livelihood as a source of water supply as well as a form of cheap energy. Nowadays, their practical importance has greatly diminished: the city gets most of its water from outside, and working watermills have all but disappeared. Nevertheless, the rivers and springs enjoy a reputation that far exceeds their utilitarian value. The local water has become a symbol of the city's rich natural endowment and a mark of quality living and discriminating taste in food and beverage consumption.

The city is fond of pointing out that until the early-twentieth century hundreds of watermills lined the rivers and produced vegetable oil, flour, and de-germinated rice for making *sake* ((Rokkō sabō 2001:15–16, Suishinka 1999, Sumiyoshigawa seiryū no kai 1999:33–34). For the modern enthusiasts of river culture, the watermill-lined rivers exemplify an ideal human–nature relationship that respects the integrity of the environment while allowing for profit making. As a visual reminder of this fortuitous synergy, watermills are making a comeback as a favored display in public places. To highlight its contribution to nature conservation, the city's sewer section has installed a watermill powered by highly treated sewage in Lovers' Cape, a park in Higashi-Tarumi.[32] Similarly, the artificial stream in Matsumoto, Hyōgo-ku, built after the 1995 earthquake, features a mini-watermill in addition to cascades and ponds.[33] In this case, too, the water is treated sewage. The city's resort-ranch in the Rokkō Range also has for display a restored farmhouse complete with a watermill, although what powers it is not clear.[34] Meanwhile, businesses are not to be outdone. The buckwheat noodle restaurant Maya near Hankyu Line's Rokkō Station has a rolling watermill by its entrance reminding customers how flour used to be made. Breweries are explicit about the contribution watermills made to their trade. Hakutsuru pays tribute to the device on its homepage by introducing the testimony of a 1907–born worker explaining the working of a mill and the production process.[35] Another company, Kikumasamune, has relocated a watermill together with its wooden shelter onto the ground of its museum. The inscription in front of the shed praises the efficiency and reliability of the technology, which guaranteed a steady supply of processed rice for making quality *sake*.[36]

While wooden wheels and mortars are mere objects of display, rivers and springs continue to deliver precious water. The local breweries especially value the spring water, known as *miyamizu*, from the foot of the Rokkō Range.[37] It is explained that the geological makeup of the hills not only allows them to purify the groundwater but also to add to it essential minerals, making it congenial to fermentation. As the special quality of this water was ascertained in the mid-nineteenth century, it gave a strong boost to the growth of a nationally famous *sake*-making industry in Kōbe.[38] As the exhibitions at Shūshōkan and Shūshinkan, two museums maintained by breweries, emphasize, there are three essential ingredients to fine *sake*, namely, brewer (*toji*), rice, and water. The first two are 'human factors' – brewer provides knowledge and skill whereas rice is the result of peasant labor – only the water is the blessing of nature.[39] In Hakutsuru's advertisement for its brand Tanrei Junmai (literally meaning 'elegantly light pure rice *sake*'), this formula is further reduced: 'This *sake*', it says, 'is made from only the water of Rokkō and rice' (*Asahi Shinbun* 2002.11.24).

This unique water has other uses as well. It continues to be consumed as drinking water. The city claims that 'Kōbe water' is known in the shipping world for its exceptional purity. It is said that in the early-twentieth century, foreign ships made it a point to fill up in Kōbe so that they would have a water that could last beyond the Equator or the Indian Ocean (Rokkō sabō 2001:15, Mainichi 1961:184–185). In 1985, the Environmental Agency included the water from above Nunobiki Waterfalls in its list of One Hundred Distinguished Waters (*Nihon hyaku meisui sen*) (Kōbe-shi shimin no mizube renraku kai 1992: 29). Nowadays, although the city's tap water is adulterated, the legendary local water is still available. The food and beverage company Hausu sells bottled water under the brand 'Rokkō's Sweet Water' (*Rokkō no oishii mizu*). Dedicated residents make daily trips to their favorite fountain in the hills to fetch free supplies for their rice cookers and teakettles. To satisfy this popular demand, one public bath operator has a pump by the entrance of his business from which underground water can be purchased on the tap. Other businesses also seek association with the local water. Two manufacturers of Chinese noodles claim to use 'the famous water of Rokkō' (*Rokkō no meisui*) and 'river water from Mt Rokkō' (*Rokkōsan keisui*) for their products.[40] The Rokkō Beer and the tea and coffee served in the restaurant inside the municipal Rokkō Kōzan Botanic Garden are said to derive their special flavor from the same water.[41] Even the 30–year-old bakery Poemu cites the water of Rokkō as one of the reasons for the gourmet quality of its bread. In short, just as the 'Kōbe brand' is supposed to confer an aura of class and elegance to a piece of fashion or accessory, adding Rokko's water to a cup of tea or a bowl of noodle is taken as a guarantee of exquisite taste.

What the exhibitions, PR literature, and advertisements purport to show is that the city has a river culture, even though some aspects of it may have been lost. Indirectly and subtly, citizens are reminded to adjust their lifestyle to preserve this beneficial and yet delicate human-nature balance obtained since pre-modern times. After the Hanshin Awaji

Earthquake, the city is eager to further consolidate this aqua-heritage through a bold new plan to bring the river into every neighborhood and the life of every citizen. The idea of a Hanshin Canal (*Hanshin Sosui*) was floated after the 1995 earthquake as a radical solution to the problem of severe water shortage in another major disaster.[42] It envisions the building of a 50–km underground tunnel to transport water from Ōsaka's Yodogawa to the thirsty rivers that flow from the Rokkō Range into the Ōsaka Bay. A secondary network of artificial streams and ponds would be built to connect existing rivers and enmesh the entire urban area in a gridlock of 'clear streams' (*seseragi*). Once in place, this system would deliver a constant flow of water to every neighborhood where it would serve two purposes.

The first purpose is to make available 'unrestricted water resources' (*mugen suigen*) for disaster relief (Keisei iinkai 1998). Immediately after the devastating earthquake, unchecked fires reduced whole blocks to ashes. The secondary damage was extensive because fire engines could not reach the fires, and even when they could, there was no water to be had from the broken pipes. By maintaining sufficient water in the rivers, and by distributing it evenly throughout the city, the proposed system would ensure that every neighborhood has access to a local source of water in an emergency. This would enable residents and the local fire brigade to take immediate act to limit the extent of damage. An effective initial response is critical since, according to official estimation, no outside help would arrive until five or six hours after a disaster has hit (Keisei iinkai 1998). This network of waterways is also expected to function as firebreaks. At the very least, citizens could use the greenbelts along them as sanctuaries. Finally, as the Hanshin Awaji Earthquake has shown, there would be a continual demand for alternative sources of water for days, even weeks, in the aftermath of a disaster. In such a situation, people would have to rely on rivers for such basic needs as washing, bathing, flushing, and cooking.

The second purpose is aesthetical and ecological, namely, to turn Kōbe into a 'millennium city of water and greenery' (*mizu to midori no sennen toshi*) (Kinki 2002). Referring to waterfront cities overseas as well as pilot projects inside and outside Kōbe, the prefectural and municipal governments and the Construction Ministry's Kinki Regional Development Bureau (*Kinki chihō seibi kyoku*) promote the canal as the cornerstone of a 'vibrant, relaxing, and ecological' future city capable of retaining its vitality and charm for a thousand years. They present images of an urban landscape embedded in a network of 'corridors of water and greenery' (*mizu to midori no kairō*), which would incorporate 'nature' – the Rokkō Range, the Ōsaka Bay, and the rivers – into the built environment. These continuous natural pathways would allow humans and other life forms to interact and to move among the hills, various parts of the city (through the streams), and the sea. The authorities optimistically claim that such a ubiquitous presence of fauna and flora, nourished by an abundance of fresh water, would help urban dwellers to 'recover their humanity' (*ningensei kaifuku*) and 'cultivate their sensibilities' (*jōcho kyōiku*) (Kinki 2002).

The obvious appeal of this vision notwithstanding, the problems involved are daunting. The most difficult issues pertain to cost and the availability of water (*Sankei Shinbun* 2002.02.28). In the current recession, the government is averse to committing to such an expensive project. It is also doubtful if Yodogawa has much extra water to give Kōbe. The city already draws 75% of its water from Yodogawa, which also supplies water to Ōsaka, the second most populous city in the country. For Kōbe to demand more from this beleaguered river would almost certainly compromise its already fragile ecology. There are other smaller but no less tricky headaches. A checkerboard of shallow and winding waterways would need constant attention to maintain its ecological viability and structural integrity. Pilot projects involving intricate hydrophilic features have achieved mixed results. Some of the miniature cascades and puddles on the newly landscaped banks of Togagawa and Ishiyagawa are either dry due to leakage or overflowing because of the accumulated rubbish.[43] Some of the ponds are lifeless and muddy puddles, their fish either lost to poachers or killed by overgrowing algae. Small though they may be, these problems would multiply manifold were the city to become enmeshed in such shallow watercourses. It would be truly ironic if neighborhood streams of the future millennium city were to degenerate into open sewers of the bad old days.

CONCLUSION

Although Kōbe's rivers still overflow from time to time, it is their benign aspect that predominates official and unofficial discourses on the subject since the early 1990s. Rather than to be feared, they are often portrayed as something desirable not just for the sake of recreation or even biodiversity but the grand purpose of 'community making'. Scholars have observed that modern Japanese social and cultural discourses tend to be nostalgic of an idealized *furusato* (hometown), which is, if not the opposite of modernity, at least free of its attendant ailments. Urban Japanese who perceive themselves to be atomized, rootless, and homogenized long to return to this hometown where they can be in touch with nature, tradition, and themselves once again. The mission of community making, through economic, social, cultural, and engineering projects, is to approximate this ideal community in the modern city where the majority of Japanese now live. On one hand, the idea of friendly rivers derives its appeal from this powerful, anti-modern notion of community, which is always imagined in a rural setting. On the other hand, it reinforces this nostalgia by giving it an explicit modern environmentalist slant. The urban *furusato* stands for not just social and psychological security but an environmentally responsible lifestyle that enables its inhabitants to regain and coexist with an abundant and near-pristine nature.

The image of benign rivers emerged in Kōbe's community making discourse at a point in time when two national trends converged. The first trend is what Broadbent (1998) has identified, namely, the country's 'transition from an environmental debacle to environmental miracle' beginning in the 1970s. In Kōbe, the dire reality of riverine ecological degradation made it apparent to officials and citizens that concerted and broad-based remedial action was necessary to stop the decline in living standards. The second trend is a gradual shift in the government's river conservation policy from exploitation and control to protection since the 1980s (Seki 1994). Having successfully reduced the threat of floods in the quarter century after the Second World War, it was ready to re-examine its priorities concerning rivers. Kōbe seized this opportunity early on and became one of the forerunning cities to re-imagine and re-engineer its rivers as a natural, human-friendly feature of the urban landscape.

However appealing the image of human-friendly rivers may be, it cannot gloss over the fact that the same rivers overflowed before and may do so again. Kōbe does not try to hide this contradiction but acknowledges them as the two sides of a coin. The municipal government's publications repeatedly point out that while the city has a beautiful natural environment the latter is also a source of grave dangers. Its community making vision for the twenty-first century, which is summed up by the four concepts of 'peace of mind' (*anshin*), 'vitality' (*katsuryoku*), 'attraction' (*miryoku*), and 'teamwork' (*kyōdō*), addresses both aspects of the natural environment (Kōbe-shi 1999:1). To deliver 'peace of mind' the city promises, among other things, to work toward preventing natural disasters, including river-related ones. Meanwhile, to increase 'attraction,' it is committed to continuing with river beautification and other urban redevelopment and environmental protection projects (1999:6, 13). But the city attempts to go further than this. Drawing on the experience of the 1995 earthquake, officials and citizens eagerly promote the river as a fail-proof 'lifeline' in an urban catastrophe. The Hanshin Canal vision is built on the latest notion that rivers can save lives. Hence, the city now lives with a memory of rivers that has three layers of meaning. The oldest layer is that of the river as the source of natural disasters, the middle layer is that of the river as eco-playground, and the top layer is that of the river as eco-refuge. Nature, in other words, has become the last resort of survival in an urban natural disaster.

REFERENCES

Broadbent, Jeffrey. 1998. *Environmental politics in Japan: networks of power and protest.* Cambridge: University Press.

Hyōgo-ken. n.d. *Kōbe: hito to kawa.* Kōbe: Hyōgoken dobokubu Kōbe doboku jimusho.

Iketani Hiroshi. 1999. *Dosekiryū saigai.* Tokyo: Iwanami.

Kamioka Namiko. 1987. *Nihon no kōgai shi.* Tōkyō: Sekai shoin.

Keisei iinkai. 1998. 21 seiki ni muketa mizu to midori no kankyō bōsai toshi o mezashite: Hanshin chiiki mizu to midori no kankyō bōsai toshi kōzō keisei Iinkai kara no teigen. http://www.kkr.mlit.go.jp/river/mizumidori/index.html. (Report available from the website of Kinki chihō seibi kyoku, accessed in July 2002)

Kerr, Alex. 2001. *Gods and demons: the fall of modern Japan.* London and New York: Penguin Books.

Kinkin. 2002. Hanshin sosui. http://www.kkr.mlit.go.jp/inaso/sosui/index.html (Document available on the website of Kinki chihō seibi kyoku, accessed in July 2002).

Kiriyama Kasane. 1991. 'Kaisetsu'. In *Shimantogawa: Atsuyoshi no natsu,* pp. 197–204. Tokyo: Kawade Shobō.

Kōbe-shi. 1991. *Kōbe no kawa to yama.* Kōbe: Kōbe-shi dobokukyoku.

Kōbe-shi. 1999. *Kōbe Shisei gaido.* Kōbe: Kōbe-shi kōhōka.

Kōbe-shi shimin no mizube renraku kai. 1992. *Kōbe-shi shimin no mizube renraku kai 10 shūnen kinen shi: Shimin no mizube o mamori sodateru tame ni.* Kōbe: Kōbe-shi shimin no mizube renraku kai.

Kōbe-shi shimin no mizube renraku kai. 1997. *Mizube o arukō.* Kōbe: Kōbe-shi shimin no mizube renraku kai.

Mainichi. 1961. *Kōbe umai mon.* compiled by Mainichi shinbun Kōbe shikyoku. Kōbe: Mainichi shinbun Kōbe shikyoku.

Mitsuoka Akira. 1985. *Yanagawa no mizu yo yomigaere.* Tōkyō: Kōdansha.

Nash, Roderick. 2001. *Wilderness and the American mind.* 4th edition. New Haven: Yale University Press.

Rokkō sabō. 2001? *Rokkōsan mo machi mo mamorimasu.* Kōbe: Rokkō sabō kōji jimusho.

Sakai Tokitada. 1973. *Midori no kairō: Hyōgo kaisō ron.* Kōbe: Nojigiku bunko.

Sasayama Kyūzō. 1991. *Shimantogawa: Atsuyoshi no natsu.* Tōkyō: Kawade shobō.

Seki Masakazu. 1994. *Daichi no kawa: yomigaere Nihon no furusato no kawa.* Tōkyō: Sōshisha.

Suishinka 1999. *Togagawa marugoto mappu.* Kōbe: Kōbe-shi Nada-kuyakusho shiminbu machizukuri suisinka.

Sumiyoshigawa seiryū no kai ed. 1999. *Sumiyoshigawa seiryū no kai 20 shūnen kinen shi.* Higashi-Nada: Sumiyoshigawa seiryū no kai.

Takahashi Yutaka. 1971. *Kokudo no henbō to suigai.* Tokyo: Iwanami.

Tanimura Kiyoshi. 1977. *Kasen kankyō: chisui, risui to no chōwa o motomete.* Tōkyō: Daiichi hōki shupppan kabushiki kaisha.

Togagawa o mamorō kai. 1997. *Togagawa o mamorō kai 20 shūnen kinnen shi.* Kōbe: Togagawa o mamorō kai.

Wakabayashi Yasushi. 1987. *Nada Kōbe chihōshi no kenkyū.* Ashiyashi: Wakabayashi Yasushi shi o shinobu kai.

Waley, Paul. 2000. Following the flow of Japan's river culture. *Japan Forum* 12: 199–217.

Yasuoka Shōtarō. 1973. Sumidagawa. In Asahi shinbun sha ed. *Ryūiki kikō,* pp.5–30. Tōkyō: Asahi shinbun sha.

NOTES

1   I wish to thank the Sumitomo Foundation, the Toshiba International Foundation and the National University of Singapore for their generous funding of research projects whose results informed this chapter.

2   This paper treats 'river culture' and 'water culture' as interchangeable. In the sources they generally refer to overlapping phenomena and similar attitudes, although they can have different emphases – the former focusing on a geographic and ecological system while the latter including not just water drawn from rivers but also rain-water, underground water, even desalinated water extracted from the ocean floor (*shinkaisui*).

3   The urbanized area refers to the seven seaboard wards of Higashinada (population: 186,313, area: 30.36 km²), Nada (population: 115,487, area: 31.40 km²), Chūō (population: 110,382, area: 25.58 km²), Hyōgo (population: 103,116, area: 14.54 km²), Nagata (population: 107,217, area: 11.46 km²), Suma (population: 169,163, area: 30.99 km²), and Tarumi. They constitute the *omote*-Rokkō or the Pacific side of Rokkō. Together with the two large landlocked wards of Kita (population: 227,927, area: 241.84 km²) and Nishi (population: 240,531, area: 137.86 km²) on the opposite side of the Rokkō Range, they make up the city of Kōbe (Kōbe-shi 1999:22–30).

4   I arrived at this number using a 1992 *Kōbe-shi sabō shiteichi zu* published by the Kōbe municipal government. The number of rivers has changed over the years as some were diverted while others were covered over.

5   It is not the intention of this chapter to suggest that Japan is unique among modern, industrialized countries in having continual problems, culturally and socially, with 'modernity'. The United States had doubts about the progress of 'civilization' and the retreat of 'wilderness' in the late-nineteenth century (Nash 2001:96–107). Cross-cultural comparisons are, obviously, beyond the scope of this chapter.

6   This applies to Kyūshū, Shikoku, and the Pacific side of Honshū. Hokkaidō and the continental side of Honshū get a lot of precipitation in the form of snow.

7   In 2000, typhoon #14 killed 10 people and injured over 100 when it

caused Nigawa in Nagoya to spill over (http://www.bousai.go.jp/kinkyu/tokai/tokai1.html).

[8] Tanimura (1977) summarizes the situation from a national perspective, speaking as an ally of the bureaucrats in the Ministry of Construction. Sakai (1973), then prefectural governor, describes the problems faced by Hyōgo prefecture's Pacific-side industrial belt, which has Kōbe as the largest city. Mitsuoka (1977) provides another regional perspective from Yanagawa city in Kumamoto prefecture, Kyūshū. Although the city is now famous for its scenic canal system, many sections of it were once so full of rubbish that the municipal authorities planned to fill them in. Yasuoka's (1973) essay touches on the pathetic situation of Tokyo's Sumidagawa, historically the city's representative river. He recalls how a national leader like Satō Eisaku, upon hearing his complaint about the river, could not comprehend the significance of protecting riverine ecology.

[9] See http://homepage2.nifty.com/tamagawa/gesam.html and http://www.keihin.ktr.mlit.go.jp/.

[10] 'Nature as it is' (*shizen no mama*) and 'pastoral' (*bokka teki*) are the expressions used by Tanimura, who argued the government's case as a member of various committees advising the Ministry of Construction (1977:18, 23).

[11] See Waley (2000) for a useful discussion of this change in national government policy. While his study 'set[s the] story within a historical context of state-led river engineering and management' (p.201), this chapter finds multiple sources of inspiration for the government's switch to a 'soft' approach to rivers. It also sees this policy correction as (partly) a response to popular demand and protest.

[12] http://www.mlit.go.jp/river/gaiyou/houritu/9705.html.

[13] Inevitably, after the 1995 Hanshin Awaji Earthquake, the 1938 flood is usually relegated to the second place in narratives of natural disasters.

[14] This month was designated the year after catastrophic floods and landslides hit Nagasaki in July 1982 (Iketani 1999:74–80).

[15] It was held in Sannomiya's Phoenix Plaza (*Hanshin Awaji daishinsai fukkō shienkan*). This place was closed in March 2002 with its functions transferred to the new Disaster Reduction and Human Renovation Institution (*Hito to bōsai mirai sentā*). Much of the same information can also be found in Rokkō sabō (2001:1–24).

[16] http://www.kkr.mlit.go.jp/rokko/inet.

[17] http://www.city.kōbe.jp/cityoffice/15/020/medium/report/1999–6/koube99–6.htm.

[18] http://www.hyogo-c.ed.jp/~maiko-hs/1.19/119kinen.htm.

[19] http://www.kōbe-c.ed.jp/mgw-ms/bousai/bousai2.htm.

[20] http://www.kōbe-c.ed.jp/mgw-ms/h12sentaku/wagamati/index.html.

[21] http://www.kōbe.coop.or.jp/anohi/anohi7.html

[22] http://www.kōbe-motomachi.or.jp.

[23] http://www.jin.ne.jp/kōbe/moto-1/index2.htm.

24 http://www.equiv.net/gp/ky003/ky003.html.
25 http://www.npo.co.jp/hanshin/1book/1–210.html.
26 http://www.asahi-net.or.jp/~de9y-httr/index.html.
27 http://www.geocities.co.jp/HeartLand/5995/.
28 Members of other river protection associations have made similar references to childhood memory. See Sumiyoshi seiryū no kai (1999:16, 49) and Kōbe-shi shimin no mizube renraku kai (1992:52).
29 http://www.ne.jp/asahi/river/project/5–12.html.
30 See the cover illustration of Kōbe-shi shimin no mizube renraku kai (1997) and pictures in Kōbe-shi shimin no mizube renraku kai (1992), Togagawa o mamorō kai (1997), Sumiyoshigawa seiryū no kai (1999).
31 The fish-grabbing event at Kannonjigawa takes place at a section of the river that is barely three meters wide. On one side of it is a vertical retaining wall over two meters high. On the other side is an even higher wall with an uninterrupted roll of buildings sitting on its edge. See the photo in Kōbe-shi (1991:49).
32 http://www.city.kōbe.jp/cityoffice/30/031/13.html.
33 http://osaka.yomiuri.co.jp/new_feature/forum/020620e.htm.
34 http://www.exd.kōbe.jp/kōbewinery/kengaku.htm.
35 http://www.hakutsuru.co.jp/know/guide/24guide.html.
36 http://www.kikumasamune.co.jp/kinenkan/tour/suisha.html.
37 http://www.hakutsuru.co.jp/know/guide/2guide.html.
38 http://www.hept.himeji-tech.ac.jp/~cpikansai/commit/publici/lett11/04.html.
39 http://www.shushinkan.co.jp/a2.html, http://www.takinokoi.co.jp/pages/mono1.htm.
40 http://www.sankei.co.jp/cooking/ffnet/index09.htmly, http://www.mizho.co.jp/y.
41 http://www.crie.net/tourcon/gu2.asp?y=2002&m=6, http://www.skfoods.co.jp/sk0503b1.html.
42 It was originally advocated by Professor Ikebuchi Shūichi, the former director of Kyōto University's Disaster Prevention Research Institute (*Bōsai kenkyūjo*), and later endorsed by a committee set up by the Kinki Regional Development Bureau (*Sankei shinbun* 28.02.2002).
43 Personal observations made in 2001.

PART 4

Conclusion

13

Social Memory and Commemoration: Some 'After the Fact' Thoughts

VERED VINITZKY-SEROUSSI

My first comment is embedded in my impression (and I may be wrong) that there is much confusion with the terminology we are using in this field. The literature and the papers here include the terms 'collective memory', 'popular memory', 'cultural memory', 'public memory', 'collective representations', 'shared memory', 'communal memory' and 'social memory', which in many ways refer to the same phenomenon. I wish to suggest the term 'social memory' not only because I believe that sharing a definition (even in the age that is perceived as post-modernist) is the first step in moving forward but also because I believe that this term is flexible enough to work with and be creative and innovative and yet bounded and thus enable us to exclude the too often tendency to perceive any mentioning of the word 'past' as an indication for the existence of memory and commemoration. By social memory I adopt Olick and Robbins' definition which consists of 'the varieties of forms through which we are shaped by the past, conscious and unconscious, public and private, material and communicative, consensual and challenged' (Olick and Robbins 1998: 112). The chapters presented here demonstrate the varieties of forms that we need to look at in order to understand the ways through which we are shaped by the past: from Ben-Ari's chapter about the rituals in Yasukuni Shrine, to the monuments and artifacts in the chapters of van Bremen, Takagi, Veldkamp and Nakamaki, political campaign in Knight's chapter, oral history in Thang's chapter, language in Bourdaghs' chapter, landscapes in Hislop's work and much more. The mnemonic practices vary but it seems that above and beyond the diversity of the practices – some common puzzles bother most of the scholars of memory of Japan (as well as in many other nations) and 'ordinary people' whose efforts and struggles we document and analyze.

The notion of social memory in general, and of commemoration as its tangible public presentations in particular, have haunted 'ordinary people,' political and social elites as well as scholars from diverse disciplines over the last two decades. This preoccupation with memory is hardly the result of a special attraction to history (although the latter's relation to memory plays a critical role). On the contrary, the effects of the use and abuse of the past on a wide range of issues attached to the present – from the formation of collective identities (whether national, local, ethnic, or gender-based), to questions of politics and power, traditions and myths, social solidarity, accuracy and authenticity, continuity and change, social order, meaning- making, and culture in general – fuel this interest.

The first issue concerns the relations between micro and macro – between 'collective memory' and 'collected memories' (Olick, 1999a) – between what is publicly enacted and controlled (mostly by elites through various agents of memory such as architects, poets, producers, play writers, designers, religious leaders, journalists, politicians, song writers, performers, museum curators, and many others) and what is personally experienced and perceived. At least four of the chapters touched explicitly on that issue (Ben-Ari, van Bremen, Thang, Hislop) while others were more implicit about it but nonetheless it was somewhere in the background. The state of the field of social memory is already at the stage where there are 'two cultures' (Olick 1999a) within it (macro and micro): these two cultures are asking somewhat different questions and are using different methods in order to know what they claim they know. In my opinion, it is about time to look for the links between micro and macro, between agent and structure, between autobiographical memories and public presentations of the past, between personal pain and national narratives.

The second issue involves the very complicated relationships between the past and the present in shaping the images of the past that later on (through convoluted ways) affect our personal perception and perhaps even behavior. This issue that was discussed by Hislop, Veldkamp, ven Bremen, Thang, Ben-Ari, Nakamaki and Bourdaghs (perhaps everybody) is a long time argument in this newish field. While so many rightly insisted that present needs and circumstances affect the way the past is presented (a claim that was first made by Halbwachs 1992, 1980 and George Herbert Mead 1938), this claim is challenged by people like Michael Schudson who argues that there are certain pasts that would not go away; there are certain pasts in which we are deeply invested. Giving up certain memories – even if they are painful – will take away parts of our identities, parts of ourselves.

I agree that without community we have no memory, that without space we have no memory but by the same token, without memory and space and time and discourse, we have no community and no identity. (Perhaps today we are witnessing a new phenomenon where one can manage to construct an identity and a community through virtual spaces and times. I'm a bit suspicious of the ability of the internet to become a real substitution for the drama and power of social life.)

Let me come back to the relations of past and present. Present needs and circumstances do indeed affect the way in which the past is shaped and presented but there are limits or as Barry Schwartz state 'the past cannot be literally constructed; it can only be selectively exploited' (1982: 396).

While during the workshop that was the basis for this book we saw that heroes and paradise are still sought after in Japan, much of the current preoccupation with the past is less about a paradise lost than skeletons in the closet. We witness this interest in many of the chapters written here. The past threatens to penetrate the contemporary social and political scene, to change the hegemonic narrative, to encourage new voices, to demand justice and recognition. In the political sphere, democratic nations see fewer politicians who believe in their ability to win campaigns or maintain world-wide popularity without apologizing for their 'fathers' sins.' The recent examples of the 'politics of regret' (Olick 1999a) include former US President Bill Clinton, British Prime Minister Tony Blair, former Israeli Prime Minister Ehud Barak and the Japanese Prime Minster Koizumi. Commemorations of the 'good old days' seem to be disappearing in favor of acknowledgments of 'difficult pasts.' In that sense, this book is not an exception. It is the rule: one can read in the book about painful memories from Kōbe's rivers and earthquake, Okinawa's traumatic past and present, untimely dead, wars and lost empires, even the wolf suffers from a bad reputation. Difficult pasts are certainly the name of the game today. A difficult past is not necessarily more tragic than other commemorated past events; what constitutes a difficult past is an inherent moral trauma (Wagner-Pacifici and Schwartz 1991), disputes, tensions and conflicts. Thus, in the case of Japan, the commemoration of the atomic bomb is not an example for a difficult past; but the way in which Japan treated some of its neighbors is certainly a difficult past to deal with (the issue of the comfort women, Nanjing massacre, the Battle of Okinawa to name only but few examples).

The interest in embarrassing pasts has become a focus of much academic work over the last decade. The literature deals with the question posed by Wagner-Pacifici and Schwartz: 'How is commemoration without consensus, or without pride, possible?' (1991:379). Now we see that this interest reached Asia. In a newish book edited by Fujitani, White and Yoneyama (2001), the editors rightly complain that 'the

Asia-Pacific War . . . for Euro-American audiences, has remained largely overshadowed by interest in the war in Europe and the events of the Holocaust.' Indeed, when asked to comment on the recent literature on 'collective memory,' Michael Schudson observed, 'there are two kinds of studies of collective memory, those that examine the Holocaust and all the others' (2001:3). The book, which is titled *Perilous Memories*, and this book certainly mark a strong and impressive beginning of this field in this area. So how do we cope with this challenge? Wagner-Pacifici and Schwartz have suggested a multi-vocal commemoration. A multi-vocal commemoration is about a shared space (as the Vietnam Veterans Memorial in Washington D.C. is) a shared time or a shared text that carries diverse meanings and thus can be peopled by groups with different interpretations of the same past. I would like to propose a different type of commemoration of a difficult past: a fragmented one. A fragmented commemoration includes multiple commemorations in various spaces and times where diverse discourses of the past are voiced and aimed at disparate collectives. We may wish to see whether Japanese commemoration can be understood within this kind of analysis. Perhaps the rites at the Yasukuni Shrine and the memorial in Okinawa where names of aggressors and victims appear together (Masaie, 2001) can serve as examples for a multivocal commemoration. Another question is of course what is the meaning of a multivocal commemoration that incorporates names of victims and perpetuators. Is it about reconciliation? Does it enhance the blurring of boundaries between good and evil?

Moreover, I wish to suggest a theoretical model within which the likelihood of the emergence of both types of commemoration can be understood, explained and analyzed. Before I discuss the model, I wish to make another comment about the framing of the narrative which is at the heart of the analysis of the problematic of the commemoration of a difficult past. In effect, the narrative is at the heart of any commemoration.

FRAMING NARRATIVES OF DIFFICULT PASTS

Narratives are never mere lists, assemblages of dates or facts, put together without logic or motivation. Rather they are selective accounts with beginnings and endings, constructed to create meanings, interpret reality, organize events in time, establish coherency and continuity, construct identities, enable social action, construct the world and its moral and social order for its audience (Jacobs 1996; Alexander and Smith 1993; McAdams 1993; Freeman 1993; McCall 1990; Mitchell 1981). Precisely because narratives are rarely naive, the way they are constructed is especially pertinent when considering the planning and enactment of commemorative practices.

Commemorative narratives – particularly the ones of painful pasts – can be understood as consisting of three components: the protagonist(s) being commemorated, the event itself, and the event's context. Examples of the first component may include, for the United States, the American soldiers killed in Vietnam. Incorporating the second component into the commemoration process changes the focus into the Vietnam War. Including the third component of the narrative implies acknowledgment of the implications of an activist American foreign policy that led to the involvement in Vietnam.

Borrowing the concept of 'framing' from Goffman (1974) and the literature on social movements, mnemonic narratives are framed through the emphasis on or absence of one or more of the three components of the narrative. Framing narratives through inclusion and exclusion of material is part and parcel of the formation and reformation of any commemoration. The significance of the framing, however, lies in the fact that the component adopted may affect the contours of the collective that is addressed. The stricter the adherence to only the first or second component of the narrative (often associated with the 'hard core' facts), the larger the collective that can gather around it. In other words, the 'thinner' the message (often associated with a consensual message), the larger the collective that can identify with it. The risk is that the makeup of the narrative can be reduced to so little that it will repel those collectives for whom the paucity of content is tantamount to an attempt to 'erase the past'. Conversely, opting for a focus on the context ensures that the collective adhering to it will be smaller, as many may find the mnemonic narrative 'too politicized'. In other words, the wider the narrative – i.e. including general issues under dispute – the harder it is to construct a commemoration without contests and tensions to which a large collective can relate. Moreover, emphasizing the context may be critical when considering a difficult past, as it may evoke the same conflict that constituted that painful past in the first place.

Narratives also contain time structures, beginnings and endings, which help in constructing a context (Olick 1999b), thus reflecting and affecting the way in which a collective perceives the past and itself (E. Zerubavel 1993; Y. Zerubavel 1995). The people of Okinawa prefer to begin their narrative in the 1945 Battle of Okinawa. But, as Masaie states, the battle has to be put in context of a war that took place for 15 years. In that war 'Okinawan soldiers were members of the same Imperial Japanese Army that invaded and occupied Korea, China and Southeast Asia . . . Manchuria and Micronesia.' Without taking away the pain that the Okinawans feel, starting the narrative earlier makes them no less aggressors than the Japanese Army (2001: 98). The American narrative which condemns 'the Japanese military's attack on Pearl Harbor . . . [ignores] the questions of how in the first place Hawaii

had come to be a US territory and why a US naval base existed there'
(Yoneyama, 2001:334). While the issue of constructing a narrative that
will be shared by a nation is quite complex, tourism and bilateral relations between nations make this ordeal even more complex. Bilateral
interests made China distinguish between the Japanese people and the
Japanese militarism regarding the Japanese atrocities in China (Yang,
2001). Japan for instance has to cope with pressures from the outside –
pressures that many nations cannot ignore any more. In a response to
Prime Minister Koizumi's visit to Yasukuni Shrine (in August 2001),
China enabled demonstrations in front of the Japanese embassy in
Beijing and the President of Korea said to the press 'how can we become
best friends of those who try to forget and ignore the pain they caused
to us?'

Another angle to the issue of narrative and time structure can be
thought of regarding Knight's work. Perhaps locating the story of the
wolf deeper and farther in history may solve the problem (assuming
that the wolf had a better reputation then). If the memories of the wolf
from one hundred years ago do not serve present needs, one may
emphasize the role of the wolf in Japanese culture and history five
hundred years ago. The Zionist movement did it with much success by
erasing 2000 years of Jewish exile and reconnected the new settlers in
Palestine to its biblical past (Y. Zerubavel 1995). The new Zionist Jew
was inspired by ancestors she or he never met, while ignoring the ones
she knew. Following that logic, the roots of the wolves need to be recovered somewhere else in order to reintroduce them into contemporary
culture.

The importance of the suggested analytic framework lies not only in
its ability to detect the heart of potential social dissensus but also in its
implications for understanding its reality and how it can be dealt with.
As noted, the more tightly a mnemonic practice is restricted to include
only the protagonist and/or the event, the larger the collective that can
share the commemoration. Concentrating on the context may draw a
smaller collective that can share the moment.

TYPES OF COMMEMORATION AND THEIR SOCIAL CONTEXT: TOWARDS A THEORETICAL MODEL

While various events in different nations constitute a similar challenge, the commemorative types that emerged are radically different:
multivocal versus fragmented. I wish to suggest a theoretical model
that may bring to light the social conditions under which the differences in the outcomes can be analyzed and understood. The proposed
model consists of three dimensions. The first dimension concerns the
political culture of the commemorating society. The second dimension
involves temporal considerations. The third dimension encompasses

the power of the agents of memory. I argue that a multivocal type of commemoration is more likely to emerge under the following complex of social factors: a consensual political culture; when the commemorated past is no longer part of the present agenda; and when agents of memory have only limited power and resources. In contrast, a fragmented type of commemoration will be engendered under the following social conditions: a conflictual political culture; a strong link between the past and present debates; the presence of powerful agents of memory. (For an elaboration, see Vinitzky-Seroussi, 2002.)

1. The political culture of the commemorating society
While societies are of course never entirely consensual or dissensual, and while it is hard to discuss political culture without essentializing it, some societies are nonetheless characterized by a more or less consensual political culture.

America copes with cultural wars, conflicts and disputes, but Alexander and Smith claim that there is 'an underlying consensus as to the key symbolic patterns of American civic society, and a relationship of complementarity between different components of the cultural system' (1993: 165). Accordingly, the United States can be said to be relatively consensual and a commemoration of even a controversial past such as the Vietnam War can therefore be multivocal – representing the product of a compromise. It seems that the political culture of Japan can be also conceived as consensual. Other nations such as Israel and Chile are characterized by a conflictual political culture.

2. Timing of Commemoration: Relevance of Past to Present
The timing of commemoration has two facets. The first one relates to cultural developments in general and to an epochal quality of memory cultures in particular. In the last decades Western nations have been characterized by what Maier calls a 'hunger for memory' (1988: 149). It seems that Japan is also part of this trend. This dimension, however, better explains the recent 'rush for commemoration' in the public sphere, rather than the emergence of a specific type of commemoration, and is thus beyond the scope of this chapter.

A second facet of timing relates to political contingencies, or in other words, the relations between the event commemorated and the current agenda of the commemorating society. To be sure, each commemoration takes places in some present and is thus affected by it (in effect, the power of the present in shaping the past, to one degree or another, is one of the few shared understandings among contemporary scholars of social memory). Obviously, if the past did not matter to anyone, probably no one would bother to represent it in any shape or form. But the point emphasized here is that certain pasts are still part and parcel of current partisan politics and social reality. A difficult past can still be a

difficult present and thus more likely to become a fragmented commemoration. By the same token, the relative irrelevance of the past to
the present agenda may enable the enactment of a multivocal commemoration.

What may intensify the likelihood of erecting a fragmented or a multivocal commemoration is the length of time that has elapsed between the
events and their commemoration (Zolberg, 1998; Irwin-Zarecka, 1994):
the longer one waits, the better the chances of a multivocal (even a consensual) commemoration. Austria waited over 40 years after the Second
World War ended to erect the Monument against War and Fascism in the
center of Vienna (Bunzl 1995). When a monument is dedicated decades
after the actual event, those for whom the memory is what Halbwachs
has defined as 'an autobiographical,' personally experienced one (1992),
are either dead or at least middle-aged, if not old. Most Austrians who
attended the dedication ceremony of the Monument against War and
Fascism were born after World War Two. Perhaps what enabled Austria
and perhaps Japan to cope with their difficult pasts is precisely the fact
that, by the time of the dedication ceremonies, the burden of those who
bore the marks of the past on their bodies and in their souls had become
the social yet once-removed memories of others. To borrow again from
Halbwachs, the memory is no longer an autobiographical one, but an
historical one, one that is mediated through documents, commemorations, etc. (1992).

But time operates neither in a linear manner (Zolberg, 1998) nor in an
empty space and thus may qualify the effect of length. Within this
context one may understand the appearance on the public scene of
events that stir much controversy hundreds and even thousands years
after they took place (see for example Kertzer's work on Joan of Arc,
1988). Those controversies have little to do with the past and much with
the present.

By the same token one may solve the puzzle of the multivocal character of the Vietnam Veterans Memorial when only nine years divided the
dedication of the monument (1982) from the death of the last American
soldier in Vietnam. In 1982, the war was over, and except at specific
points in time (such as prior to the Gulf War – see Beamish, Molotch and
Flacks 1995), the Vietnam War was no longer part of the American
agenda. Such relative irrelevance of the past to the present may have contributed to the construction of a multi-vocal commemoration.

In the case of the assassination of Rabin, Israel's Prime Minister, the
commemoration began within a week! The people who lived through the
trauma and those who were accused (rightly or wrongly) of responsibility were, and are, very much alive. More important yet, the peace process
with the Palestinians which Rabin had led and which was at the heart of
the conflict, has not ended and is still at the center of the Israeli agenda.
A current agenda coupled with virtually no time elapsed between the

event and its commemoration is certainly difficult ground for a multi-vocal commemoration. Okinawa is also a case in point. The presence of American bases since the war there and as Masaie says 'the military role Okinawa has since played serves as a constant, painful reminder' (2001:95) of the past. 'As much as people may want to forget, circumstances do not permit' (ibid). The time between events and their commemoration is critical in the analysis of the types of mnemonic outcomes, but only if the length of time affects the agenda of the commemorating society. In other words, it is the relevance or the irrelevance of the past to the present that generates a fragmented or a multivocal commemoration, respectively.

3. The Agents of Memory
Determination obviously characterizes all agents of memory. Moreover, current agents of memory are aware today that 'whoever controls images of the past shapes the present, and possibly the ideas of the future' (Levy 1999: 51). More important, the power of agents of memory varies. The type of commemoration enacted depends considerably on the relative power of those who 'do commemoration'. What kind of political, economic, social, symbolic and cultural capital do the JWA hold? What kind of capital do the witnesses of the earthquake hold? When agents of memory hold significant political, economic, social, cultural and symbolic capital, it is likely that what will emerge is a fragmented type of commemoration. When the resources are more modest, people may need to compromise.

Furthermore, state support and recognition (Wagner-Pacifici and Schwartz 1991; Schwartz and Bayma 1999) is not necessarily the ultimate and sole goal; sometimes, it is only the beginning. While in all likelihood Jan Scruggs and other American Vietnam veterans could never have built a memorial without the assistance of the state and other organizations, other (more powerful) agents of memory may form voluntary associations, raise substantial amounts of money, and appropriate public spaces and times in which their narrative could be heard outside the official framework.

In addition, the composition of commemorative committees may send a message regarding the tone of the desired outcome. The men and women 'who differed visibly and widely on many political issues but shared the desire to honor the Vietnam veterans' (Wagner-Pacifici and Schwartz 1991: 389), and who were all uncontroversial figures, transmitted a significant message of consensus and sharing to the rest of the American public. How different this is when the agents of memory share the same political views and interpretations of the commemorated event.

CONCLUSIONS

Mnemonic practices and sites as 'a cultural force in [their] own right' (Schwartz 1997: 488; see also Olick and Robbins 1998; Y. Zerubavel 1995; Cressy 1994) may themselves become an arena through which social conflicts and the identities involved may be constructed and defined. Both types of commemoration (multivocal and fragmented) do not resolve social conflicts but rather represent and express them. A multivocal commemoration has the potential to attract people with diversified views of the past memorialized in a shared space or time, and thus is about building and enhancing social solidarity despite disagreement. In that sense, a multivocal commemoration can be understood within a Durkheimian perspective (1965). In contrast, fragmented commemoration which consists of multiple and diversified times and spaces in which different discourses of the past are enacted and expressed, each appealing to diverse groups, does not enhance social solidarity. More than just representing social conflicts, it may sharpen them by offering contentious collectives what they scarcely could have laid a claim to before the monuments were erected and the memorial days were set: a place to meet, a time to share, and a discourse to cherish. A fragmented commemoration thus sharply deviates from the Durkheimian perspective as it is about reinforcing, even building, dissensus. While memorial rituals and monuments may enable a society to come to terms with its past (Bunzl 1995), resolve contradictions and confusions (Schwartz and Bayma 1999; Ducharme and Fine 1995), provide reassurance of solidarity and equilibrium at a time of chaos and uncertainty (Kertzer 1988; Koselleck 1994; Schwartz 2000), terminate social dissent (Polleta 1998), legitimize the continuation of exploitation (Nakamaki), take the burden of memory away from the people (Young 1993), or replace it altogether (Nora 1989), they may also enhance social conflicts.

More than understanding the emergence of a specific type of commemoration and its social significance, from the standpoint of social memory and commemoration, the importance of polarization, timing and agency resides in their impermanence. In future days, social conditions may change and in turn the mnemonic practices and their narratives may change. A consensual political culture, for instance, will interpret an event differently from the way a conflictual political culture defined it, and this different interpretation – combined with the disappearance of specific agents of memory and the a change in present agenda, may lead to further consensus in its commemorative forms, which may lead to further consensus in the society. This is what happened to the commemoration of Abraham Lincoln (Schwartz 2000); it may also happen to in other places. The model presented is thus neither static nor closed-ended.

My comments are partially aimed at demonstrating the value of explanatory models consisting of a dynamic interplay of agent, culture and structure (which in themselves are rarely static) as a principle for the study of many sorts of cultural productions: museums and exhibitions, text books, constitutions, parades, ceremonies and other cultural practices that are as shaped by the social context in which they emerged as are commemorative practices. To be sure, social memory and commemoration are processual, unpredictable, partial, usable, negotiable, dynamic and dialogical (Olick and Robbins 1998; Zelizer 1995). But before we can rightly ask how collective memory or cultural productions work (perhaps even transform the very same conditions from which they emerged), we must look at their founding moments. Many of the chapters here are about such founding moments. It is vital to uncover the social conditions that affect its emergence, not only because commemoration is a cultural agent in its own right and thus may strengthen or weaken social solidarity, but also because any future cultural production will have to take it into account.

While it is difficult to call for a general model based on only a few case studies, I view this exercise as an opportunity to open doors for future systematic comparative research of other cases, whether inter- or intra-societal, where a different combination of the proposed social factors operates (or even where the social factors themselves are less binary in their nature). A good starting point may be by examining the mnemonic reality in Japan. Is Japan at the stage of dealing with its difficult past? The answer seems to be positive. What is the mnemonic reality look like in Japan? How can its political culture be defined? Is it changing? Are the events or people commemorated still part of a conflictual agenda? How powerful or powerless are the agents of memory in the various cases? The assessment of the model may also require future investigation of cases in which attempts to commemorate failed or never took place; an inquiry into those 'failures' may reveal as much about the relative importance of the dimensions that affect the construction of collective memory in general, and commemoration in particular, as successful mnemonic practices. To cite only two examples, France may be 'the queen' of national memory work, but the Algerian War is virtually nonexistent in French collective memory (Prost 1999). The same may be said for the Civil War in Spain (Aguilar 1999; 1997). Are there major events in Japan's history that remain in the darkness? And if so, how can one explain that?

American society may never reach consensus on the Vietnam War (Tatun 1996; Ehrenhaus 1989), but its dissensus shares the same commemorative space. Such commemorative practice may even imply that, in one way or another, American society has in fact come to terms with its difficult past. Those who want (or are obligated) to remember

Rabin hardly share the same space, time or discourse, except as prescribed by state protocol and law. There is no sense of healing the nation. When dedicating the Korean War Veterans Memorial, President Clinton said, 'from many we are one' (Schwartz and Bayma 1999). The appropriate dedication in cases of a fragmented commemoration might be, 'from many we are even more.' The question is, at the moment, can we discuss, analyze and understand commemoration in Japan in the same terms? What can be learned about this society from the way it chooses to remember or to forget its past; difficult or honorable or both.

The past seems to be an unfinished business. From the point of view of scholars of this intriguing field, I hope it will never become a finished ordeal.

REFERENCES

Aguilar, Paloma. 1997. 'Collective Memory of the Spanish Civil War: The Case of the Political Amnesty in the Spanish Transition to Democracy.' *Democratization* 4:88–109.

Aguilar, Paloma. 1999. 'Agents of Memory: Spanish Civil War Veterans and Disabled Soldiers.' Pp. 84–103 in *War and Remembrance in the Twentieth Century*, edited by J. Winter, and E. Sivan. Cambridge, England: Cambridge University Press.

Alexander, Jeffrey C., and Philip Smith. 1993. 'The Discourse of American Civil Society: A New Proposal for Cultural Studies.' *Theory and Society* 22:151–207.

Beamish, Thomas D., Harvey Molotch, and Richard Flacks. 1995. 'Why Support the Troops? Vietnam, the Gulf War, and the Making of Collective Memory.' *Social Problems* 42:344–60.

Bunzl, Matti. 1995. 'On the Politics and Semantics of Austrian Memory: Vienna's Monument against War and Fascism.' *History and Memory* 7:7–38.

Cressy, David. 1994. 'National Memory in Early Modern England.' pp. 61–73 in *Commemorations: The Politics of National Identity*, edited by J. Gillis. Princeton, NJ: Princeton University Press.

Durkheim, Emil. 1965. *The Elementary Forms of the Religious Life.* New York: Free Press.

Ducharme, Lori J. and Gary A. Fine. 1995. 'The Construction of Nonpersonhood and Demonization: Commemorating the Traitorous Reputation of Benedict Arnold.' *Social Forces* 73:1309–31.

Ehrenhaus, Peter. 1989. 'Commemorating the Unwon War: On *Not* Remembering Vietnam.' *Journal of Communication* 39:96–107.

Fine, Gary A. 2001. *Difficult Reputations: Collective Memories of the Evil, Inept, and Controversial.* Chicago, Ill: University of Chicago Press.

Freeman, Mark. 1993. *Rewriting the Self: History, Memory, Narrative.* London, England: Routledge.

Fujitani, T., Geoffrey M. White, and Lisa Yoneyama. 2001. (eds). *Perilous Memories: The Asia-Pacific War(s).* London: Duke University Press.

Goffman, Erving. 1974. *Frame Analysis.* New York: Harper and Row.

Ha'aretz service. 2002. 'Japanese Prime Minister Expressed Regrets over his Nation's Deeds during World War Two' (in Hebrew). *Ha'aretz,* 16 August, p. A11.

Halbwachs, Maurice. 1992. *On Collective Memory.* Chicago, IL: University of Chicago Press.

Halbwachs, Maurice. 1980[1950]. *The Collective Memory.* New York: Harper and Row.

Irwin-Zarecka, Iwona. 1994. *Frames of Remembrance: The Dynamics of Collective Memory.* New Brunswick, N.J: Transaction.

Jacobs, Ronald N. 1996. 'Civil Society and Crisis: Culture, Discourse, and the Rodney King Beating.' *American Journal of Sociology* 101:1238–72.

Kertzer, David I. 1988. *Ritual, Politics, and Power.* New Haven, CT.: Yale University Press.

Koselleck, Reinhart. 1994. 'Introduction.' pp. 9–20 in *The Political Cult of the Dead: War Memorials in the Modern Era* (in German). edited by R. Koselleck, and M. Jeismann. Munich, Germany: Wilhelm Fink Verlag.

Levy, Daniel. 1999. 'The Future of the Past: Historiographical Disputes and Competing Memories in Germany and Israel.' *History and Theory* 38:51–66.

Maier, Charles S. 1998. *The Unmasterable Past: History, Holocaust and German National Identity.* Cambridge, MA: Harvard University Press.

Masaie, Ishihara. 2001. 'Memories of War and Okinawa.' 2001. In *Perilous Memories: The Asia-Pacific War(s).* Edited by T. Fujitani,., Geoffrey M. White, and Lisa Yoneyama. 2001. (eds). London: Duke University Press. pp.87–106.

McAdams, Dan P. 1993. *The Stories We Live By: Personal Myth and the Making of the Self.* New York: William Morrow.

McCall, Michal M. 1990. 'The Significance of Storytelling.' *Studies in Symbolic Interaction* 11:145–61.

Mead, George Herbert. 1938. *The Philosophy of the Act.* Chicago: University of Chicago Press.

Mitchell, William J., ed. 1981. *On Narrative.* Chicago: University of Chicago Press.

Nora, Pierre. 1989. 'Between Memory and History: Les Lieux de Memoire.' *Representations* 26:7–25.

Olick, Jeffrey K. 1999a. 'Collective Memory; the Two Cultures.' *Theory and Society* 17:1–16.

Olick, Jeffrey K. 1999b. 'Genre Memories and Memory Genres: A Dialogical Analysis of May 8, 1945 Commemorations in the Federal Republic of Germany.' *American Sociological Review* 64: 381–402.

Olick, Jeffrey K. and Joyce Robbins. 1998. 'Social Memory Studies: From 'Collective Memory' to the Historical Sociology of Mnemonic Practices.' *Annual Review of Sociology* 24:105–40.

Polleta, Francesca. 1998. 'Legacies and Liabilities of an Insurgent Past: Remembering Martin Luther King, Jr., on the House and Senate Floor.' *Social Science History* 22:479–512.

Prost, Antoine. 1999. 'The Algerian War in French Collective Memory.' pp. 161–176. in *War and Remembrance in the Twentieth Century*, edited by J. Winter and E. Sivan. Cambridge, England: Cambridge University Press.

Schwartz, Barry. 1982. 'The Social Context of Commemoration: A Study in Collective Memory.' *Social Forces* 61:374–402.

Schwartz, Barry. 1997. 'Collective Memory and History: How Abraham Lincoln Became a Symbol for Racial Equality.' *The Sociological Quarterly* 38: 469–96.

Schwartz, Barry. 2000. *Abraham Lincoln and the Forge of National Memory*. Chicago, IL: University of Chicago Press.

Schwartz, Barry and Todd Bayma. 1999. 'Commemoration and the Politics of Recognition: The Korean War Veterans Memorial.' *American Behavioral Scientist* 42:946–67.

Schudson, Michael. 1989. 'The Present in the Past versus the Past in the Present.' *Communication* 11:105–13.

Tatun, James. 1996. 'Memorials of the American War in Vietnam.' *Critical Inquiry* 22:634–80.

Vinitzky-Seroussi, Vered. 2002. 'Commemorating a difficult past: Yitshak Rabin's memorials.' *American Sociological Review* 67 (February): 30–51.

Wagner-Pacifici, Robin and Barry Schwartz. 1991. 'The Vietnam Veterans Memorial: Commemorating a Difficult Past.' *American Journal of Sociology* 97:376–420.

Yang, Dazing. 2001. 'The Malleable and the Contested: The Nanjing Massacre in Postwar China and Japan.' In *Perilous Memories: The Asia-Pacific War(s)*. Edited by T. Fujitani, Geoffrey M. White, and Lisa Yoneyama. 2001. (eds). London: Duke University Press. pp. 50–86.

Yoneyama, Lisa. 2001. 'The Transformative Knowledge and Postnationalist Public Spheres: The Smithsonian *Enola Gay* Controversy.' In *Perilous Memories: The Asia-Pacific War(s)*. Edited by T. Fujitani, Geoffrey M. White, and Lisa Yoneyama. 2001. (eds). London: Duke University Press. pp. 323–346.

Young, James E. 1993. *The Texture of Memory*. 1993. New Haven, CT: Yale University Press.

Zelizer, Barbie. 1995. 'Reading the Past against the Grain: The Shape of Memory Studies.' *Critical Studies in Mass Communication*. 12:214–39

Zerubavel, Eviatar. 1993. 'In the Beginning: Notes on the Social Construction of Historical Discontinuity.' *Sociological Inquiry* 63:457–59.

Zerubavel, Yael. 1995. *Recovered Roots*. Chicago, IL: University of Chicago Press.

Zolberg, Vera L. 1998. 'Contested Remembrance: The Hiroshima Exhibit Controversy.' *Theory and Society* 27:565–90.

Index